Millionaire Dreams: African Schemes

*Turning pocket change into profits:
Joe's Hilarious guide to wealth and wisdom
from Liberia to Australia.*

By

Joe Robert Saye Komandan

Published by:

Dedication

I would like to dedicate this book to my late friend, Rufus Dokie, who was a true friend to me throughout. He believed in me, even when I couldn't see things in myself. He always used to tell me, "You need to be careful with your life. You're a lucky man, and your dreams will come true one day. You'll be the millionaire you wish to be, but remember."

We would laugh it off. Unfortunately, I lost Rufus while I was here in Australia. He didn't live to see me return to Africa.

Miss you, mate.

Table of Contents

Chapter 1:
From Nimba To Prosperity

My Humble Beginnings in Nimba:

Growing up in Nimba County, Liberia, was like being part of a real-life comedy show, where the punchlines just kept coming. My family wasn't rolling in money, but we had something far more valuable: an abundance that makes for good storytelling today. My parents, Mr Saye Luk Komandan and Ma Zogbelee Saye, raised us with the wealth of culture rather than cash. To this day, I'm convinced that laughter was our family's main currency, and we didn't even need a bank.

Every morning, you could find me running around barefoot, chasing chickens—those feathery little tyrants. I swear they had a mind of their own, strutting around like they owned the place. I learned early on that if you wanted to eat, you had to be faster than the chicken and quicker than your siblings trying to catch it. My parents had a humble farm, but in our eyes, that farm was nothing short of Disneyland. We didn't have cotton candy stands, of course, unless you counted the occasional sugarcane. But we had dreams there. Oh, the dreams! Dreams of moving away from the daily grind of farming and the comedy of errors that came with it.

My siblings and I became entrepreneurs—even before we knew what that word meant. We thought about how to turn pocket change into something substantial, without knowing it would become the title of my future book! I remember one bright afternoon; while trying to sell firewood to passersby, I set up my stall next to the most enormous mango tree on the farm. I declared myself the 'King of Firewood,' and soon, I was selling twigs and branches until even the chickens were raising their eyebrows. The customers? Mostly my family, who would pretend to haggle with me to make me feel like a successful businessman. Through it all, I learned that if you stomped your feet while arguing about prices—whether you were selling or simply reminiscing about Aunt Cee-Yalamah's bitter stew—people would take you more seriously.

Of course, my childhood wasn't just about entrepreneurial exploits and chicken chases. It was steeped in life lessons—sometimes delivered with a hefty dose of humour. Take, for instance, the time my mother attempted to teach us the value of hard work by making us plant cassava. She would say, "Everything that comes easy is not worth having." So, there we were, her little workers in the hot sun, planting cassava while she lounged under the shade, sipping her palm wine. I could hear the cackles of laughter echoing from the neighbouring villages as we stumbled our way through the dirt, trying to figure out what went where. I remember my younger sister, Irine, who, in defiance, decided she would rather take a nap in the sun than plant anything. By the time my mother caught her, the plot had turned into an agricultural disaster area, with plants going every which way like a confused chicken on caffeine.

These experiences instilled in me a robust work ethic and an understanding that nothing worthwhile comes without effort. It was all fun and games until you realised that those funny stories were backed by grit and determination. My family taught me the importance of resilience—not with fancy quotes or motivational speeches, but through doing. It was in those sun-soaked fields, with dirt under my fingernails and laughter in the air, that I learned to embrace the struggle. Those lessons shaped my character and are still relevant today as they were back then.

And as our days blended into one another in a delicious mixture of absurdity and love, I remember thinking that life in Nimba was its own peculiar gift. We may not have had much, but there was rich diversity in our community. It wasn't unusual for someone to show up at our door with a gallon of palm wine in one hand and a goat or chicken on a leash in the other, ready to barter whatever we had on offer—often resulting in some hilariously awkward exchanges where no one really understood the other's intention. I swear that's where I first learned the fine art of negotiation. In retrospect, those humble beginnings provide rich fodder for humour and wisdom. Each moment, each winding path, all of it prepared me for the journey ahead, from Nimba to a world beyond, where the opportunities might be grander, but the essence of joy and laughter remained a treasured constant. And who knew? One day, I would fill the pages of a book about it all, with a twist of satire that turned pocket change into something much more meaningful.

The Turning Point: Dreaming Big:

As I navigated through life in Nimba, there came a point when I realised that there was more out there than chasing chickens, bargaining for firewood, cutting palm, and pretending to understand the value of cassava farming. I mean, who knew what was happening beyond our little patch of paradise? It was time for me to expand my horizons and dream a little bigger. You could say it was my "giant chicken" moment, where you realise that the tiny, feathered tyrants might just be a little too small for your aspirations.

This epiphany didn't come as a bolt from the blue but rather as a series of astonishing revelations that coalesced into my desire for something larger than life. I will never forget the day one of my older siblings, Alfred, brought home a worn-out, second-hand book from a friend. It was a curious object, a portal to a world I had hardly imagined. The pages were yellowed, with dog-eared corners, and filled with tales of success, wealth, and the glamorous lives of millionaires (not even the "rich" sides of my family could rival that!).

Looking back, the irony of reading about wealth while squatting in a grass hut surrounded by goats wasn't lost on me.

After flipping through the pages of this book, I noticed that dreams weren't just for the privileged or the adventurous; they were for anyone willing to chase after them, even if it meant running barefoot through thorny paths—paths that could lead to unknown episodes of hilarity. Suddenly, the thoughts of becoming a millionaire weren't just slogans on my t-shirt, but they were actually tangible goals that sparked excitement within me. I remember thinking, "If those people can make it, why can't I?" The reality of my circumstances didn't seem so confining anymore. It felt like I had donned an optimistic superhero cape, shaped out of my childhood t-shirt.

Conversations with family members, like my father, often took a delightful turn toward the absurd. He'd joke about being "too rich to be poor" while adjusting his old, tattered sandals. His style of humour was like magic that was constantly transforming mundane discussions about money into side-splitting banter. He'd joke that if we ever became millionaires, he would buy a mansion that had a swimming pool made entirely of beer (with strict 'no-swimming' rules, of course). It was in these moments that I started to visualise the impossible—a future that intertwined laughter with success. What if I could turn those concepts into true reality and not merely comic fantasies?

With my newfound vision, I began to take my destiny into my own hands, albeit with the clumsiness of a toddler learning to walk. School became a different world for me. I was no longer just a student—I was a dreamer on a mission! I took every lecture on maths and economics, swirling them around in my head like a delicious concoction, never realising how crucial they would be to our financial escapades. I would imagine myself as the lion-hearted entrepreneur, swaggering in and dramatically transforming our family farm into a fragrant garden of wealth. I envisioned barbecues on the lawn, laughter echoing as family and friends mingled, all while I stood there in a suit, a glass of palm wine in hand—my very own fortune fireworks show!

Yet, in the pursuit of these dreams, I often tripped over reality. The disconnect between farm life and this newfound ambition became clearer each day. I attempted to apply some half-baked financial strategies, like combining cassava and chicken sales to boost my revenue. Spoiler alert: it resulted in a lot of chickens clucking their dissatisfaction and cassava turning into "root vegetables with potential." My family stepped in like the cast of a sitcom, with Ma Zogbelee shaking her head, giggling about her son's bizarre 'money-making schemes,' reminding me that ingenious ideas often live in the land of hilarity.

But even among the blunders, I held on to my dreams with a persistence that bordered on comical obsession. I began enlisting my siblings in "Get Rich Quick (But Please Don't Cluck)" initiatives. We laughed, brainstormed, and occasionally failed spectacularly at convincing our village that fresh goat milk was the key to youthful vitality. The turning point was visible; I wasn't just dreaming—I was dragging others along in our whimsical waddle toward entrepreneurship.

And so the journey began. I learned to embrace the hilarity of failure, realising that every "how-not-to" moment was just another chapter in my story—a tale swirling with humour and humility. I discovered that dreaming bigger didn't mean leaving my roots behind; instead, it meant cherishing them while reaching out for the stars. It was a delightful dance, one that shaped my identity—a blossoming young man from Nimba, determined to craft a future painted not by limitation but by laughter, ambition, and the delicious aroma of drumsticks and dreams.

Lessons from My Family: Work Ethic and Values:

Family! The origin of jokes, wisdom, and, of course, my remarkably efficient attempts at becoming a millionaire. Growing up with the Saye Komandan family meant being exposed to a masterclass in work ethic and values, all wrapped in a delightful paper of laughter. Our household may not have been Pinterest-worthy, but we operated on the unspoken principle that everything could be achieved through hard work and a healthy dose of humour.

Take my father, man of many hats, even if those hats were often metaphorical. He was the king of making us understand that idleness was an enemy best suited for the lazy. Whenever he caught one of us lounging around, he'd strike a classic "proud parent" pose, hands on hips, eyebrow raised, and deliver his favourite line, "The lazy stomach eats the hardest! You don't want to be all bark and no bite." Of course, what he meant was that you can't just sit idly dreaming of being rich—one must hustle, which we did, albeit with varying degrees of success.

His punishments for idleness turned into opportunities for hilarity. One instance stands out: one sunny afternoon, I was caught daydreaming (which I preferred to call "strategic planning") instead of working on the farm. My punishment? I had to carry a bucket of water uphill while reciting a tongue twister about cassava. "Cassava seems to sap sweetness when served too simply!" I stammered, while the laughter of my siblings echoed around me like a cheering crowd. That notorious bucket became a symbol of tenacity; if I could handle that steep hill while battling words, surely I could face the world. The lesson? Hard work doesn't have to be miserable; it can be hilariously creative.

Then there's my mother, the indomitable Ma Zogbelee Saye, who infused her work ethic with a fierce sense of practicality. She believed doing things with pride and purpose was key to our family survival. Even when preparing a simple meal, she'd weave entertaining tales about our favourite goats—like the time one of them successfully evaded capture by performing what could only be described as the greatest escape act in history. Each dinner was not only a meal; it was an opportunity to enjoy priceless family anecdotes, all whilst practising the art of appreciation for hard work. The beauty was in the details—our food reflected our labour, our conversations reflected our love, and all of that was combined with a hefty sprinkle of wit.

Mom would often instil in us the idea that "money cannot buy rice." This was her way of teaching the importance of self-sufficiency and making the most out of what we have. The humour in her statement was palpable, as each time we faced a particularly lean season, she would concoct an outrageous recipe using anything she could find, turning our pantry into a culinary version of *Chopped*. To this day, I still can't decide if her "slippery GB" was a miracle or a crisis, but one thing was sure—it taught me resilience. If you can't buy a fancy rice cooker, just use your resourcefulness!

My siblings and I continually learned the value of collaboration through family endeavours. We'd band together like a team of superheroes (the kind without capes or cool powers) to take on chores. Whether we were lifting heavy sacks of rice or pulling stubborn goats by their tails, every task became a bonding experience, complete with laughter, scuffles, and my younger self allying with goats as if they were his secret friends in this epic saga we called life. It was then that I recognised that support from family often outweighs individual challenges, especially when everyone's busy improvising solutions to laughably chaotic problems.

Perhaps the most profound lesson of all was about integrity. My family carried values as rich as the soil in Nimba and more potent than any palm wine. When faced with tough decisions, my parents often reminded us that while money might come and go, one's integrity shouldn't be up for sale. I remember a moment when we found a lost goat that belonged to a neighbour. Instead of enjoying our surprise feast, my parents took the effort to return it. My siblings and I watched in awe; they transformed our simple act into a valuable lesson that our reputation and honesty are worth more than a plate of stolen rice.

Through laughter, hard work, and memorable experiences, my family shaped my views of success. They cultivated not only my ambitions but also taught me that wealth is not just the accumulation of money, but the richness of our relationships, shared stories, and resilience. So, as I journeyed the rich soil of Nimba to the grander dreams of my youth, I knew the heart of my values would accompany me, reminding me to hustle with humour and embrace every lesson learned on the way. The life we lived may have been humble, but through the values instilled by my family, we became stewards of joy, working hard not just for wealth but also for the delight that stitches us together as a family.

Overcoming Adversity: The Strength of Resilience:

Adversity! That persistent little rascal who loves to trudge through life unannounced, just when you think you've got everything under control. I learned early on that life is like a game of whack-a-mole—just when you bat one problem down, another pops up with an attitude! In my journey, from the dusty paths of Nimba to the grander aspirations I dared to dream, resilience became my trusty sidekick, helping me navigate through hilariously unfortunate moments while solidifying my character.

One of the most memorable challenges came knocking when I was blissfully unaware of my "future millionaire" ambitions. Our family experienced a series of setbacks that would make for splendid material in a comedy show—only instead of laughter, we had to muster up resilience. I remember a miserable rainy season when our humble farm was on the verge of becoming a water park for reluctant frogs. The cassava crop we had painstakingly nurtured looked more like a soggy sponge than the bountiful harvest we anticipated. As the skies wept day in and day out, I could almost hear the "splash" of our burgeoning wealth disappearing into the mud with an unceremonious gurgle.

Instead of sitting around and sulking about how the rain turned our fortune into a comedy of errors, my family decided it was time to regroup and strategise. My mother, with all the wisdom and flair of a seasoned general, organised an "emergency family meeting" over what had become an unfortunate daily ritual: swapping soggy staples for afternoon snack ideas. "We may be drowning in water, but let us not drown in despair!" she declared, her voice betraying just the right amount of drama. It was that moment of collective earnestness, woven with humour, that ignited our resilience.

In true Saye Komandan fashion, we put our heads together to hatch a plan. We transformed our waterlogged land into a makeshift ice-skating rink— okay, so maybe it wasn't the Olympics, but it did provide some diversion! My little siblings, with their feet adorned in ill-fitting flip-flops, learned to skate on mudslides while I perfected the art of "graceful falls." Each slip, tumble, and the subsequent eruption of giggles became a reminder that while we were immersed in discomfort, we could create joy amid the chaos. Those hilarious afternoons stitched our familial fabric tighter, and every fall was accompanied by cheer, nurturing our spirit of resilience.

As the rainy season reluctantly pulled back to reveal the sun, we faced the daunting task of reclaiming the farm. Armed with humour as our shield and hard work as our sword, we embarked on the restoration journey with the conviction of clumsy warriors on a mission. The land that once seemed lost became an opportunity for growth—and I don't mean just cassava. We punted new seeds, not only in the ground but in our lives. Each seed became a symbol of hope and the belief that with hard work, we could rise from muck to miracles.

Amidst these challenges, there were certainly moments that veered sharply towards the absurd. Like the time I attempted to carry a heavy bucket of water on my head, channeling the ancestors, but instead became a human hydropower plant, soaking my brothers as they heroically tried to dodge my clumsiness. In between helping to plant crops and fending off brotherly attacks, I gained clarity—it wasn't about perfectly fulfilling tasks. It was about empowering one another, getting through it together, with the laughter to accompany our efforts.

Then came the inevitable awkward lessons. Much later in life, I would look back on these adversities and laugh at those unforgettable moments, recognising that even missteps can take you on extraordinary paths. Resilience, to me, means that failure is merely a rehearsal for success, and like my confused chickens fleeing from a perceived disaster, I had learned to either sprint, fiercely evade adversity, or create such a scene that laughter would break the tension instead.

Every time I found the humour amidst the trials, I strengthened my resolve. Resilience is not about merely surviving—it's about living life with an open heart, allowing the inevitable mishaps to teach us how to navigate forward. It's about embracing trials as the universe's way of ensuring we learn and grow. In many ways, it's like walking through a mud puddle—stumbling at times but ultimately finding joy and balance in the messiness of life.

Today, as I stand on the other side of those experiences, simplicity glows brighter than gold. The laughter and camaraderie forged in adversity transformed each challenge into a delightful comedy—a reminder that every stumble can be the stepping stone to success. Life absurdly threw difficulties our way, but every laugh tickled our spirits and cemented resilience in our hearts. So let's raise a glass of fresh palm wine to adversity; may it always come with a side of resilience, laughter, and the charm that life is best lived with a heart full of humour, no matter what mud puddles await!

The Role of Education in Shaping My Path:

Education! That magical wand that shifts the trajectory of young lives, often accompanied by searching too far for pencils that decided to hide and teachers who seemed to live for giving pop quizzes at the worst possible moments. I dare say, education in my life has been nothing short of a colossal adventure—one filled with hilarious mishaps, pivotal insights, and sporadic moments of pure enlightenment that ignited the flame of possibility within me.

In my upbringing in Nimba County, education was regarded with a seriousness that desperately clashed with the frolicking spirit of youthful mischief found in the hearts of my siblings and me. We'd stumble into school every day, a bit like a herd of confused goats, eyes wide with wonder and minds ready to wander. Our classrooms were far from luxurious, often resembling a vibrant circus tent where learning was accompanied by spontaneous outbursts of laughter. You couldn't say we weren't invested in our education; we participated wholeheartedly, often ending up with our names written on the blackboard for "extra credit" on shenanigans instead of actual assignments.

The schoolyard antics served as a vivid backdrop for my first lessons. My teachers, those brave souls, became the unsung warriors battling for our attention. I will never forget Mrs Johnson, my lovely yet formidable teacher, who had a preference for dramatic storytelling. Her history lessons were less about dates and facts and more about epic reenactments that included imagining the sounds of cannon fire (not to mention her impressive sound effects). One day, as she passionately narrated the tale of an ancient kingdom, I couldn't help but imagine her as a queen on a peculiar quest for knowledge, fighting the dragon of ignorance with nothing but her trusty chalk. Through her, I learned to appreciate education as a portal to creativity and possibility.

However, like many youths longing for a little mischief, my heart held dreams that exceeded the borders of our village. While my peers dreamed of career paths that included herding goats or crafting the finest palm oil, I set my sights on visionary pursuits. I craved knowledge beyond survival. I scoured the library, which could hardly be described as extensive but offered a collection of books that simply begged to be devoured. The power of words fascinated me, so much so that I'd bribe friends with cassava to exchange their books for just a few hours. Little did they know that exposing me to new ideas was akin to letting a monkey loose in a banana factory—utter pandemonium was imminent!

From science to arithmetic, every subject slapped me like a splash of cold water of realisation. I learned about crafting equations. My love for numbers came alive until puberty hit, and then I would discover that solving "X" didn't give me any answers about the chaotic happenings in life. But the lesson remained: education teaches you to think critically, even if it means occasionally questioning the universe while fumbling through a maths exam. Looking back, I chuckle at the moments where I grappled with the mysteries of algebra, understanding now that the real formula was learning to balance and struggle in everything we pursue.

Our academic progression triggered many poignant events, the most memorable being the day I completed a big project—a presentation on the economics of cassava farming, somehow managing to turn it into a goofy musical number that set my classmates into laughter. But while my melodious mermaid rendition of *The Cassava Polka* may not have won me any accolades, it taught me a valuable lesson on the importance of creative thinking. Education isn't just about memorising facts; it's about understanding that creativity can be as powerful as the textbooks that weigh down your backpacks.

As I moved forward into high school (where I was grateful for a semi-proper chair instead of benches), I noticed education took on a more profound seriousness, yet the laughter and camaraderie remained. I had mentors, people who believed in my potential, and they started awakening my thirst to learn not just for myself but for the community around me. Here, I recognised that education was more than just a series of tests; it was a gateway to self-discovery, a chance to learn to lead, and an opportunity to give back.

Ultimately, the role of education in shaping my path became clear: it was the guiding light in my quest for growth, packed with valuable lessons that echoed laughter and joy. It transformed a young dreamer from a humble village into a young man prepared to embrace the wider world with the grit of a warrior and the heart of a jester. The gates of opportunity opened wide; I would harness my education to venture beyond the horizon of my humble beginnings and launch myself into the realms of dreams, equipped not only with knowledge but with an unshakeable resilience bubbling with humour. And so I ventured forth, knowing that whether I was walking down the path of liberation or diving into the depths of success, the lessons learned from education would be my eternal compass.

Setting My Sights on Prosperity

As I ventured through the winding paths of education and life in Nimba, I found myself standing at a peculiar crossroads armed with a vision—the vision of prosperity! That shining beacon of success called to me like a greedy chicken to a feast, promising riches, laughter, and perhaps a hint of overly ambitious daydreaming. I firmly decided that it was time to set my sights firmly on prosperity, not simply for myself, but to uplift my family and community. So, manifesting my inner "we can do this" mantra, I set out concocting my master plan for financial victory.

The first step in my grand adventure involved liberating myself from the shackles of self-doubt. I had spent years tossing and turning over endless possibilities, feeling like a fish out of water trying to choose between becoming a fisherman or starting a goat yoga studio (just kidding; goats aren't great at following strict exercise routines). But through the laughter and absurdity of my earlier endeavours, I learned that one must engage with ambition and embrace it like a long-lost friend. It was time to stop waiting for fortunes to fall from the sky like ripe mangoes. No more daydreaming! I was going to turn those dreams into actionable goals, actionable strategies, and perhaps even some actionable pizza (because who doesn't operate better with a full stomach?).

Once I hatched my illustrious plan, I began collecting information like a squirrel hoarding corn. I dove into books on finance and entrepreneurship as if they were my survival guide through the jungle of adulthood, turning my humble living room into a makeshift research laboratory. Mum would poke her head through the doorway, eyebrow arched, and ask if I was diving deep into the realities of wealth or merely from chores. Little did she know that balancing financial advice with household work was just another form of multitasking! "It's called innovation, Ma!" I'd respond, juggling the task at hand with delightful enthusiasm.

Every nugget of wisdom I absorbed led me to conclude that prosperity required a mindset—the "millionaire mentality." I flipped through pages, emphasising success habits, pushing past the ghost of instant gratification. Financial gurus claimed things like "wealth is a marathon, not a sprint," which made me ponder who would want to run a marathon in place! While I couldn't imagine jogging anywhere longer than to the local market, I found humour in the idea that perseverance is the key. I knew I had to lace up my metaphorical running shoes, even if my feet were firmly planted in the soft soil of Nimba.

With my power-packed strategies mapped out, I began taking calculated risks like an acrobat on a tightrope. I dabbled in mini-entrepreneurial ventures, creatively trying to generate income regardless of setbacks. Picture this: a young man trying to sell artisanal palm oil while imitating a professional salesperson, complete with exaggerated gestures and questionable narration about the oil's magical properties (it may have unexpectedly promised to clean your dishes and boost your mood at the same time). Each attempt filled my heart with dread yet ignited my determination. If I could survive the embarrassment of funny faces and awkward exchanges, I could survive anything, including the daily hustle in the bush.

As I stumbled—and I mean truly stumbled—through a series of comical entrepreneurial adventures (including, yes, a failed attempt to sell handmade bookbags), I began to craft a community out of my network. I realised that prosperity isn't a solo journey, but a collective pursuit enriched by relationships. My family, friends, and neighbours rallied behind me, sharing advice, resources, and their tales of resilience. There's something magical about a vibrant community that allows everyone to shine; it's like constructing a surprising puzzle made of laughter instead of sharp pieces.

No matter how wacky the approach, I was gradually moving toward my goal. I took every laugh-filled setback as a stepping stone, understanding that failure is simply a comedic ally. One particularly hilarious episode involved mispricing my farm produce and getting swindled by my mum during a sales chit-chat—she insisted on haggling for flour that I had accidentally mixed with dirt. It turned out to be the best lesson on pricing strategy I could have asked for.

Taking my sights beyond the immediate community, I pursued opportunities to engage with mentors in various fields. I realised success isn't just about wealth; it's also about wisdom, and what better way to gain wisdom than learning from those who've turned their dreams into reality? Every time I reached out for guidance, I found doors swinging open. It's not just the accumulation of money; it's the richness of experiences, relationships, and lessons learned along the journey. So here I stood, a future millionaire in the making, filled with laughter, determination, and a determination to embrace prosperity as a multi-faceted journey. With my sights set high, I was off to conquer the world, not just as a dreamer, but as a joyful participant filled with the promise of endless possibilities!

Chapter 2:
The Millionaire Mentality

Defining the Millionaire Mentality:

The millionaire mentality! You see, it's not just about having a fat bank account or flaunting a golden watch that shimmers brighter than a Liberian sun. No, my friends, the millionaire mentality is a state of mind, a quirky little place where dreams dance with possibilities while sipping on coconut water. It all begins with a shift in perspective—a realisation so profound that it can make your great-grandma's head spin in her grave. You might even say it's the mental equivalent of trying to catch a goat running wild during a celebration; chaotic yet thrilling!

First, let's establish what I mean by the "millionaire mentality." It's not about counting your coins and daydreaming about Ferraris while watching reruns of that '70s show. No, it's a mindset that embraces abundance rather than scarcity. Oftentimes, people focus on what they lack—money, connections, or maybe a decent haircut—but millionaires see opportunity everywhere. Think of it like the difference between a chicken and a rooster; one lays eggs while the other struts around like it owns the yard! Millionaires strut their potential like roosters, confidently presenting themselves to the world, ready to capitalise on every opportunity that comes their way.

Another key ingredient in this millionaire recipe is the ability to take risks. And I'm not talking about the "Let's jump off the roof and see if we can fly" kind of risk; no, my dear readers, I am speaking of calculated risks, the kind that makes you feel alive and perhaps a bit tingly in your toes. Many folks fear failure like it's a rabid dog on the loose, but millionaires realise that failure is merely an uninvited but necessary guest at the party of success. In fact, they sprinkle their speeches with quotes like "I have not failed; I've just 10,000 ways that won't work!" (Thank you, Thomas Edison). They march forward, knowing that the path to wealth is littered with mistakes, more than a dancer's feet are with corn during rehearsals.

Now, let's not forget about creativity—the secret sauce that spices up millionaire mentality stew. Millionaires are not just conformists who follow the crowd like sheep headed to the slaughterhouse. No, they're the adventurous goats that leapt outside the fence, exploring new pastures and contemplating whether they can make a profit from organic, free-range banking. Think outside of the proverbial box—squirt mustard on it, set it on Liberian, then dance around it! Innovation is your best friend in this journey to quirky. It's what allows you to take an idea and twist it until it's something that people didn't even know they needed, like a pocket-sized African drum that can fit in your back pocket yet still brings the vibe of a Liberian beach party.

Community matters, too. This one might come as a shocker, but hear me out. The millionaire mentality is fuelled by building connections. It's about surrounding yourself with like-minded people who inspire you to dream bigger and laugh louder. Ever met someone who sucks the fun out of life like a vacuum cleaner on steroids? Kick them to the curb! Millionaires thrive on a support network that lifts them higher, like a group of friends that lifts you into the air during a wedding celebration. You're going to need support when you hit roadblocks because every millionaire has a story of getting stuck in traffic on the road to financial freedom.

Now, let's sprinkle a little laughter on top of this serious mentality cake! Humility and humour go hand in hand in the millionaire world. It's the recognition that you can dream big and still not take yourself too seriously. Ever seen a millionaire cringe at a bad joke? No way! They can laugh at themselves, learn from their blunders, and embrace that sometimes, life is a big old comedy show. So, my fellow dreamers, let your hair down, put a whoopee cushion on that business partner's chair, and remind yourself that wealth is as much about joy and laughter as it is about bank statements.

So, there you have it—the painting of the millionaire mentality on the canvas of your mind. It's vibrant, wild, and a little wacky, but oh-so enticing.
Embrace this mentality, and you, too, may find yourself skipping along

the road to prosperity, scattering confetti and laughter along the way. Get ready; the journey is about to get hilarious.

Common Myths about Wealth and Success:

The myths surrounding wealth and success! Honestly, they might as well win an Oscar for Best Fiction. Strap in, my friends, because I'm about to take you on a wild ride through the land of ludicrous lies that prevent many from achieving their millionaire dreams. These myths are like mosquitoes at a barbeque—buzzing around your ears, making you uncomfortable, and possibly ruining your chances of enjoying that steak! So, let's bust these myths wide open like a ripe plum left out in the sun too long.

First up, let's tackle the biggest myth that's been sticking around like an unwanted houseguest: "You need a mountain of cash to start building wealth." Listen, if I had a dime for every time I heard that, I'd be a millionaire playing a ukulele on a beach in the Maldives. The truth is that wealth doesn't magically appear like a fairy godmother waving her wand; it is built from dreams, ideas, and, most importantly, action. Many people walk around thinking they need a secret treasure chest to start, yet all they need is a bit of creativity and some pocket change—don't worry; I'm not suggesting you break open your piggy bank here! Even my grandmother would tell you that starting small can lead to big things. You can buy some mangos from the market, sell them to your neighbours, and before you know it, you're on the path to being Liberia's next most prominent mogul!

Oh, and let's talk about the myth surrounding education and success; it's about as overstated as a chicken claiming it can fly. You see, in many places in life, there's this sweeping belief that having a formal education and a pile of degrees is the golden ticket to success. Yes, education is essential, but it does not guarantee you a comfortable seat on the millionaire express! I've met plenty of folks with fancy degrees struggling like a cat trying to swim, while others with barely finished high school are out there making bank. The truth is, a lifetime of learning comes from experiences, curiosity, and occasionally face-planting into the grass of life. Trust me; there's no classroom for that kind of wisdom!

Then there's the infamous myth that wealthy people are "greedy or selfish." This one makes me roll my eyes more than my friend Joseph when he attempts to dance. While it's true that some wealthy individuals may closely guard their nacho cheese like it's the secret to the universe, the majority of affluent folks believe in giving back. They understand that the more you receive, kinda like returning that borrowed cup of sugar, but instead, you bring them a whole cake. Philanthropy isn't just for celebrities; everyone can do their part, and many rich people are doing just that. After all, who could decline an opportunity to contribute to the community while raking in some sweet karma?

Now let's straight talk about the belief that "success would come easy if you just put your mind to it." It's a comforting thought, isn't it? If only success were as easy as reciting a monologue from your favourite movie! I hate to break it to you, but chasing your dreams often feels more like working out with an angry hippo. When you have to work hard for something, your dreams become more meaningful. Please don't fall into that trap of thinking it should be a breeze! But you know what? Put in the effort; strike when a bit of opportunity knocks—uninvited, of course— and success will reward you handsomely. Just don't forget to bring your sense of humour along, trust me, you'll need it during those late-night brainstorming sessions that could rival a soap opera for drama!

Let's not ignore the myth that says money is the root of all evil. Good gracious, you'd think money was the actual devil with how it is talked about! The truth is, money is like a multiplication table—it's a tool that amplifies whatever is already inside of you. If you are a kind and generous person, wealth will allow you to positively impact lives. But if you're a grouchy troll who lives under the bridge, then money will amplify that, too! So, let's get it straight—cash itself isn't to blame; it's the character of the person wielding it.

So, as we wrap up our amusing journey through the world of myths about wealth and success, step back and reflect on what you've learned today. The real value lies in shifting perspectives, smashing societal myths to bits, and allowing yourself to dream—even if a goat wanders into that dream now and then. Embrace the fun in your pursuits, gather your courage, and never let the myths of others dictate your version of success. After all, the millionaire mindset is half the battle, and with the right attitude, you'll be on your way to creating your own success story!

The Importance of a Growth Mindset:

The growth mindset! It's the golden ticket to personal development, success, and all the joy in life. Picture it like a garden of delicious vegetables; if you just plant the seeds, water them a little, and swear to cut out the weeds (and occasional wayward goats), you'll soon have the lushest botanical paradise on your hands. What a sight to behold! Seriously, if you're looking to achieve your dreams (or at least get out of the rut of watching Netflix in your pyjamas all day), embracing this mindset is the ticket.

Let's first clarify what a growth mindset really means. Developed by psychologist Carol Dweck (bless her heart!), the concept embodies the belief that your abilities and intelligence can be developed through hard work, dedication, and innovation. Essentially, you can grow smarter, better, richer, and perhaps even incorporate more dance moves into your routine! On the other hand, some people walk around with a fixed mindset as if they were training for the Olympics in "Unyielding Games." They believe that their abilities are set in stone, like the pyramids of Giza. So rather than trying new things, they clutch their old comforts as if they were Grandma's last cookie. But here's the kicker: with a growth mindset, every failure is an opportunity in disguise, lurking in the corner like a ninja waiting to pounce on your insecurities!

What's the secret sauce behind this mindset? It's about embracing challenges, leaning into discomfort, and being willing to fail. Now, I don't mean to imply that everyone should start signing up for extreme sports, such as skydiving while blindfolded. No, that would be absurd! But what I am saying is that the willingness to step beyond your comfort zone is where magic happens. Just like when I ventured into Australian markets for the first time, bewildered by all sorts of strange vegetables and confused salespeople, I embraced the chaos and learned a thing or two! You see, it isn't always smooth sailing, and sometimes you must *ride the raging waves of uncertainty—think of it as sailing a ship named "Intrepid Fool."*

With a growth mindset, you begin to view challenges not as roadblocks but as opportunities for growth. Picture yourself at an old-fashioned crossroad, where you must choose between two paths: the easy, familiar road, which leads to another boring day of scrolling social media, and the steep, rocky mountain trail that promises breathtaking views. A nagging fear may suggest you stick to the gravel, but with growth, you'll bravely lace up your shoes and take on the climb! Each path brings you closer to new experiences, and maybe a summit selfie that leaves your friends green with envy. Don't fear the unknown; it's the perfect opportunity to find out how strong your inner goat really is.

Now, you might be wondering how this growth mindset translates to building. Well, grab a chair and let's dive into the nitty-gritty! The journey to financial success is riddled with hiccups, potholes, and the runaway chicken. Millionaires don't just spring from the ground like mushrooms after rain; they cultivate their skills, learn from mistakes, and persist in the face of failure. Imagine trying to invest in the stock market and seeing your first investment drop like a rock thrown into a pond. A person with a fixed mindset might lament, "I'm just terrible at investing!" while the growth-minded individual shrugs, analyses the situation, and asks, "What went wrong, and how can I do better next time?" That's the name of the game!

And here's a tasty titbit: a growth mindset is infectious! Surround yourself with growth-minded individuals, and you'll find yourself infected with ambitious thoughts and daring endeavours, much like a joyous choir singing hymns of success. Sharing experiences, goals, and encouragement creates an environment where everyone thrives and takes their dreams seriously—imagine a community as vibrant as a festival in Liberia! Trust me, your inner circle has a significant impact on your aspirations, so be intentional about who you let into your life (and your business)!

In closing, a growth mindset is the bedrock upon which true wealth—whether financial or personal—is built. With this mindset, the limitations of a fixed perspective crumble like stale crackers, making room for personal development, laughter, and a trove of opportunities. So go forth, my friends, and water the garden of your potential! Dance in uncomfortable circumstances, embrace life's little challenges, and you may just stumble upon an unexpected fortune (or at the very least, discover that you're a great dancer after all). Here's to expanding, growing, and shaking off the burdens of that fixed mindset—one joyful leap at a time!

Building Resilience and Embracing Failure:

Building resilience and embracing failure are like the peanut butter and jelly of financial success! You can have one without the other, but together, they create a delightful combination that sticks to the roof of your mouth and makes life oh-so-tasty. Imagine trying to bake a cake without flour—sure, it might look pretty on the outside, but we all know it's going to taste like dried leaves! Resilience is the flour, and learning from failure is the sugar; both are essential to create something as delightful as your dreams coming true.

Now, let's get right to it—failure! The dreaded F-word that causes many to cringe, squeal, and dive under the nearest table. But here's the scoop: if you're not facing failure, my friend, it means you're probably not taking enough risks, and that's a greater tragedy than imagining a world without ice cream. Picture this: every millionaire you meet has a closet full of failures that could rival a long-forgotten sitcom's blooper reel. Even the great geniuses, like Albert Einstein and, well, maybe my neighbour who keeps trying to invent the next best thing in lunchbox technology, faced their fair share of missteps. Each tumble is a stepping stone to success, or as I prefer to think of them, delightful piñatas just waiting for you to swing a bat at them to find the goodies hidden inside.

Building resilience requires a mindset as tough as a Liberian warrior, ready to tackle whatever life throws at you. That means accepting that adversity is not a wall to stop you but a trampoline to bounce off. You see, life will throw unexpected challenges your way—like the time I thought I could impress my family with an extravagant dish, only to end up serving a burnt offering that had my cousins questioning my culinary skills. But here's the secret: the more you experience setbacks and choose to rise above them, the stronger your resilience becomes. It's like doing push-ups for your mental muscles, and trust me, I'm still struggling to push through a single one!

But let's delve into the glorious realm of embracing failure. The way I see it, failure is like a comical friend—it can either ruin your day or teach you the most valuable lessons of your life. When I failed at my first investment, I had a moment of despair, followed closely by a wave of excitement as I realised I had loads of newfound wisdom! I had tripped, bundled myself up in a metaphorical banana peel, but then got back up, laughing and ready to learn. Every failure showcases your capacity for growth and adaptation, just like a wise old tortoise with a delightful sense of humour, eager to tell tales of perseverance to the eager little rabbits zipping past.

People often ask me, "Joe, how do you embrace failure?" Well, let me tell you, I've crafted my very own dance with failure! It starts slow, with a little to the left as I analyse what went wrong, then a big twist as I let go of blaming factors outside my control. Finally, with a leap and a twirl, I proudly seize the lessons learned to forge ahead with gusto—and possibly a confused goat in tow. This dance ensures that failure is not a final bow but rather a reminder of why I'm on this journey in the first place. You see, failure isn't something to be ashamed of; it's a necessary ingredient in the recipe for success.

Now, here's a spicy tip: share your failures with others! You might think that talking about your blunders will invite pity, but no—it's a celebration of resilience! Like last week when I decided to share my investment blunders over a feasty family dinner. Everyone laughed, and a few shared their own stories in return. We bonded over failed attempts to cook edible food and passed the mashed potatoes aimed at minimising the taste of embarrassment. The humour lightens the burden, making it easier for others to see failure as a shared experience rather than an isolated catastrophe. Plus, it serves as a reminder that we're all in this wacky world together—like a tribe of resilient jellies in a giant peanut butter jar.

As we wrap this delightful section about resilience and embracing failure, remember that every setback offers a unique lesson waiting to peek out from behind the curtain for you to discover. Resilience is built by nurturing the mind with perseverance, humour, and the occasional dance party centred around failure. You are much more likely to achieve your goals when you learn how to bounce back after being knocked down! So, let's grab our metaphorical dance shoes, crank up the tunes, and learn to embrace failure together—it's time to get that wiggle on the resilience dance floor, my friends!

Surrounding Yourself with the Right People:

Surround yourself with the right people! It's like choosing the perfect ingredients for a delicious African jollof rice—get it right, and you've got a flavour explosion; get it wrong, and you might find yourself with a pot of dubious mush that even the goats wouldn't touch! It's no secret that the company you keep can either propel you toward greatness or drag you down faster than a lead balloon caught in a torrential downpour. So, let's dig into why surrounding yourself with those sparkling gems of humanity is crucial for achieving your millionaire dreams!

First, let's face the music—negativity is like a bad dance partner. You know the type, the one that steps on your toes, trips you up, and leaves you feeling like you just performed a solo at a wedding no one wanted to attend. You've got to watch out for those negative Nancy types who will gladly tell you why your dreams are foolish and unachievable. Listen, if I had listened to every naysayer, I'd be stuck in a cycle of watching reruns of bad soap operas rather than writing my epic journey! Surround yourself with people who lift you, cheer you on, and make you want to reach for the stars. Trust me, you want the hype squad at your side—these folks will be your biggest supporters while reminding you that even the quietest peanut butter jar gets opened up for some jelly now and then!

Next up, let's talk about collaboration. It's nice to surround yourself with like-minded individuals, but it's even better to hang out with people who challenge you and bring diverse perspectives. Just like a healthy pot of soup, true richness comes from blending various ingredients to create something beautiful. Look for those who spark ideas in your mind like fireworks on Independence Day! Surround yourself with people from different backgrounds who can offer wisdom, experience, and possibly an excellent recipe for sweet potato pie. It's the variations in your circle that will help you grow, learn, and flourish like the finest mango trees in all of West Africa.

Now, here's a juicy truth: successful people generally gravitate toward each other. It's like watching a pack of cheetahs hunting together—there's power in that chemistry! When you are exposed to the energy, creativity, and ambition of others chasing their dreams, it becomes contagious. You can learn so much, from practical advice to vital tips about investment opportunities and which restaurants serve the best fufu. Just hang around these go-getters, and soon you'll find yourself inspired and motivated to chase your dreams fiercely enough to outrun a cheetah!

Emotional support is essential, too. Building your dreams can sometimes be like climbing a hill while carrying a bag of palm nuts on your head—challenging and exhausting! You need people to catch you when you stumble or yell, "You've got this!" when you reach the slippery slope of despair. Your journey may consist of challenges, and having reliable friends with whom you can share your highs and lows makes all the difference. Think of them as your cheerleaders, except instead of pom-poms, they come with coffee cups and hugs (lots of them!). They remind you that you are not alone in this quest for success—and that failure is just part of the rollercoaster ride. Helping each other navigate the hurdles in life makes it much easier to keep your balance while tackling your goals together.

Let's sprinkle some humour into this, shall we? Picture yourself in a room filled with successful people; it can feel like a wild celebration. You've got throw pillows filled with inspirational quotes and enough laughter to make even a grumpy lion smile! Having that inviting camaraderie not only boosts morale but also encourages everyone to brainstorm ideas without judgment (unless one of them proposes that pineapple belongs on pizza—then there may be a corporate intervention!). Remember, humour is a great connector; it lightens the atmosphere and invites fresh perspective. So foster connections that not only provide inspiration but also unleash giggles along the way!

In conclusion, surrounding yourself with the right people is vital for building wealth and nurturing your dreams. Don't shy away from forming connections with those who will lift you, inspire you, and challenge you positively. Ignite your circle with diverse perspectives, create a network that fuels your ambition, and fill your journey with laughter and emotional support. After all, success doesn't have to be a lonely road trodden in isolation—let it be an exhilarating adventure shared with friends, a wild party filled with camaraderie, laughter, and the occasional goat prancing through the mix! So, go forth and build that tribe—because the right people can turn your dreams into reality, one laughter-filled adventure at a time!

Creating Daily Habits for Millionaire Success:

Creating daily habits for millionaire success! Now, before you imagine a group of millionaires sipping green smoothies at dawn while practising yoga on top of a mountain (with the delightful sound of rainbows in the background), let me tell you that it doesn't have to be that extravagant! Nope, daily habits that lead to success can be just as straightforward and earthy as planting cassava tubers in rich soil. Let's dig in, roll up our sleeves, and uncover the amazing daily rituals that can boost your journey to wealth like a hot bowl of Liberian pepper soup on a foggy morning.

First and foremost, let's talk about the power of routine. You see, millionaires often thrive on structure and consistency. Think about it: routines help you cultivate discipline, create predictability, and fortify your mental state like a well-constructed fortress. I know, you're thinking, "But Joe, routines can be boring!" And well, yes, they can! However, sprinkle a little creativity into your morning coffee, and add a glam dance party at the same time as you brush your teeth, and suddenly, you've got the adrenaline of a Saturday night out while still having a firm grip on your daily targets. Find what routine works for you, be it morning meditation, writing down your goals, or perhaps conducting an impromptu living room karaoke session while looking over your progress from the day before.

Next on our millionaire menu is the art of goal setting. I can't stress how important it is to set clear, actionable goals—akin to planting seeds for delicious watermelon down the line. It's not enough to dream of becoming a millionaire; you need to define those dreams into tangible goals! "I want to be rich" is excellent, but it won't build your empire! Get specific! Aim: "I will save $200 a month to start a small business", or "By next year, I will launch my online store selling artisanal soap." Setting specific, measurable goals is like turning on a GPS for your financial journey, and trust me—who wants to wander through the deserts of uncertainty? Not this guy!

Let's not overlook the necessity of regular reflection. Millionaires aren't just on a fast train to success; they pull into the station regularly to evaluate their route. Reflecting daily on your achievements, setbacks, and some bizarre goat-related experiences ensures that you keep learning and adjusting. Create a special time, perhaps during your evening cup of tea or while listening to your favourite tunes, to assess your day. What worked? What flopped like a newly introduced fish in hot water? This reflection solidifies lessons learned, allowing you to pursue your goals with renewed determination. If something didn't work as planned, figure out what went wrong and how you can do it differently next time. Think of it as polishing a gem until it shines bright enough to be featured on a fashionable jewellery ad!

Next up is the habit of lifelong learning. The world is a buffet of knowledge—so grab your plate and fill it up! Successful people recognise that continual learning is essential for growth, so expand your mind like a blooming flower! You don't have to enrol in a university filled with stuffy professors, though. There are resources available everywhere, from audiobooks to podcasts, online courses, and even those weirdly informative TikTok videos that show you how to fold a T-shirt like a ninja! Engaging with new information keeps your neurons firing, and who knows? You might discover a new passion or a hidden talent for crafting miniature sculptures out of marshmallows.

Don't forget the importance of networking, too! Establishing connections with others in your field or those who share your interests can be instrumental in paving the path to your millionaire dreams. Schedule time in your daily routine to reach out to an acquaintance for coffee or attend webinars and workshops, even those that sound like a complete snoozefest at first (you might find the next brilliant idea hiding within!). These interactions not only cultivate freedom and inspiration but also help solidify your position within your community, kind of like getting a personalised VIP badge for dreamers.

Lastly, let's put a cherry on top of this delicious habit sundae: self-care. Yes, you heard me right! Taking care of yourself is as crucial as getting your daily dose of wisdom. It's easy to focus solely on hard work and neglect your health, but maintaining a balance ensures a sustainable journey toward success. Make time for exercise, whether it's dancing like nobody's watching or braving the outdoors with a brisk walk while humming your victory anthem. Don't forget to laugh—laughter is an excellent source of inspiration and motivation. It's like the secret ingredient that keeps your spirit flying as you navigate through the ups and downs of life.

In conclusion, creating daily habits for millionaire success is about merging structure, creativity, reflection, learning, networking, and self-care. It's assembling a vibrant tapestry of practices that bolster your desire and readiness to chase your dreams. As you embark on your journey, remember that little daily actions can lead to enormous results over time, transforming you into the empowered millionaire you aspire to be. So, lace up your shoes, gather your beautiful dreams, and let this journey unfold one colourful habit at a time!

Chapter 3:
Turning Pocket Change into Gold

Understanding the Importance of Investing Early

Investing early is like planting a mango tree in your backyard—the earlier you plant it, the sooner you get to enjoy those juicy, delicious fruits (and let's be honest, who doesn't want to be the friend with mango trees?). Imagine waking up to find your friends swinging by for brunch, and you pull out fresh mangoes like some kind of frugal god. The secret is simple: delay gratification today for bigger rewards tomorrow. This mindset doesn't just apply to fruit—it's about building the wealth you need to live your dreams.

Investing early is my passion, and there's a good reason for it—it boils down to three things: time, risk, and the undeniable power of compounding.

Now, I know what you're thinking: "Joe, investing early? But I'm just trying to figure out how to pay for my morning coffee!" Trust me, I've been there too, scrutinising my wallet like it might reveal the secrets of the universe. But consider this: while those coffee beans give you energy for a few hours, investing the same amount can give you compound growth—the eighth wonder of the world (and let's be honest, that's a strong argument for buying a fancy coffee maker).

Imagine putting aside a small portion of your income each month— perhaps the cost of that overpriced latte we all secretly love. Over time, with a little patience and consistency, those pennies can turn into dollars. If only getting my family to agree on dinner was this simple! The ultimate financial secret recipe is this: start early, stay consistent, and let those dividends do their magic while you binge-watch your favourite shows.

Investing early also reduces financial stress. It's like walking into an IKEA showroom with everything perfectly in its place—pure bliss. When you've started early, you can afford to take calculated risks because time is on your side. Young Joe used to procrastinate, delegating household chores instead of making early investments—but I've learned that the earlier you start, the less you worry about market fluctuations over the years. If only our relationships had that kind of confidence! You could weather arguments over missing socks, perfectly knowing your bond would ultimately weather through.

Now, let's chat real talk. There's this undeniable thrill that comes from seeing your investments grow. It's like receiving random texts from family members reminding you to eat healthy—the urgency! The beeping notifications of my investment app made me feel like a stock market tycoon or the hero in a superhero movie (maybe a less polished version of Iron Man). Seeing your money multiply is downright addictive! And if you can start with just a small amount—maybe even a nice trip to your local market instead of splurging on internet wealth can grow like that mango tree!

In a nutshell, investing early is crucial for long-term financial health. It's about creating a future where your dreams aren't limited to bottomless coffee cups or family debates over whether to vacation in Africa or Australia. Every dime saved, every dollar invested, is a step toward that mango tree of your own—one you can pass along to your kids, or at least ensure you have a buffet of mangoes to accompany your brunch plans. So, my friends, let go of that fear, grab some resources, find the right investments, and start sowing those seeds today. In the world of finance, the real magic happens for those who embrace the present with tomorrow's goals in mind

Identifying Opportunities in Everyday Life

When it comes to spotting opportunities, I like to think of myself as a treasure hunter—not the pirate kind, but the savvy type with a worn-out notepad and an insatiable curiosity. In my humble journey from the dusty roads of Nimba County to the bustling urban streets of Australia, I've discovered that opportunities can hide in plain sight—like that one piece of laundry that refuses to leave the laundry basket, no matter how many times you wash it!

Let me tell you, opportunities are everywhere! Sometimes, you just have to look hard enough to spot them—like trying to find the mixtape of my Alfred that somehow went "missing" after the last family function.

Whether you're strolling through the market, snacking on grilled plantains, or waiting for your bus, everyday life is a gold mine of possibilities! You just have to train your eyes to recognize them. I mean, after all, the best investment advice is the one you get while standing in line for your morning coffee, right? (Or at least that's what I tell myself to justify my caffeine addiction.)

One of my favourite ways to identify these gems is by keeping my senses wide open—much like how I am at family gatherings, trying to avoid being the primary target of my Helen's questions about when I'll finally settle down. You know that awkward silence that fills the room after you say "I'm dating my career"? That's actually an opportunity in disguise! Instead of giving in to societal pressure about marriage or work trajectories, I found ways to leverage that moment to explore side hustles, honing or perhaps buffing up my kidney bean recipe for the next Liberian feast competition!

In daily interactions, ask questions, engage, and listen intently. You never know when the person next to you at the bus stop might reveal the secret to a thriving business, or at least a witty joke that makes the commute more enjoyable. While I was pondering whether I should invest my spare change into a new video game or stocks, I had a chat with a gentleman who turned his hobbies into a full-time gig! He went from being "that dude with the bonsai tree" to a local legend selling them for a pretty penny. Bonsais! My friends, who knew such adorable plants could turn into dollar bills? There lies the beauty in recognizing

Recognising the needs of others is key. People crave unique experiences or products, and you can be the one to provide them. Even the mundane can spark ideas. Think about your last grocery shopping experience. You know how every item in the supermarket has a price? Well, there's a classic entrepreneurial rule that says, "Find a cheaper way to deliver value, and you've got a business." I mean, isn't someone destined to create the ultimate "discount shopping app that alerts you to the best prices on your favourite snacks? Imagine sharing that find with friends while discussing the latest gossip—making savings and connections simultaneously! Talk about hitting two birds with one stone, only more ethically and without the Yoko Ono-inspired protests. Then there's the importance of embracing innovation with a twist of creativity! Have you ever considered becoming a "problem solver"? Each day presents challenges that need fixing, whether it's creating an easy meal prep subscription service for busy families or proposing a plan for the best Local trash collection to handle those errant potato chips that fall beneath the couch that no one dares to retrieve. Embracing this role can inspire Lovely new opportunities that turn everyday annoyances into thriving ventures!

In my quest for opportunities, I also learned to take the less traditional routes to scout those hidden gems. Perhaps hosting an open-mic night in your backyard featuring select cousins with questionable musical talents is a way to gather money for worthy causes. Not only do you inspire your community, but you also open doors by marketing yourself to potential investors who might stop by for a slice of your famous avocado toast. On the surface it may seem absurd, but who knows what a simple gathering of like-minded folks can inspire?

So, my fellow aspirational millionaires, let us remember to see everyday experiences as opportunities waiting to be seized. Life is a continual classroom filled with spontaneous lessons, from grocery shopping to those awkward family dinners, and each moment holds the potential for brilliance. With sharp eyes and open hearts, we can transform our mundane routines into thrilling financial adventures that rival the treasure hunts of our youth. Happy searching, and may your opportunities be ever plentiful.

The Art of Budgeting: Keeping Your Eyes on the Prize

Budgeting. The noble art of tracking your finances like a hawk soaring above the lush, green plains of opportunity, or perhaps more like an old aunt persistently searching for the last piece of okra at family dinners. Some folks see budgeting as a tedious chore, dragging those coffee-stained spreadsheets around like an anchor weighing down their dreams. But let me tell you, my friends, mastering the art of budgeting is your ticket to financial freedom. It is like getting the golden ticket to Willy

Wonka's chocolate factory, except instead of Oompa Loompas, you will meet wealth in its various delicious forms.

The fundamental truth about budgeting is that it gives you control. It allows you to rise above the chaos of everyday life, like Johnny Bravo trying to find his hair gel. When you create a budget, you establish a clear pathway to your financial goals. And let me tell you, without a budget, it is like descending into a chaotic disco party where no one knows the dance steps. Everyone gets lost in their spending, and nobody clearly remembers who paid for that last round of drinks (or more likely, the last round of overpriced guacamole).

So, how do you get started on this wonderful budgeting journey? Well, it all begins with the classic "Know Thyself" mantra. Understand your spending habits. Take a hard look at how you allocate your resources. List out your fixed expenses, such as rent, groceries and Hunter's weekly dose of video games, and those pesky variable expenses that seem to appear out of nowhere, like someone deciding they want to treat you to a spontaneous pyjama party. Trust me, while pyjama parties are fun, they should not come at the expense of your rent money.

Once you have outlined your expenses, it is crucial to set realistic goals. Think of them as your financial GPS, guiding you toward your destination, whether that is a dream vacation to the beaches of Australia or that shiny new car that will make driving home a little more enjoyable. Remember, having eyes on the prize means knowing what you are aiming for. The last thing you want is for your budgeting journey to be sidelined by an unexpected impulse buy, like those inflatable flamingo floats that seem cute until you realise they dominate your backyard.

With well-defined goals in place, it is time to take a look at your earnings, that sweet pay cheque that drops into your account. Create a plan that includes savings, bills, entertainment and, of course, the indulgences we cannot resist. After all, for me it is all about finding balance, a little fun mixed with some financial strategy. Allocate portions of your hard-earned money toward savings, responsibility and essentials.

Think of budgeting like cooking your favourite stew. You need a hint of spice, a generous chunk of vegetables and some time to let everything simmer. Skimping on any of these may leave you with a disastrous concoction that ultimately leads you to regret your culinary choices.

As you begin to hone your budgeting skills, it is essential to keep a clear track of your progress. I suggest fiddling with budgeting apps or simple spreadsheets. It is your classic game of "See Who Can Save the Most". But a fair warning, the Achilles' heel of many budgets lies in those unplanned expenses that crop up when we least expect them, like that rogue family member who suddenly shows up for dinner uninvited. Do not let those random surprises derail your budgeting efforts. Instead, build a little wiggle room, a cushion for those unexpected visits or late-night cravings for extra cookies.

The secret sauce to successful budgeting is flexibility. Famously known as the "waterbed approach", allow your budget to flow and adapt based on circumstances. Sometimes life throws you a curveball, much like how Rebecca, one of my sisters, almost took out the fence with her driving skills. You need to adjust your budget accordingly. If it means cutting back on that expensive lunch for a week or two, then so be it. You will thank yourself later when the fruit of your labour appears as the luxurious life you have envisioned.

And finally, I cannot stress this enough: keep your eyes on the prize. Your budget is a tool designed to steer you toward your dreams. Celebrate small victories along the way, whether saving up for that new gadget you have been eyeing or enjoying a night out guilt-free after hitting your savings goal. With a little dedication and a dollop of discipline, you will tune into the harmonious rhythm of budgeting in no time. Before you know it, the art of budgeting will become instinctive, guiding you toward the wealth and happiness you deserve. Now go out there, my budgeting warriors, and conquer your financial universe.

Creative Ways to Save Money

Saving money, the art so rarely mastered, kind of like trying to find a decent parking spot in the city or keeping plants alive in your home. Many people assume saving is a dull endeavour, rife with coupon clipping and calculator-use-induced migraines. But, dear friends, let me assure you that saving money can be a riot, filled with creativity and laughter if you choose to approach it that way. Picture it as a scavenger hunt, with hidden treasures waiting to be found behind every corner. So, grab your imaginary binoculars and let us dive into some creative ways to save money while keeping the fun meter soaring.

First up on our money-saving adventure is the fabulous world of meal prepping. Now, I know what you might be thinking: "Joe, meal prepping sounds as exciting as watching paint dry." But hear me out. When you take the time to plan your meals for the week, you not only save money by avoiding those overpriced takeaway lunches, but you also get more chances to channel your inner culinary genius. Trust me, nothing says "financial wisdom" like showing off your week's stash of colourful containers filled with deliciousness that even Gordon Ramsay would be proud of, perhaps minus the swearing.

Next, why not tap into your artistic side? By that I do not mean sketching portraits to hang in the Louvre, but rather turning your home into a sanctuary of upcycle art. Have an old ladder collecting dust in the garage? Put it to use as a stylish bookshelf instead of letting it gather cobwebs. You will save a few dollars on furniture while impressing friends with your newfound boho chic vibe. What a win-win. Similarly, old T-shirts can be transformed into reusable shopping bags or, if you are gifted enough, fashionable outfits that will elicit jealousy from everyone at the family picnic. Who knew being frugal could make you the talk of the town?

Next, let us explore the world outside our doors, nature's bounteous buffet. Being outdoorsy does not just provide thrilling adventures; it is also an excellent chance to save on groceries with foraging. Now, let us be clear, we are not talking about diving into someone's backyard and plundering their tomatoes like an overly ambitious raccoon. Instead, we can gather seasonal fruits and vegetables, with permission of course, from local parks, friends with gardens or farmers' markets. Rock those local produce stands like you are on a mission to command the food pyramid. Not only will it be fresher and probably tastier, but it will also add impressive nutritional value to your meals without emptying your wallet. May your smoothie game remain strong and bursting with flavour.

Having fun does not always mean you have to spend loads of cash. I have learned that hosting game nights can breathe some excitement into your life. Since your last epic family battle, these nights can turn into priceless memories. Who needs pricey entertainment when a simple round of charades can lead to uncontrollable laughter and wildly exaggerated impressions like sister Helen's legendary chicken curry? It is all about finding joy without tossing cash into a black hole.

Now, let us rewind to the beauty of technology, specifically budgeting apps and cashback rewards. This is not just for finance gurus. Many apps let you track your spending, and some even give you cashback on purchases made with participating retailers. Picture yourself going through life effortlessly racking up cashback on your essential groceries, only to find yourself treating friends with your newfound savings. Whether you have a deck of cards or a dusty board game gathering wealth, you can play the hero in their life: yes, I shall treat you to a round of fruit, courtesy of my savvy savings.

Ah, and let's not forget one of my absolute favourites: DIY gifts! Handmade gifts can save you a fortune while showing that you genuinely care. Create personalised photo albums stuffed with memories, or bake delicious treats wrapped in recycled packaging that may or may not include questionable doodles. Inevitably, you may find that people appreciate the effort behind the gift more than another bland store-bought candle that might go unappreciated. Trust me, we all know that "burnt" scent isn't worth it.

In the end, creativity unlocks a treasure chest of possibilities for saving money without sacrificing fun. From meal prepping to romantic evenings over board games, you can save a boatload without feeling the pinch. The beauty of it all lies in how resourceful you can become while keeping your sense of humour intact. So go on, embark on your money-saving adventure, and embrace creative ways to stock up your savings while crafting joyful memories along the way. Every dime saved is a step closer to that million-dollar dream, and I say, bring it on!

Building a mindset for wealth accumulation is a bit like preparing a feast for a family gathering. There's a recipe, a sprinkle of creativity and that essential dash of determination that keeps you coming back for seconds. When I first arrived in Australia from Liberia, I quickly realised that accumulating wealth wasn't just about saving coins and waiting for them to magically multiply. No, my friends, it was about cultivating a solid mindset that could weather any financial storm, much like how my late friend Rufus would confidently handle those unpredictable tropical rain showers, never missing a beat and wading through puddles like a boss.

First off, let's get a handle on what it means to have a wealth mindset. I remember my younger self frantically counting every penny like it was a lottery ticket, convinced that one day I'd hit the jackpot just in time for the world's best sale. But wishing for wealth won't get you far on this journey. Instead, we need to adopt a proactive approach, understanding that building wealth is a marathon, not a sprint. Rather than fixating on the dollar signs, start focusing on the opportunities that each day brings. This kind of mindset shift can be a game-changer, just like how Oretha disregards the old saying "slow and steady wins the race", opting instead for rapid-fire attempts to finish in record time. Sometimes you just need to embrace spontaneity.

Now let's talk about the infamous abundance mentality. You see, it's all about believing that there's plenty of wealth to go around. This perspective can feel like lifting a burden off your shoulders. For years, I wrestled with a scarcity mindset, convinced that money was like the last piece of pie at dinner, and there just wouldn't be enough for me. But once I started operating from an abundance mentality, it became easier to spot opportunities. I enjoyed life's little deals, whether it was snagging a quirky second-hand book at a thrift store or discovering an unexpected sale on mangoes that sent shivers down my spine. Old worries quickly vanished. After all, if there's one thing I learned from communal meals in Liberia, it's that no one leaves the table hungry if they eat with open hearts and a little creativity in crafting those family recipes.

Speaking of recipes, let's dive into the ingredients for the wealth mindset medley. The first must-have is a touch of long-term thinking. Remember that every small decision you make today adds to your financial future, like those tiny sprouts of my avocado plants that I nurtured until they outgrew their pots. Consider how compound interest works; the earlier you invest, the more your wealth expands. It's as if you plant a seed and wake up to find a little avocado tree doing the cha-cha in your backyard. This leads to the veritable grocery shopping experience with endless possibilities. While many people are tempted to splurge on their desires today, remember to set aside that little nugget for tomorrow. Even my cousin Alfred, who couldn't resist indulging in mind-boggling knick-knacks at thrift shops, eventually learned there's more joy in envisioning future wealth when you resist temptation in the moment.

But what about action? Taking action is your secret weapon. Part of building a wealth mindset means embracing discomfort and kicking procrastination to the curb. It's like trying to convince Oretha that staying up until dawn binge-watching shows on Netflix might not be the best use of his time. Taking action means tackling tiny goals first, like setting up an emergency fund or practising thrift shopping instead of aimless spending. Through these gradual accomplishments, the confidence to take bolder leaps begins to take root.

Now don't forget the delightful power of gratitude. You might wonder how gratitude fits into the wealth mindset equation, but trust me, it's the secret ingredient that turns ordinary into extraordinary. When you adopt a grateful attitude, you begin to see the abundance all around you, appreciating the hard work that brought you to your current financial state and celebrating the efforts of those along the way. I often thank the diligent folks who tend to local markets for their fresh produce, ensuring I have delicious meals and invigorating entertainment during my culinary experiments. Gratitude turns what we have into enough, strengthening our mental resilience and fuelling our momentum.

In conclusion, building a wealth mindset opens up a realm of opportunities that can enrich your life and prepare you to accumulate wealth effectively. With a sprinkle of long-term vision, a dash of abundance, a commitment to action and a generous serving of gratitude, you will find yourself well on your way to carving out a bright and beautiful future. So, dear reader, embrace the journey and remember: the feast is waiting, and it is yours for the taking. As long as you approach wealth with determination, creativity and an attitude as refreshing as a mango on a hot day, you will find that the treasure you seek is well within your grasp.

Chapter 4:
Lessons from My Family

The Wisdom of Family: A Legacy of Hard Work

Growing up in Nimba County, Liberia, family was not just an essential part of life; it was the whole enchilada, the taco supreme, if you get my drift. My family lives by the motto, "Work hard, play harder," which was often followed by the universal truth that sweat is the perfume of success. Coming from a lineage of hustlers, yes, I'm talking about the kind that can turn palm oil into profit while simultaneously cooking a feast fit for a chief, I learned at a very young age that hard work was non-negotiable.

My father, the late Saye Luck Komandan, was a remarkable man and my first inspiration. He had a peculiar wisdom that could make even the most mundane tasks sound profound. One day, while digging in the backyard to plant cassava, he said, "Son, the deeper the hole, the bigger the harvest." Now, I was but a child and rather sceptical. I was convinced that I'd rather dig a shorter hole and hop off to the river to catch fish. But lo and behold, years later, I understood the profound significance behind his metaphor about digging deep. It was about investing time and effort for long-term gain, kind of like trying to save instead of blowing your pocket change on hot pepper soup, which, I must admit, is sometimes worth the splurge.

Then there's my mother, the unwavering Ma Zogbelee Saye Vaye, known in the neighbourhood as "Ma Lainkpor." There's a special power to a mother's love, especially when it comes with a wooden spoon and a stern gaze that could make even a mischievous monkey reconsider its choices. My mother could invoke a hunger-induced miracle, transforming leftovers into gourmet dishes. Her hard work in the kitchen was not just about food; it was a lesson in persistence. "Own-dad" (meaning my father), she would say, "if you want to eat well, you have to cook well."

So naturally, family gatherings were less about kinship and more like a competition to see who could wolf down dinner the fastest while still bidding for the biggest piece of palm butter chicken. I can still hear the roars of laughter and the wisecracks flung around like old rubber bands, echoing the sentiments of our childhood: laughter is as much a part of labour as the sweat pouring down your brow.

Alongside my parents, my siblings were like the cheering squad and mischievous sidekicks wrapped in one. Alfred and Rebecca not only made great gaming partners, think playing football with a raggedy ball made of discarded plastic bags, but they also taught me the art of teamwork. We spent so many hours launching into what we thought were high-stakes competitions, ranging from who could sell the mat (don't tell Ma) to who could persuade our neighbours to donate food for "our business venture." Spoiler alert: it mostly ended up as a way to get snacks without spending our allowance. Ah, the wisdom of the streets!

You see, family gatherings weren't confined to the household. The Saye Komandan family turned the entire neighbourhood into our playground. One pivotal lesson learned was how to negotiate. My uncle, Mr Joseph Tokpah, if you caught him in the right mood, which is to say if he wasn't napping, was a master of persuasion. Armed with charm and sometimes a strong preference for jollof rice, his words danced through the air, convincing anyone that buying his homemade produce was like investing in a goldmine, even if the only mining was getting out of the kitchen to watch a football match.

In these moments, I began to weave my tapestry of life, learning that every family interaction, every bit of labour, every laughter shared through hot and sweaty days was a stitch in my journey towards prosperity. It's the bedrock of my past and the scaffolding for my future dreams. And believe me, if I could somehow convoy that energy into a money-making scheme, like a "Saye Komandan Work Hard, Laugh Harder" seminar, I might finally figure out this millionaire game!

The wisdom of family, wrapped in hard work and humour, continues to be the guiding compass for navigating life's overwhelming seas. So perhaps the biggest lesson they've imparted to me is not just about rolling up your sleeves for the job but also about rolling with laughter when things don't go as planned. Because in the end, if you can't laugh at yourself, you might just be stuck digging that same hole for a lot longer than needed.

Lessons from My Parents: Sacrifice and Perseverance

If there's one thing I learned from my parents, those modest titans of toil, it's that sacrifice and perseverance are the secret sauces in the recipe for success. My mother, who is now 101 years old, and my late father, Saye Luck Komandan, epitomised what it meant to put in the grind for a better future. Their lives weren't just stories of struggle; they were epic sagas seasoned with lessons that I, often rather humourously, interpreted through the lens of my youthful ignorance.

Picture this: my father, a man known for his impressive moustache that could rival even the finest of horses, didn't just have that charm about him; he was the king of compromises. Though he had ambitions of being Liberia's next great entrepreneur, maybe even starting a company that sold palm-oil-infused cologne, he often found himself in the neighbouring villages sourcing ingredients for the local market. It wasn't glamorous, and trust me, those trips often involved dodging more mosquitoes than money, but he embraced the grind with a smile, as if each mile walked was a step closer to wealth, or at least to a well-deserved meal.

Now, let's talk about my mother, who I like to think could single-handedly fuel an entire army with her cooking skills. My mother is no stranger to sacrifice. She worked day and night, pouring every ounce of energy into nurturing not only our physical well-being but also our spirits. There were times when we had too little food, but you wouldn't hear complaints from her. Instead, the kitchen would be filled with the aromas of creative recipes worthy of a Michelin star. "Own-dad", she would say, wielding a sweet potato like it was a baton of encouragement, "you can make a feast from the tiniest of ingredients if you have the heart." And lo and behold, that heart, and those sweet potatoes, really did produce culinary miracles.

You know, it's easy to take these lessons in sacrifice for granted, especially during those days when I was convinced my path to becoming a millionaire was through winning the next village-wide chicken race. But looking back, those daily displays of perseverance offered me a treasure trove of insight. My parents taught me that success often comes wrapped in a bundle of hard choices, like giving up a night of chatting with my friends to finish my homework. Only in adulthood do you find that those minutes add up to considerable returns, unlike that fleeting laughter shared with buddies over an endless bowl of jollof rice.

Then there was that infamous day when the rains came pouring down and flooded our tiny village. Instead of cocooning themselves in a storm of worry, my parents charged forth like warrior poets, rolling up their sleeves to help their neighbours. "We can't let the rain drown out our spirits," my dad declared, an apparent contradiction to the river cascading down the street. They taught me that in the face of adversity, when everyone else might be hiding under tables, it's essential to stand tall, even if all you have is a flimsy umbrella that looks more like a broken leaf than adequate shelter.

In some wild moments, I marvelled at how my parents managed to balance the seemingly absurd chaos around them. Between their duties as parents caring for nine children, working and participating in the local gossip mill, they somehow made it work. They showed me that sacrifice isn't merely about hardship; it's about harnessing those experiences to uplift everyone involved. If two people can turn a single bucket of cassava into a family feast, imagine what happens when a community unites, like a formidable business coalition fuelled by common goals.

So, as I tackle my goals, often with more laughter than seriousness, I carry the legacy of their perseverance with me. Each time I face setbacks or when my plans go askew, like when my "brilliant" idea for a banana stand was met with more banana peels than buyers, I hear my parents' voices resonating in my mind. They're reminders that, just like the sweetness of ripe bananas, success might take a little time to ripen, but while waiting, it's perfectly okay to make merry and laugh at life's absurdities.

Sacrifice and perseverance are potent allies on the journey towards wealth. Still, it's also about finding joy in the sweat, sharing a laugh amidst the chaos and embracing the absurdities of life with an open heart. After all, success is much sweeter when you can chuckle at the hard work that led you there.

Siblings' Support: The Power of Unity

Growing up in the bustling household of the Saye Komandan family, I learned early on that the bond between siblings was as vital as the palm tree to the village economy. With my siblings, William, Helena, Alfred, Rebecca, Oretha, Eric, Irine and Everlyn, by my side, we forged an unbreakable alliance that paralleled the fierce loyalty of a pack of hungry hyenas. Sure, we might have bickered, argued and staged dramatic reenactments of various soap operas during our time together, but we also shared laughter, support and countless adventures that turned our humble upbringing into a real-life sitcom full of unpredictable plot twists.

For us, life was a competition. Any mundane task quickly morphed into a sibling showdown. The moment we were tasked with washing dishes, a Herculean struggle would ensue, bubbles flying faster than our bargaining skills when it came to "who gets the biggest piece of fish at dinner." I distinctly remember one epic dishwashing duel where Rebecca, armed with her trusty sponge, claimed that she had surpassed the limits of human capability. "Look! I can wash more dishes in a minute than you can comprehend!" she boasted, while Alfred frantically swung the water hose around like he was leading a water ballet. It might have seemed like chaos to outsiders, but underneath it all, that spirited rivalry forged not just fun but deep bonds of unity.

We learned early that unity was a powerful force. Yes, there were days when I felt that my siblings were deliberately plotting to foil my plans, like that time I convinced them that we'd become millionaires selling palm oil, only to have them lick it and sing off-key songs that would make even the animals cringe. Yet, in the face of adversity, we stood shoulder to shoulder. When it was time to tackle the tough challenges life threw our way, we became like a delicious Liberian cassava pie, tightly packed and perfectly combined.

Now, let's talk about the awkward family photo sessions, because nothing screams "bonding experience" quite like attempting to fit nine children into one frame without uproarious laughter and someone falling into the mud. Oh, you better believe that our brightest smiles were flanked by some questionable poses that could end up in a comedy hall of fame. But those moments, filled with our collective foolery, taught me the value of laughter in unity. When one of us fell flat on our back trying to strike the perfect pose, it was a wave of collective giggles that would both rally and rejuvenate us.

As we aged, those silly moments transformed into a strong sense of responsibility among us. From trading notes during school exams (hey, it's called teamwork!) to brainstorming innovative ideas for funding that ended with more laughter than cash, we were driven by a collective ambition. I recall one brainstorming session where we founded the "Saye Komandan Young Entrepreneurs Club", which underscored our ambition to start our paltry versions of businesses with ideas ranging from selling handcrafted necklaces made from coloured beads to hosting overpriced storytelling sessions featuring the "legendary Nyan-quoi-Ceegbay", our wise stepfather.

Despite the ineptitude of our business ventures, having that sibling support system made everything more bearable and even enjoyable. Our countless brainstorms were peppered with inside jokes and conspiratorial laughter. Those gatherings transformed into scenes where we could imagine ourselves as powerful moguls, with the younger siblings claiming they would one day own entire supermarket chains, and me flip-flopping between my aspirations of being a wealthy author, interpreter and chef. As we nurtured those dreams, we reminded each other that every incredible journey began with bizarre, albeit humorous, ideas.

Now, here I stand, thousands of miles away from Nimba County, reflecting on those memories of insight and hilarity. Every ounce of success I have achieved is interlaced with the threads of sibling support. Those chaotic family dinners where we argued about who would clear the table, while also training for imaginary Olympic events, laid a foundation for courage and resilience. So, as I carry this philosophy into my current gigs, both as a clinical nurse and aspiring author, I celebrate the power of unity.

As I pen this tantalising journey toward my millionaire dreams, I can still hear echoes of my siblings' laughter, reminding me that the road is better travelled together. And as I like to say jokingly, when one sibling lacks motivation, the others pull together like a troupe of clumsy acrobats, helping each other perform and swing through the messy circus we call life. Now, how's that for sibling power?

Tradition and Values: Shaping My Entrepreneurial Spirit

In the rich tapestry of my upbringing in Nimba County, Liberia, tradition and values played an invaluable role in shaping my entrepreneurial spirit, a sort of mystical potion concocted by the ancient recipes of my ancestors and the whims of comically absurd family quirks. You see, I grew up steeped in the vibrant traditions of the Mano tribe, where I often felt that every lesson was accompanied by a drumbeat and a good dose of laughter. It's fascinating to think about how the wisdom of tradition intertwines with that familiar challenge of "let's see if this doesn't make you run faster than a goat!"

My parents, like diligent guides, introduced me to the time-honoured principles of hard work, integrity and community consciousness. I can still recall my father's laborious tales under the flickering oil lamp, recounting how our ancestors made a living through their resourcefulness. "Son," he would say, plucking a mango from our tree as if it were a gleaming golden coin, "it doesn't matter how many suckers you meet in the market; what truly counts is turning that mango into something more than a snack." Sprung from these archival wisdom nuggets was the understanding that anything could become profitable given a dash of creativity, a hint of risk and a bag full of guts.

With such traditions at play, my siblings and I partook in a perfectly choreographed festival of responsibilities within the household. By day, we were the cutest little labourers this side of the river, grinding cassava and collecting firewood, inevitably igniting yet another sibling rivalry. However, the real excitement happened every Saturday when we took that labour and transformed it into a full-blown entrepreneurial expedition. Armed with a steaming pot of palm oil soup, we would enthusiastically set up our makeshift market stand. Picture this: seven underage entrepreneurs hustling as if we held the winning lottery ticket to riches, all while shouting "Palm oil soup! Get your palm oil soup!" like a chorus in a peculiar play.

In hindsight, this wasn't merely about peddling soup. It was a crash course in tapping into the power of community. We had our loyal customer base, mostly friends and relatives who likely bought our "delicious" concoctions out of pity more than anything else. But we learned the importance of building strong relationships in business: knowing your clientele's tastes, adapting to feedback (also known as the polite "this is not my favourite, but thank you"), and networking, because if there was ever a family function, this was a ready-made market for next week's profit review.

Moreover, the values centred around hospitality loomed large in our family ethos. Our home was an open door for all, creating an innate understanding that in our culture, your best assets, whether in business or life, were the relationships you cultivated. I fondly recall the days when everyone in the village would gather for feasts under the stars. While traditional recipes simmered in pots, the aroma of community and laughter wafted through the air, planting a seed in my entrepreneurial spirit. After all, who wouldn't want to monetise those gatherings? Ah, if only I had thought of opening a restaurant back then, maybe I'd be serving palms in my cathedral of culinary wonders!

As I made my way to Australia in search of greener pastures (and perhaps a better Wi-Fi signal), I began to see how these traditions and values translated into new opportunities. Adapting to life down under wasn't without its challenges, like mastering the fine art of understanding the many ways "how's it going, mate?" can be used. However, my roots anchored me, reminding me that resourcefulness, community focus and the underlying theme of laughter were universally understood languages.

In this journey, I learned that heritage isn't just about dusting off old family tales. It's a legacy that fuels the future. Today, when I think about starting my ventures, I hear echoes of my ancestors reminding me to adapt while remaining steadfast to my roots. Those tales of soup stands have morphed into a different market entirely. Still, the underlying values remain, a recipe for success that includes the simple truth that building a business is as much about delighting the heart as it is about filling wallets.

So here I am, navigating the entrepreneurial waters with the buoyant spirit of tradition as my lifebuoy. And as I continue to find ways to turn pocket change into profit, whether through online platforms or brainstorming sessions with friends, you can bet your last meal that I'll be doing it with a hearty laugh and the unwavering influence of my family's legacy swirling around me. Tradition and values, like an intricately woven basket, shape the fabric of my journey and will carry me through the winds of entrepreneurship better than any tutorial on Google.

As I sit here reflecting on the whirlwind of my life and the legacy that my family instilled in me, I can't help but feel the weight, yet also the joy, of responsibility to keep our family's story alive. My parents, with their roots profoundly embedded in the rich soil of Nimba County, taught me that an enduring legacy isn't just about holding on to the past. It's about nourishing future generations with tales, experiences and the lessons learned from the unending dance of life. After all, if we aren't passing down a bit of wisdom and a ton of laughter along the way, then what are we even doing here?

Growing up, I never imagined that the colourful anecdotes spun by my father and the values imparted by my mother would lead to what I can affectionately call my life's mission, which is to inspire future generations. It's a funny thing, really. As kids, we often roll our eyes at our parents' seemingly cliché sayings, like "hard work pays off", while simultaneously plotting how to navigate our next grand adventure. But oh, the irony. Now, those same sayings echo in my ears, nudging me to impart what I can to the younger generation, and while I hope they grasp the gravity of my stories, I now see it isn't just about the serious stuff. It's also about keeping the laughter alive.

Imagine a circle of giggling youngsters gathered around me as I regale them with tales from our family history, stories that are equal parts absurdity and truth, like that time someone claimed he could outrun a windmill during a storm. I see their eyes light up as I weave in the ridiculousness, enriching the lessons with levity. It's in those moments that I realise tradition isn't dusty relics from the past. It's a living, breathing entity that thrives on being shared with gusto. And when they laugh, when they embrace the hilarity of our family's quirks, it's like igniting the spark of curiosity and resilience in their hearts.

I have come to appreciate that the act of storytelling is much like planting seeds that may one day flourish into a vibrant garden of knowledge. Think of it this way: every tale shared, from the grandeur of fishing mishaps to the courage of my ancestors, becomes a stepping stone for the next generation. They grow inspired by the perseverance and the laughter-filled bravery my family has always shown.

However, keeping a legacy alive is not just about tucking stories away in comfortable corners of the heart. There is a deliberately playful angle to it as well. Much of what we inherited cannot simply sit on a shelf gathering dust. I believe in involving children in activities that spark creativity and resourcefulness, qualities that run strongly through our family. As they learn and mature, the threads of our legacy are woven even tighter. This is where the real joy lies, watching them adapt, experiment and rise to challenges with the same spirit of thinking outside the proverbial palm oil box. Host workshops, adventures and even cooking sessions, because if any family can squeeze wisdom out of a bowl of cassava, it is us. I am convinced that when children experience something dynamic and fun, they are far more likely to take in the heart of what we are teaching.

As I move through both clinical nursing and writing, I often meet remarkable young minds eager to connect with their cultural heritage. So I take it upon myself to lead with intention, weaving our family's hardworking energy into many community projects. Whether I am running a sustainable farming workshop or working with local mentors to support young entrepreneurs, I hope our story spills over into the lives of others. It is about fostering a collaborative ecosystem and showing them that entrepreneurship does not need to come from polished suits and boardrooms. Sometimes it is a creative journey born from laughter in a modest kitchen.

In embracing our family legacy, there is a lasting message that can echo for generations to come: success finds you when you combine effort, togetherness and a hearty sense of absurdity. It reminds me, and hopefully them, that while ambition can guide our direction, it is the shared laughter during challenges and mischief that truly binds the fabric of family and culture.

Ultimately, the lessons I hope to pass on are intertwined with humour that will ring through the laughter of children and inspire them to share their own stories while honouring the one they came from. And who knows, perhaps one day someone will tell a tale about a clumsily ambitious writer who taught kids through storytelling while trying not to spill the palm butter soup, a legacy well worth laughing about and carrying forward.

Chapter 5:
Embracing Change: My Move to Australia

The Decision to Move: A Leap of Faith

Making the decision to move was like choosing whether to leap off a diving board or tiptoe into a pool. I was standing on the edge, heart racing and all. There I was in Nimba County, Liberia, surrounded by the warmth of my family. The decision itself came with all the drama of a soap opera twist. One moment I was living comfortably enough, nibbling on GB, cassava and soup, and the next I found myself contemplating a fresh start Down Under. It was an exciting thought, but honestly, it felt like swapping my treasured palm wine for a foreign drink that looked suspiciously as if it came from cheerful kangaroos.

So why did I take this leap of faith? Naturally, bright dreams of being a millionaire swirled around in my imagination, wearing sharp suits, sipping tea like royalty and laughing at my own success story while wearing a shirt that boldly announced I Want to Be a Millionaire. The promise of opportunity was as intoxicating as the aroma of roasted cassava drifting through my mother's kitchen. As I pictured a life where I could turn loose coins into profit, the next logical step seemed to be exploring new horizons filled with kangaroos and koalas. Do not let their cuteness fool you though, there is mischief behind those fluffy ears.

Of course, the decision did not come without some comedic turmoil. Enter my family, a talented troupe of characters in my personal drama. My mother was certain that moving to Australia was a perfect recipe for disaster. She would look at me as though I had just announced that I planned to wrestle a lion. You want to go that far? Are you not worried you will forget how to cook? she would ask. Meanwhile, my late father, Mr Saye Luck Komandan, would probably be shaking his head from the other side, reminding me to stick to safer ventures like running a bar or starting a goat farming empire. Joe, goats will never leave you, I can almost hear him say.

Then there were my siblings, each with their own bold ambitions. William wanted to be a pastor, Alfred a teacher, Oretha dreamed of fame and Rebecca was plotting global dominance one sewing class at a time. With all that ambition bouncing around, I felt like a lone ship at sea with no map. It was a full circus. So I gathered my courage, filled my heart with hope and clicked confirm on that visa application with the precision of a tightrope walker juggling flaming torches. Saying goodbye was just as dramatic, with tears, laughter and reminders not to forget my roots echoing behind me as I headed towards potential million dollar opportunities.

Packing my bags became an adventure of its own, climbing over piles of clothes, sentimental treasures and a collection of self help books. My arrival at the airport felt less like a grand Hollywood moment and more like the opening scene of a comedy series. I could not decide which luggage to bring or whether I needed my lucky charm. Do they even have palm butter in Australia? Should I bring my own or prepare to make grapes and salami my new best friends?

With warm hugs, tearful farewells and half serious promises of regular calls, I finally boarded the plane. Flying over oceans and continents, excitement surged through me. This was more than a physical relocation, it was the beginning of a personal adventure where every mishap would become a lesson and each step would take me closer to my millionaire dream. Leaving Liberia behind meant saying goodbye to everything familiar, but it also meant stepping into the chaos that would shape my Australian journey. Little did I know that the kangaroos and I would become quick rivals, especially in our favourite game of Keep Joe's Lunch. Migration truly has its own comedy.

Cultural Shock: The Good, the Bad and the Hilarious

When I landed in Australia, I felt like a baby elephant taking its first steps, wobbly, excited and completely clueless about this strange new world. I stepped off the plane and onto terra firma, which seemed firm enough, but the entire experience felt like diving into a pool full of jellybeans. Ladies and gentlemen, welcome to culture shock. It is a curious blend of delight and confusion, where you feel both enchanted and bewildered all at once. It is like biting into something sweet only to realise it tastes like toothpaste.

Let us start with the positives. The scenery. Have you ever seen a place where the sky is bluer than a flashy parrot and the grass greener than an eager gardener's pride? I felt like I had injected joy straight into my veins the moment I saw the stunning beaches. I had only ever seen beaches in films and suddenly there I was, ready to play in sand as fine as powdered sugar. It took me a little while to learn proper beach etiquette though. Discovering that wearing sandals without socks was normal took a few very sunny hours. Who knew that socks could fry on hot sand like plantains on an iron pan?

Then came the food. Let me tell you now, I am a GB lover through and through. Shifting from a rich Liberian meal to unfamiliar Australian dishes was like trading a thick novel for a children's picture book. I walked into my first barbecue expecting grilled goat and cassava only to be greeted by kangaroo steaks and something called pavlova. I had come seeking culture and instead found pavlova staring at me like a sugar dusted alien. Where is the peanut butter for my GB soup? One unfortunate experiment with local cuisine resulted in a dish that could only be described as what is left in the fridge on a Tuesday.

Now let us turn to the awkward side of cultural shock, wrapped in a deliciously funny bow. My first day at the local grocery store was nothing short of a spectacle. There I was, holding two avocados and staring in utter confusion at the endless range of products. How many types of milk can exist? Almond, oat, soy, coconut. The mind truly boggles. I started to wonder if I had stumbled into a dairy paradise or some kind of alternate universe. And the checkout process? Oi vey. It felt like watching a slow motion sprint. Do you have a loyalty card? Would you like a bag for that? Pressing this, tapping that. All I wanted was my milk and a chance to escape from that cosmic supermarket labyrinth.

And how could I forget the moments that have permanently etched themselves into my memory as classic Joe moments? Picture this: my first encounter with the delightful Australian way of speaking, which I realised was less a language and more a verbal roller coaster. I confidently asked a shopkeeper if they had adamant apples, only to be met with a stare that suggested I was performing Shakespeare in a tutu. What I meant to say was apples, but after a jumble of words and nerves, all that came out sounded like a confused cry for help. Before long I learned that g'day mate and fair dinkum were staples, and I had better master them before being permanently labelled the tourist.

Navigating local customs became a hilarious adventure. On one outing, I mistakenly decided to sit on the grass, imagining it was a brilliant idea. The locals stared at me as if I had started an impromptu dance routine. What are you doing, mate? That is not how we do it here. Perhaps sitting like royalty on my family's land back home was a bit too informal for the lawn lovers of Australia. All these moments wove themselves into an unforgettable tapestry as I navigated unfamiliar cultural norms with equal parts laughter and confusion.

In the end, the whirlwind of cultural shock taught me more than any textbook ever could. It became a vibrant blend of the good, the bad and the hilariously unexpected. From beach mishaps to culinary surprises, I found the humour in each awkward step as I learned to embrace the unfamiliar. I may have left my palm wine behind, but I gained a treasure chest of stories and friendships, proving that humour truly is universal, even among kangaroos and kookaburras.

Finding Community in a Land Far Away

Finding community in a faraway place can feel like trying to fit a square peg into a round hole while riding a unicycle. It is a balancing act that is both exhilarating and utterly absurd. When I first landed in Australia, the thrill of new adventures buzzed in the air, but the ache of loneliness gnawed harder than a hungry kangaroo after a hidden stash. There I was, a Liberian wandering through a land of surfboards, didgeridoos and endless sunscreen. It felt like being an extra on the set of Survivor: Australia Edition.

My mission began with a marathon of Googling that led me to local cultural events. If you are going to learn how to fit in, you may as well do it surrounded by people who are just as quirky as you. Armed with a dash of confidence and questionable optimism, I attended my first gathering of fellow expats. My motto was simple. When life hands you lemons, find a lemon meringue pie recipe. Off I went, imagining an open hearted gathering filled with laughter and deep conversations. Spoiler alert, it was a bake sale.

The moment I arrived, I was met with a flood of warm smiles and a buffet that made me wonder if I had wandered into a five star restaurant. I stood there trying to blend in, nibbling my first Lamington, a sponge cake coated in chocolate and coconut. Tasty, yes, but my heart still longed for palm butter soup. I quickly befriended the woman beside me, who proudly claimed to make the best sausage rolls in town. Her name was Darlene and she became the Australian version of my mother, handing out advice and snacks with equal enthusiasm.

As the evening wore on, I realised I had not just made friends. I had accidentally volunteered to join a choir. Out of nowhere, someone announced they were looking for participants for the community choir. Fuelled by enthusiasm and a misplaced belief in my singing skills, I raised my hand like the keenest student in class. Can you carry a tune? they asked. I said, Well, I can carry a GB pot, so how hard can it be? Little did I know that my off key renditions of African folk songs would become my signature move. Before long they were calling me the Harmony Ambassador, which was generous, but I embraced it with pride.

In the days that followed, I gathered the courage to join groups tailored to expats, including the Adventurous Eatery Club. That was where I discovered that food truly is a universal language. More than once we tried to organise tasting nights that ended in chaotic cooking battles, lovingly testing each other's skills or lack of them. The spread included dishes labelled mystery meat and too spicy to function. There should have been a trophy for the best culinary disaster. My hanafuda inspired soup nearly sent my new friends into full Mayday mode.

Building friendships took time, of course. My many social blunders became a source of laughter. I tried dropping cultural references, only to learn that throwing shrimp on the barbie was just a saying. I thought it meant hosting a beach party filled with coconut palms and palm wine, only to discover it simply meant cooking on the barbecue. What is a barbie? I asked, much to everyone's delight. Soon they all accepted me as the joyfully naïve one, and they loved me for it.

Through these misadventures I discovered the heart of community, a beautifully messy mixture of cultures coming together. I somehow became Joe the Connector, a title I claimed with pride. Embracing and celebrating our differences became the threads that tied us together, woven through laughter, music and even the occasional culinary catastrophe.

Before long Australia felt like home. I rejoiced in the colourful patchwork of friendships that reminded me of the rich fabric of my roots in Liberia. In finding community so far away, I learned to let go of perfection, embrace the unexpected and appreciate the hilarious friendships that will stay with me for life. Here is to the joyful chaos of belonging in the land of kangaroos, because honestly, who would choose anything less than a hearty laugh while navigating this wonderful pandemonium called life?

Learning the Lingo: Lingual Laughs and Mishaps

Learning the lingo in Australia was like trying to untangle a giant ball of yarn while blindfolded, frustrating and hilarious all at once! I showed up to this enchanting land full of hope and dreams, armed only with my swagger but severely lacking a solid grasp of their distinctly Australian dialect. If I had a dollar for every time I heard a phrase that sounded like someone had just sneezed in the middle of a sentence, I could buy my own koala! Imagine my bewilderment when I first heard "arvo." We were sitting around sipping drinks, and someone said, "Let's meet this arvo." My first thought was, "Is this a new form of avocado? I didn't think we were that close yet!" I panicked for a solid minute, pondering whether I should be on the lookout for a new trend or consulting my avocados back home. It turns out arvo" was simply short for afternoon! Who knew the Aussies had a preference for syllable chopping like they were prepping for a cook-off? If efficiency was a dish, Australians served it with a side of "simplify the language!"

And my day-to-day interactions became this beautiful song of miscommunication. I remember vividly my attempt at ordering breakfast at a local cafe. With my stomach grumbling louder than a marching band,

I confidently approached the counter and said, "I'd like a bushy latte and a meat pie, please!" That subtle moment of triumph came crashing down. Then the cashier looked at me like I was reciting Shakespeare in Klingon. Turns out, I had muddled up "bushy" and "flat white", which, for the record, was crucial for my status as a coffee connoisseur! All I wanted was caffeine reinforcement, but instead, I might have triggered an existential crisis for the cashier.

Things only got better, or worse, when I had the courage to join a footy match with my new mates. Saying I was clueless was putting it mildly. It was like asking a fish to shoot hoops. The moment I turned up, they greeted me with a cheerful, "You alright, mate?" and I clearly caught the word "footy." A thousand thoughts started sprinting through my mind. Was it a foot race? Did I need to give foot massages? Was it soccer with an Australian twist? I replied casually, "I'm actually feeling more like a leg bloke today." My new friends burst out laughing, and I realised I had officially stepped into the strange and wonderful world of Australian sporting slang. Turns out footy was simply the local version of rugby. Who knew my calves would be aching after all those so-called footy magic moments?

Keeping up with their love of slang became a full-time job. Bogan, bloke, battler. The embarrassment I faced whenever a new word popped up left me blushing harder than a ripe tomato. During one conversation, people were chatting about their weekend plans. I jumped in enthusiastically with, "I, too, am a battler!" You could have heard a pin drop. I had never seen a group exchange looks that clearly said, "Does he think he's some kind of warrior?" A battler actually refers to someone who struggles along in a tough but often endearing way, while I ended up sounding like I was trying to build some heroic alter ego.

Then came the endless stream of one-liners, the famous Aussie-isms. Every time I learnt a new phrase like "Don't come the raw prawn with me" which basically means "don't try to pull a fast one on me" I felt like I had been handed a key to their secret comedy club. I merrily greeted people with "G'day!" like an overexcited kangaroo, only to learn that saying it in the wrong situation felt as out of place as shouting "Surprise!"

in a hospital ward. My heart nearly stopped when a friend affectionately called me "a bloody legend." I didn't realise it meant "you're fantastic." It sounded more like a colourful insult at first.

Eventually, I learnt to welcome the slip-ups, and they became my favourite tales to share. My mistakes helped dissolve any awkwardness around my arrival. The best thing was that Aussies adore a good laugh. Listening to them share their own language blunders made me feel like I belonged, even if it seemed like I had been tossed into a comedy sketch without warning.

By the end of it all, I became both the punchline and the one delivering it, forever known as "that guy" who tried to verbally tango with the locals. The laughter echoed through my bones, and slowly, learning Aussie slang became less about perfecting the language and more about joining a warm, wonderfully eccentric family. I stumbled often, but each mix-up helped me build friendships that felt like discovering hidden treasures, one G'day at a time. It has been a wild ride, and I wouldn't trade it for anything.

Lessons Learned: Adapting and Thriving

As the excitement settled from my hectic transition to Australia, I found myself reflecting on the many lessons life had thrown at me. They say life is a collection of experiences that shape who we are, and mine had grown into a vibrant patchwork of chaotic patterns and colourful misadventures that could make even a seasoned traveller laugh.

Adapting and thriving in this new world was not just about survival; it was about growth, and I was ready to embrace every bit of it.

One of the first lessons was the value of flexibility. Back home in Liberia, everything moved with a familiar rhythm, like a gentle breeze. Everyone knew the pace. But in Australia, chaos seemed to run the show. If flexibility were a dance move, I felt like I was attempting a moonwalk while balancing a pot on my head. Whether it was the traffic, the weather, or a pancake recipe that unexpectedly required a whole bottle of maple syrup instead of a drizzle, I discovered that adaptability was my closest ally. The moment I let go of the need for perfection, a wave of relief swept over me. It felt as though I had declared peace with the chaos, and suddenly, I found myself laughing at the absurdity of it all.

Take my experience in Australian workplaces, for instance. When I got my first job, I was eager to excel with a blend of charm and professionalism. Imagine my shock when I realised casual Fridays were a lifestyle, not a weekly treat. I walked into the office wearing business casual, only to find my colleagues comfortable in thongs, shorts and T-shirts covered in slogans like "Life's a beach." I became the office's accidental fashion icon, and it didn't take long to learn that embracing the laid-back Aussie attitude was essential for fitting in.

Then came the deeper lesson of vulnerability. Yes, vulnerability. Something I once thought suited only superheroes or dramatic soap operas. Moving to a new country stripped away every bit of pretence. I found myself constantly needing help or guidance. From figuring out how to fix my boiler which, by the way, ended in a spectacle worthy of a comedy show to openly admitting my confusion about Aussie slang during group outings, I realised there was real strength in acknowledging what we don't know. This vulnerability became a quiet superpower. It allowed me to connect more deeply with people, who were far more likely to share a laugh with me than judge my unfamiliarity with phrases like "fair dinkum."

As the weeks turned into months, I also learnt patience, the slow-cooked virtue that teaches you to wait your turn without complaining, even when the café staff decides to debate the origins of coffee while I'm standing there craving caffeine. Patience helped me form friendships while navigating the maze of misunderstandings and the occasional footy disaster. I came to see that thriving in a new environment is not just about adjusting to your surroundings but also about giving yourself room to grow. Each misstep became a stepping stone to understanding and acceptance, both of the culture and of myself.

A major lesson within this delightful chaos was discovering joy in simplicity. While I was busy chasing dreams of becoming a millionaire, I stumbled upon laughter, companionship and small, beautiful moments that settled into my heart like a perfectly placed bookmark in a beloved novel. I learnt to savour the flavour of friendships, the charm of flower stalls at local markets and the magic of impromptu beach gatherings. These simple interactions enriched my life far more than millions ever could.

In the end, I embraced the idea that being a work in progress is a beautiful thing. Triumph makes no sense without tales of the awkward moments that lead to it. Like the time I told a driver to "cut me off" when I meant to ask for directions. They looked at me as though I had come from another planet. Life, I realised, is not only about getting from point A to point B but also appreciating point Z, even if the journey takes you on a few unexpected detours.

So there I was, Joe Robert Saye Komandan, adapting and thriving in a foreign land with a heart full of funny stories, shock, laughter and precious memories. Embracing chaos and vulnerability made me richer than I ever imagined. In every struggle, I found joy, and in every hilarious mishap, I discovered the real essence of living. I may not have become a millionaire yet, but I've gathered a wealth of wisdom worth more than gold. Here's to thriving with a good laugh through the ups, the downs and everything in between.

Chapter 6:
Rufus and the Gift of Friendship

Reflecting on the Unforgettable Moments with my late friend, Rufus

Thinking back on the unforgettable moments with Rufus feels like flipping through a photo album filled with hiccups, laughter and the occasional facepalm. We were like peanut butter and jelly, a pair that seemed almost too good to be true. If you needed a mate to plan an over-the-top adventure in Nimba or come up with a strategy to convince our mothers that we were responsible adults, Rufus was definitely the man for the job. I still laugh at the time we tried to invent a "secret" handshake to impress some girls. It turned into something closer to a wrestling match, ending with Rufus tumbling into a ditch. The girls were not impressed, but I went home that day believing we were the coolest guys in the world, even if only in our own minds.

One unforgettable moment came during our silly attempts to start a small business selling whatever we could scavenge from the local market. Picture this: two young dreamers with dreams bigger than our wallets, trying to sell "vintage" flip-flops, mind you, they were someone's trash! As days passed, our grand idea caught attention like a chicken laying an egg in the middle of a bustling marketplace. We managed to roll in some customers, but they quickly fled once they realised that the flip-flops were fused with dirt and a few seed pods. Rufus and I just looked at each other, eyebrows raised in disbelief. We soon learned that just because something is "vintage" doesn't mean it's sellable. Still, every misstep was painted with laughter, and every failure resonated with the joyful spirit of our friendship.

Rufus's love of mischief ensured that my life, despite the seriousness of being a clinical nurse, was sprinkled with spontaneous adventures. I vividly remember the day we planned a "nature exploration" hike. I thought we were going on a serious quest, but with Rufus, things took an unusual turn. Instead of trekking through the scenic paths of the jungle, we ended up chasing after this goat, which incidentally wore a mischievous glint in its eyes. I questioned my sanity, two grown men chasing a goat, while Rufus laughed the entire time as if it was the most hilarious pursuit in world history. It felt as if the universe was orchestrating its comedic symphony at our expense. I had never been so elated, nor so confused, all at once!

One thing about Rufus was his unwavering belief in my dreams. He always said, "My man, you want to be a millionaire. Just remember to smile like you already are one." His words became a soundtrack to every wild idea I had, whether it was writing books or starting small ventures. Sometimes his support took interesting turns. I remember him encouraging me to sell my family recipes, including my mother's famous GB's soup. While the idea might have made money, his suggestion that we dress up in potato suits for marketing was far less appealing. The world was certainly not ready to see a group of Liberians promoting food while dressed as vegetables, but his enthusiasm was always heart-warming.

Losing Rufus felt like a sudden downpour, a storm that left puddles of grief along my path of self-discovery. Every shared laugh now carries a bittersweet note. It feels like coming home to a place that holds both comfort and an echo of absence. My mother once asked why I still didn't have a million-dollar idea. I realised then that every moment with Rufus was a reminder of how humour can transform ordinary experiences into stories worth sharing. I now seek inspiration in our memories, turning grief into motivation, exactly as he would have wanted. These days, I honour Rufus by living boldly, making people laugh and embracing every chance to carry his spirit forward.

What keeps me going is the thought of inspiring others through his legacy. I often share the stories of our peculiar adventures, turning them into lessons and laughter-filled anecdotes. Every little segment of his spirit can wow and uplift, ensuring his vibrant essence remains in our lives.

It seems I'm never short of quotes, often weaving them into my narrative: "If you want to chase goats and dreams, always take a buddy who's as juvenile as you!" And with every laugh I spread, I carry on as Rufus's sidekick in this great adventure called life, showcasing that although he may have left this world, the beautiful chaos of our friendship will forever echo in my heart and bring joy to every life I touch.

Lessons in Laughter: The Humour that Bonded Us:

Lessons in Laughter: The Humour that Bonded Us is one of the most joyful themes of my journey with Rufus. If laughter is the best medicine, then Rufus was my personal pharmacy, dispensing doses of hilarity strong enough to cure even the hardest days and lighten the heaviest grief.

One vivid memory that comes to mind involves a simple game of football that spiralled into what felt like an Olympic event. I still laugh when I think about the day we gathered on the local field, eager to show off our so-called skills. What should have been an exciting match turned into a scene straight out of a comedy show where the laws of physics seemed optional. Rufus found humour in everything, from someone's undone shoelaces to the dramatic dives people attempted while going for the ball. His exaggerated reactions to the ball were so theatrical that he could lay the foundation for a sketch!

That day, I ended up on the wrong side of a friendly match while trying to impress a group of girls. I spotted Rufus, my opponent, and instead of focusing on the game, I let my ego take over. I attempted an impressive backflip. Spoiler alert: gravity still existed. I landed flat on my back. Rufus erupted with laughter, saying it looked like a fish trying to do gymnastics. I lay there groaning dramatically, and instead of hiding in embarrassment, we both laughed until our stomachs hurt. Who knew a fall could create a bond stronger than steel?

Rufus had a unique ability to inject joy into every moment, even the unfortunate ones. He loved saying, "If you can't laugh at yourself, you might miss life's best punchlines." Those words became our guiding light, especially when life felt heavy. I still remember the day I accidentally walked into a fence after getting distracted by a buzzing hornet. Rufus turned it into an entire performance, dubbing me "the great entertainer" who could collide with anything for comic effect. Before long, we were reenacting the incident with ridiculous sound effects, leaving everyone around us in disbelief.

Humour, perhaps, was most critical during our attempts to tackle life's Best. As we both pursued our aspirations, such as my dream of becoming a published author and his pursuit of running for student (naturally, both of us going head-to-head), there were times we felt overwhelmed, burdened by the weight of expectations. But we quickly learned that laughter could be the remedy. One day, in the middle of an _intense study session, accompanied by heaps of anxiety and caffeine, Rufus devised a "sing-off" competition that turned dire studying sessions into uproarious events. Students would poke their heads through the door only to see us belting absurd tunes, one even punctuated by a dramatic duet about our deep misunderstandings of calculus. It was educational chaos wrapped in hilarity, and before we knew it, we had formed a whole crowd of onlookers who joined in the laughter.

Every inside joke became a brick in the foundation of our friendship, a lasting testament that endured over time, even when life threw us curveballs. Whenever I think back to Rufus and the laughter we shared, I realise that humour is not simply fleeting; it's an enduring gift that carries within it the lessons of resilience and friendship. Even in our darkest times, comedy became our saving grace, and every shared moment wove tighter threads of connection.

Now, whenever I reflect on our adventures, it is clear that laughter was the invisible glue that held our friendship together. After his passing, I made a promise to become a source of humour for others, ensuring his legacy continues. Sometimes I laugh so hard it feels like he is right beside me, nudging me to lighten up and keep going.

So, to all of you on this journey, take a page from our book: never underestimate the power of laughter, for it is among life's greatest treasures that can turn trials into triumphs and friendships into cherished legacies.

Rufus's Unwavering Support: A Cornerstone of My Journey

"Rufus's Unwavering Support: A Cornerstone of My Journey" sits deep in the story of my life, a heartfelt reminder of the extraordinary bond we shared, a friendship filled not only with laughter but with steady encouragement. From our childhood days running wild in Nimba County to our adult ambitions, Rufus always backed me, often taking on the role of my personal cheerleader, without the pom-poms but with a great deal of enthusiasm that would put any marching band to shame. There was never a time I felt discouraged because he was not right there, tying together makeshift pom-poms from whatever he could find. The boy knew how to improvise.

One of the moments I treasure most is the day I decided I wanted to become a published author, a dream that felt a long way off. I still recall the conversation we had under the stars as we lay on the grass, pretending we were philosophers discussing life. Little did I know, Rufus was already planning a way to push me towards that goal. Instead of brushing it aside, he said with excitement, "Jay, do you know what you should do? Write your book about our adventures. I'll even help with the marketing. It will be a bestseller, just like that T-shirt I designed that said, 'My life is a sitcom!'"

Rufus had a gift for making me believe anything was possible, even if it meant sticking some glue on a hope and high-fiving a dream that felt far away. My early attempts at writing resembled a classic sitcom misfire. With every blank page, doubt became my unwanted companion. "What if no one wants to hear about my life?" It was Rufus who pointed out that people love awkward moments when they are presented with flair. He kept saying, "If you tell them about how we got lost in the woods on that ridiculous scavenger hunt, they will be in stitches!" And who could resist an episode about thirty confused kids trying to navigate nature with a mascot that turned out to be a tree? He encouraged me to embrace my unique experiences, and before I knew it, I was tapping away at my keyboard, lighting my creative spark.

Beyond encouragement, Rufus offered a wealth of support during life's inevitable bumps. There were times when my plans faltered, leaving me questioning whether any of it mattered. During one particularly difficult period, when balancing responsibilities felt like riding a unicycle while a swarm of bees followed me, I considered giving up. Rufus arrived like a superhero without the cape. He knocked on my door holding a huge "Get Out of Bed" sign and a large kala, the African homemade bread. "Jay," he shouted, "if life gives us lemons, we will sell them as organic lemon juice!" He waved the sign as though he were leading a parade. That kala became more than a meal; it became a symbol of absurd support that reignited my determination.

Rufus also had remarkable patience and often offered advice wrapped in humour. "You know, Jay," he would say, laughing, "every time you stumble through an opportunity, you add another chapter to the 'Life of a Legend' book!" I understood that he valued imperfection. If he got knocked down, he would be there lifting me up, brushing off my knees and reminding me with an exaggerated eye roll that "this is all part of the plan." I am not entirely sure what plan he meant, but I appreciated the constant push forward.

While I pursued my studies in public health, Rufus remained genuinely interested. He would text me during late night study sessions with poorly timed puns about diseases. "Did you hear about the infectious disease that didn't feel welcome at the party? It just couldn't get any invitations!" There I was, trying to absorb important information while suppressing laughter, grateful to have someone who could turn the academic grind into a brief moment of comedy. It was support wrapped in humour, another example of how he brought joy into every part of our lives.

Now, as I continue my journey without him physically beside me, I carry the torch of his support. Whenever challenges arise, I think of the goofy kid who always saw opportunity in chaos. His spirit lives on in my desire to uplift others and encourage people to embrace their own paths. Rufus taught me that support is not just standing on the sidelines; it is being there to laugh, to lift spirits, and sometimes to offer a pizza. For that, I remain grateful.

The Impact of Loss: Turning Grief into Motivation

"The Impact of Loss: Turning Grief into Motivation" explores the emotions that followed Rufus's passing. It is a bittersweet mix of sadness and nostalgia, with memories swirling together in a rhythm of reflection. Losing Rufus felt like having my favourite pair of shoes disappear overnight, shoes that were not only comfortable but symbolised a life filled with laughter and adventure. In the quiet that followed, I found that grief could become a source of motivation, turning painful tears into fuel for my dreams.

Initially, the universe seemed to turn grey. I questioned everything—the meaning of our shared moments, our dreams, and the inside jokes that rested between us. It felt like a cosmic joke had been played. My once-robust now echoed emptiness, and every memory we built felt tinged with it. I wandered through the day like an awkward zombie, with thoughts, "Why did he leave me to navigate this plot twist on my own?" On certain days, I found solace in the belief that my grief had the right to exist, though I often flailed through it like a fish attempting to ride a bicycle. Yet deep down, I understood that this feeling of loss serves a greater purpose.

After a particular tough day, feeling like a balloon deflated in slow motion, I sat down on my porch, my head whirlpooling with memories of Rufus. As if on cue, I could hear his voice in my mind: "Jay, don't let this bring you down! Get up and create something that would make even a potato laugh!" That quirky phrase of his popped my melancholic balloon, and I realised that turning the pain into something remarkable was within grasp. If nothing else, Rufus would want me to flourish—to share our misadventures and the lessons learned through setbacks! So, armed with remnants of his encouragement, I decided to redirect my energy into my dream of writing, hoping to immortalise our humour in the most distinct way.

With renewed determination, I began drafting an anthology of our experiences called "Light-hearted Adventures in the Life of Joe and Rufus." Each draft flowed vibrantly, highlighting the quirky antics and pulling in tales filled with mischief, like our legendary attempt at baking that resulted in a 'flour tsunami' in my kitchen! The more I poured my heart into the stories, the more it felt like I was sharing my grief with Rufus under the stars once again. It was cathartic, a way to conjure his spirit into a world that desperately needed to read about laughter, friendship, and unpredictability.

As I continued, I connected with others who understood the pain of loss and the comfort of humour. We shared memories and laughed together, turning gatherings into lively sessions that felt like impromptu comedy nights. What I once saw as a burden became a circle of reflection, showing how Rufus's spirit lived on in every shared smile.

Turning grief into motivation was not a simple path. There were moments when doubt slipped in, often at unexpected times. Thoughts such as "What if my writing is not good enough?" surfaced. In those moments I could almost hear him say, "Just focus on the fun, Joe. If you think it is good, it is good!" Eventually I learned that success is shaped by intention, and if I approached the work with joy, I had already achieved something.

As I close this chapter of turning grief into motivation, I smile despite the sadness. Rufus may not be here in person, but he remains woven into my experiences. Every story I write carries a spark of his energy, and every laugh honours his legacy. Instead of sinking into despair, I channelled that grief into storytelling, creating a collection that celebrates joy, friendship and resilience.

In this wild ride, I learned that loss, while excruciating, can spark the Eames of creativity. It is undeniably an emotional journey, woven with laughter, memories, and determination. Rufus might have taken his exit, but survived to motivate me in more ways than I could have imagined. Life taught me that grief can be a stepping stone to something magnificent, a rather inconvenient but magnificent fable, just like me. The world needs humour, and while I carry the weight of loss, I'll also embrace the joy €sharing Rufus's wit with everyone. Who would have thought? Life's experiences, be they filled with laughter or sorrow, become beautiful tales that unite us through their absurdity. And as long as I breathe, Rufus will be right here, laughing with me in every endeavour I undertake

Building New Friendships: Continuing the Spirit of Connection

"Building New Friendships: Continuing the Spirit of Connection" reflects the value of human relationships, especially during times of loss. Since Rufus passed away, I have thrown myself into the world of friendships, knowing that the joy he brought should not only remain in my heart but spread like confetti across the world. Picture me as a social butterfly with a touch of awkwardness, drifting from one opportunity to another while carrying Rufus's lively spirit in every interaction. It has been an exciting journey filled with laughter, tears, and, let's be honest, more than a few cringe-worthy attempts at connection.

After Rufus's passing, I felt stuck in a strange limbo, swinging between moments of solitude and memories of our escapades. I reflected on how each friendship had added flavour to my life, more than a pinch of salt. Each interaction revived wild memories but also stirred a hint of loneliness. While I treasured the bond we shared, I realised that forming new friendships was essential. It kept Rufus's legacy alive and expanded a network of laughter and support. So I let go of hesitation and began seeking new friends, determined to keep the spirit of connection alive.

Adjusting to new friendships felt like riding a unicycle for the first time, except I had two bananas in my hands while attempting a juggling act. I joined various community gatherings, events, and even enrolled in acrobatics (yes, I was serious about that circus metaphor). And you know what? Being vulnerable. Another magical layer became evident when we decided to embark on community outreach activities, including hosting "Joyful Noise" events—components of open-mic nights filled with laughter, music, and often led to some of the most entertaining situations. During one small get-together, I awkwardly introduced myself to the group by saying, "Hey! I'm Joe, and just like a banana, I'm quite a-peeling!" The silence that followed felt deeper than the void left by Rufus, but after a beat, we erupted in laughter. Turns out, that was the spark to ignite genuine connections.

Rufus had a way of recognising people's individuality, and in honour of him, I adopted that trait. I began collecting stories from new friends, each with their own unusual experiences. You'd be amazed at how many people have incredibly bizarre tales— like the guy who accidentally put his hand in the "free samples" section at the grocery store and ended up getting tackled by a confused store manager! As we shared our tales of mishaps and fumbles, the barriers between us crumbled—and suddenly, friendships blossomed like spontaneous wildflowers after a rainstorm. I discovered that our shared laughter made each connection deeper, transforming what could have been superficial exchanges into heartfelt bonds.

One remarkable aspect of natural friendship formation emerged when we discovered our shared acknowledgment of Rufus's charm. Many new friends, though not directly acquainted with him, shared a spark that captivated the essence of laughter and enthusiasm for life, reminiscent of my escapades with Rufus. It was from them that I began to realise that each person brings a unique spark to the table. Our gatherings became pillow fights of laughter cushions, where we embraced both old and new memories while creating a collective human spirit that honoured the lost, the present, and one another.

Another magic layer became evident when we decided to embark on community outreach activities, including hosting "Joyful Noise" events, components of open mic nights, filled with laughter, music and hilarious performances. The scheme allowed our connective quirkiness to shine and encouraged others to share their experiences, talents, and absurd stories. Far more than a comedy club, it became a sanctuary where the collective warmth and genius turned evening into special celebrations. The spirit of connection, reminiscent of the camaraderie I share with Rufus, seemed to blanket the entire gathering, creating an atmosphere so contagious it felt like a well-crafted sitcom.

Throughout the journey of building new friendships, I have learnt that vulnerability, honesty, and most importantly, an appreciation for laughter are the bedrock of strong connections. Friends have shared how honest expressions of gratitude can transform even fleeting acquaintances into cherished relationships. I have found therapy within silly games at gatherings, where everyone became part of the legendary tale. One of my favourite traditions is "Impromptu Story Hour," where we take turns crafting ridiculous stories based on random phrases. Creative dancing together, birthing hilariously absurd narratives worthy of a sitcom pilot and a form of these shared laughs, the connection grows, transforming mere acquaintances into family.

Honouring Rufus's spirit, I realised that building new friendships is not about replacing the past but expanding the space for joy. Each connection

I make evokes a touch of his essence, enriching my journey with new camaraderie and enriching lives alongside mine. With a laugh, I invite Rufus's legacy to live on through our shared experiences. All the more friendships we forge, the brighter the light becomes—a joy illuminating the extraordinary beauty of human connection. The world is expansive, the motives are bright, and as long as we continue to celebrate laughter and the bonds we share, Rufus's spirit will soar in each moment of connection!

Chapter 7:
Wit and Wealth: Harnessing Humour

The Power of Laughter in Tough Times

If there is one universal language that cuts through culture, background and even the awkward silences at family gatherings, it is laughter. My experiences from the busy streets of Liberia to the quieter corners of Australia have shown me one truth: when life becomes difficult, laughter can be your most dependable tool. Picture me, a clinical nurse in Australia, standing before a ward of patients facing uncertainty. What do I do? I make a joke. "Why did the doctor carry a red pen? To remind them to draw blood!" You see, laughter isn't just a delightful escape; it has transformative powers that help us find light even in the darkest hours.

Now, don't get me wrong! I'm not suggesting that laughter is some magic wand that banishes all your problems. If only it were that easy! I can't tell you how many times I've tried to laugh my way through a particularly stubborn bureaucratic form; the only outcome was a series of headaches and phrases that would make my late friend Rufus laugh to the point of spilling his tea. But humour does have a unique quality of unearthing resilience within us. It tells our brains, "Hey! Even though life's throwing all these curveballs, we can still chuckle over it.

There were many days during my journey from Nimba County to land down under where struggles seemed to pile up higher than the mountains surrounding my homeland. When I first arrived in Australia, I was haunted by cultural missteps and the infamous "Kangaroo Tango", I mean, who needs a wombat as a pet? I faced hurdles so high I needed an oxygen tank just to think about climbing them! But I learned that while a walking, talking spectacle made for humbling moments, sharing a laugh with friends and strangers alike was the salve for my aching pride. Whatever the situation, humour created a bridge, allowing me to connect with others who felt just as out of their depth.

Every day at work, I'd see patients yearning for hope and connection, and I'd realise that laughter could be an antidote to discomfort. Whether it was a patient chuckling at my futile attempts to pronounce "Wellington Sellington" or riffing on how dressing up in a hospital gown makes one like a superhero, albeit one without the cape, those moments of levity dominated the sombreness in the room. This taught me something profound: laughter creates a cocoon of camaraderie.

And oh, the timeless wisdom from my family! I remember my mother saying, "A smile can disarm the harshest of critics." This wasn't merely a saying; it was a way of life in my family. Even when we were recounting stories of our struggles, you could almost expect a comedic twist at the end. "Oh, so you thought the goat ran away? Nah! It was merely creatively navigating the hill!" Those moments taught me that while trials and tribulations are inevitable, how we react to them is where we find our power.

Moreover, I have come to realise that in tough times, embracing laughter can be strategic. It's like using humour as raw material to craft our narratives. When we share stories that make others laugh, we take control of our journey, turning the mundane drama of life into something that feels like a sitcom episode. I can't tell you how many opportunities came my way •x: because I managed to host a mini comedy show at the local café or just spun a tale that had everyone gasping for air from laughter. People _resonate with warmth and authenticity, and nothing disarms tension quite like a hearty laugh.

In conclusion

Whenever you find yourself overwhelmed by despair, remember that laughter is like a small spell that brings lightness to the heaviest moments. Wear your sense of humour with pride and know that every chuckle, every giggle and every burst of laughter is more than a coping mechanism. It is a demonstration of resilience. It is a light victory over the weight of adversity. Let us not only face life's challenges but move through them with laughter, leaving a trail of smiles behind us. In the end, laughter is our heartbeat. It connects us all and turns even the most daunting barriers into manageable steps.

Building Genuine Connections through Humour

Building genuine connections is an art, much like shaping a sculpture. You need the right tools and the right mindset. And nothing softens an introduction quite like humour. After all, who does not enjoy a laugh or at least a knowing eye roll in awkward social moments? My journey from the rolling hills of Nimba County to the busy streets of Australia shows this perfectly. With every cultural misstep, I discovered that humour was my golden ticket, my VIP pass into people's conversations.

Imagine me at my first Australian barbecue. I strolled in with the confidence of someone who just won the lottery, but what came next was a reality check sharper than a knife through a watermelon. There I was, greeted with an explosion of jargon about "snags," "thongs," and how to cook a prawn properly. (Spoiler alert: it doesn't involve a microwave.) As the jokes flew past me in rapid fire, my smile started to resemble that of a confused cat. You could practically see the light bulb flickering above my head, dimming by the second. That's when instinct kicked in. I chuckled, tossed in references to my misadventures with snails in Liberia, and watched as the tension melted away faster than butter on a hot pancake.

What I discovered was that humour creates real connections, kindling bonds that might otherwise remain untouched. In that moment, I was no longer a stranger fumbling through a cultural minefield; I was the guy whose nail stories transformed curiosity into conversation. It broke the barrier and connected me to everyone around the grill, enabling authentic dialogue over charred sausages and discussions on who really invented the "Aussie wave" (I maintain it's an ancient Liberian art form). That experience made one thing crystal clear: laughter lowers our defences, inviting others to join the humour and, by extension, share their own stories.

Fast forward a few months, and I found myself working as a clinical nurse. Here, I confronted a parallel universe where every patient had shoulders. I casually proclaimed, "Life is like a medical dart, full of unexpected turns and a few baffling annotations! Ever read one? It's like deciphering ancient hieroglyphs!" With that simple quip, I •ached his stony exterior crack open like a piñata, revealing the treasure of laughter he had stored inside.

I soon understood that humour not only builds connections but encourages vulnerability. When I laughed at myself, especially during chaotic moments like when my stethoscope decided to hide, I invited colleagues and patients to join in. "If my stethoscope is trying to escape," I joked, "it must want me to take a break. Like any overworked employee." Laughter spread through the room and softened the atmosphere, opening space for real interaction.

Humour is universal and timeless. You know how Liberians can link any situation back to a story about sitting around a fire chewing sugar cane? The same applies here. By using humour, I opened conversations across cultures. Stories about my mother's spicy soups and their culinary mishaps became common ground for chats over coffee, leading to deeper connections. Humour became a secret handshake, a passport into conversations that built bridges rather than walls.

Looking back, humour was not just a pleasant companion but a driving force in my relationships. As I adjusted to a new culture, it made me approachable and warm. Laughter does not mock or belittle; it celebrates our shared human experience. As I continue my journey, I hold onto this lesson: humour is not only about evoking laughter, it strengthens genuine connection. The next time you face an unfamiliar situation or a challenge, use your humour. You may come away with more friends and stories than you expected.

Using Wit as a Cultural Bridge:

Navigating cultural differences can be like attempting to dance while blindfolded, it's confusing, hilarious, and often downright awkward. Each step feels like a gamble, but if you can do it with a sense of humour, you might just end up stepping on fewer toes and making some unforgettable friends in the process. As I embarked on my journey from Liberia to Australia, I quickly learned that wit is one of the most powerful tools at my disposal to create a cultural bridge that was both fun and insightful.

Imagine this: I'm at a community event in Australia, happily sampling some "fairy bread." As I take my first bite, I can't help but find it hilarious that this common snack consists of simply buttered bread topped with colourful sprinkles. I mean, as someone raised on the rich, zesty flavours of my mother's Liberian soups, adding some sprinkles on bread sounds like a culinary prank! So, there I was, raising an eyebrow and uttering something like, "Who knew I could have dessert before I even finished my main meal? In Liberia, we save the best for the last, but here, it seems it's on the bread first. My witty comment instantly sparked laughter from everyone nearby. Suddenly, I was no longer a newcomer; I was Joe, the guy who had brought laughter into the fairy bread conversation. Now that is how you start conversations.

The beauty of using wit as a cultural bridge lies in its versatility. With each comedic observation, I found an opportunity to introduce others to culture while also embracing theirs. Just picture me at a potluck, looking at a dish called "pavlova" with puzzled curiosity. With my wit fully engaged, I casually exclaimed, "Is this an Australian cake or just someone's attempt at cloud art gone wrong?" The room erupted into giggles, and as I made them laugh, I opened the door for them to share the backstory of the infamous dessert. Those moments became delightful exchanges of cultural knowledge, with the stab of humour acting as the lubricant that eased all Ears of miscommunication and misunderstanding.

Then there were those cringeworthy moments where I had my little Slip-ups. Like the time I compared kangaroos to goats, proudly declaring they both could leap fences without a second thought. This amusing analogy earned me a chorus of laughter and a gentle tease, reminding me to think twice before brazenly redefining the Australian fauna. But instead of relating to the comfort of my Liberian roots, I leaned into that wit. Well, if these kangaroos can create such headlines, we should give them awards for best performance!" Now, that sparked a lively discussion about which animal deserved the title of a national treasure, while leaving with the inside joke about how I could never trust a leaping animal on a farm again.

But using wit as a cultural bridge is not just about the laughter shared; it also involves dissecting the cultural misunderstandings in ways that encourage learning. Humour has that splendid ability to serve as an icebreaker for difficult conversations. For example, once I joked about how in Liberia, a handshake is a sacred ritual, while in Australia, it sometimes feels more like an extreme sport with all the possible variations! By following each quip with genuine curiosity about their cultural norms, I allowed those around me to reflect on their behaviours openly without feeling defensive. It's incredible how a simple twist of wit can create an inviting space to discuss deeper topics, transforming what could have been an awkward moment into an educational exchange.

What I discovered became my compass in an unfamiliar landscape. Each joke and playful banter helped chart my course toward understanding the subtleties hidden within the shared human experience. As I navigated through cultural barriers, I realised that making people laugh doesn't just break down those walls; it reminds us of the joy in our differences while revealing how connected we truly are.

In a world increasingly driven by divisive narratives, my trusty companion, humour, has been a guiding light. Whether it's using a spritz of laughter to ease discomfort or sparking lively discussions through amusing comparisons, I've felt the power of wit weave our distinct narratives into a cohesive whole. Remember, it's not just about the stories we share, but also the bonds we create and the laughter that flows through them. As I continue to traverse this journey across cultures, I hold tightly to this essential truth: humour is our secret weapon, our common language, and our most effective bridge, turning every cultural exchange into an adventure waiting to be explored!

Comedy as a Confidence Booster

If there's one thing I've learned through my whirlwind adventures from the rugged hills of Nimba County to the expansive beaches of Australia, it's this: comedy wields a remarkable power to transform the meekest mouse into a roaring lion. Yes, that's right! The same me who once stood nervously at the back of the classroom, sweating like a snowman in the sun, discovered that comedy could be my magic wand, my secret ingredient for conjuring up confidence.

Now, let's be honest, stepping onto new terrains, both geographical and social, can be like bungee jumping without a safety cord. You might feel like you're plummeting at light speed, unsure of where you will land.

For example, I remember my first stand-up attempt at an open mic night with Australians expecting jokes seasoned with local humour. I walked onto the stage, trembling more than a leaf on a windy day, worrying whether my accent sounded like a delightful addition or a sputter of confusion. But as I stood there, I quickly realised that this was not just an opportunity to laugh; it was a golden chance to let that comedy be my safety net.

When I delivered my first line about being an "African explorer trying to navigate the galactic world of avocado on toast," I felt the shift immediately. Laughter rose from the crowd, and the nerves that had threatened to overwhelm me slipped into the background. Instead of feeling like a fish out of water, I felt buoyant, riding waves of camaraderie. It was as though I had put on an invisible armour stitched together with humour. With every chuckle and every burst of laughter, my confidence climbed higher than my childhood dreams of becoming a millionaire.

Comedy creates a kind of alchemy that allows you to own your story. I recall my childhood gatherings back home, where storytelling involved generous exaggeration. Those tales, filled with vivid detail, brought smiles and laughter, and it was in those moments that I learned a fundamental truth of comedy: it is not only about the punchline, it is about the boldness to step into the spotlight. By embracing my experiences, I turned my journey into something relatable.

One night, while sharing stories of cultural mishaps, such as confusing "Australian bushfires" with a "unique barbecue strategy" while speaking to a slightly horrified stranger, I understood something important about confidence. The audience found a place to relate, and eventually, the absurdities of our collective experiences sparked a genuine connection. That act of sharing, combined with a sprinkle of humour, left me feeling empowered and authentic. Their laughter gave me a sense of triumph. I was placing my cards on the table regardless of the outcome.

Moreover, comedy isn't merely about making others laugh; it's a thrilling journey toward self-acceptance. Many may not realise it, but cracking self-deprecating jokes can actually kickstart the process of breaking down those insecurities that have seemingly buried themselves deep within us. As I riff on my lesser moments, like the time I showed up to a formal setting wearing two mismatched shoes (hand to heart, it's a real story), I turned an embarrassing experience into a triumphant moment of clarity. Not only did I elicit laughter from the crowd, but it also helped me embrace the unpredictable side of life. I learned to be comfortable with who I am, even if it sometimes came with a side of chaos.

At times of unease, comedy became my secret weapon to illuminate my path. I recall vividly my first clinical shift as a nurse in Australia, where uncertainty buzzed around like bees. Equipped with quick humour, I would make little anecdotes about the chaos of finding lost supplies in the mystical land of the "Storage Closet." Each quip transformed my anxiety into a light-hearted moment that relaxed not only me but also my colleagues, who were equally petrified! That subtle shift allowed me to emerge victorious, proving that laughter wasn't just a release; it was a gateway to forged connections and newfound confidence.

As I continue with laughter guiding my path, I find joy in knowing that every smile I inspire creates ripples far beyond the moment. Comedy has woven a tapestry of grace over my insecurities, turning fear into fuel for confidence. So, to my fellow dreamers and lovers of laughter, remember that humour is not merely an art form. It is a life enhancing force. When you shine a light on your quirks and imperfections, you reveal the true magic of being unapologetically yourself. And trust me, every laugh shared makes the journey richer and more memorable in the grand adventure of life.

The Legacy of Laughter: Lessons from Rufus:

There are certain people who come into our lives and leave an indelible mark on our souls. My late friend Rufus Dokie was one such person. He was the kind of guy who could turn even the most mundane moments into epic tales of hilarity. Rufus had a unique gift. He was a walking comedy show, never one to shy away from a chance to bring laughter to the table, or indeed, wherever life took us. Losing him was like losing a vibrant light in my life, a constant reminder of the power of humour and its ability to heal, inspire, and forge connections.

Rufus and I shared a bond that only those who appreciate the absurd can understand. I still remember our long evenings back in Liberia, sitting under the stars, our backs against the rough ground, as Rufus spun lavish tales about everything from runaway goats to incompetent politicians. His exaggerations had everyone in fits of laughter, and my family often commented that they could hear us guffawing three compounds away. But those laughs were not merely for entertainment. They were a bonding experience that etched memories into our souls, serving as a testament to the weight that humour can carry in our lives. This life we live is all about the moments; make the best of them.

One of the most valuable lessons I learnt from Rufus was the importance of perspective, not only on life but on ourselves. He had an uncanny ability to laugh at his mistakes, which I admired. I remember a time when he accidentally spilled palm oil all over the door of our favourite gathering spot. Instead of sulking or getting angry, Rufus stood up, pointed at the slick floor, and said, "Well, I guess we're about to do the smooth cha-cha-cha dance!" Suddenly, everyone was on their feet, slipping and sliding, laughing harder than we had in months. That simple act of turning a blunder into a roguish dance party taught me that life can be both messy and joyful, and humour can ease the ride.

Rufus also had a remarkable knack for using humour to defuse difficult situations, something I hold dear as I navigate my clinical nursing role. He could walk into a heated discussion and make a comment so amusing that it immediately eased the tension. During a particularly tense hall meeting, I remember someone made a scathing remark, and I could feel the collective jaws dropping in shock. Without missing a beat, Rufus raised his hand and said, "Surely, we can all agree that even shadows deserve a break from the drama!" The entire room erupted in laughter, and just like that, tensions evaporated, allowing for calmer dialogue. That reminder that a touch of laughter can ease conflict remains one of my guiding principles.

While I cherish all the memories, the lessons Rufus imparted through laughter did not stop there. He always reminded me that life is too short for indecision. "You see that tree by the river?" he would say. "You either climb it or you sit under it. Just don't waste time wondering if the climb is worth it. Climb first, worry later!" His comical view on life made even the most daunting challenges feel surmountable. When I left Liberia for Australia, I held onto that notion: I was going to climb, and climb high, no matter the doubts swirling around me.

Then there was Rufus' understanding of the ultimate human condition: that we are all wonderfully flawed creatures. He believed that embracing our peculiarities is the key to an extraordinary life. I remember sitting with him as he passionately recounted his grand plans to impress a lady by flipping a pancake with flair. He ended up flipping it straight onto his neighbour's terrace, but instead of shying away, he proclaimed, "It's not a pancake, it's a culinary missile!" The laughter that followed lingered long after that absurd evening. Rufus taught me that life's awkward moments and our imperfections are the crux of truly living. Engaging with them can create beautiful connections that bind us together.

As I continue my journey through life, with all its ups, downs, and moments of laughter, I often find myself whispering, "What would Rufus do?" Remembering him reminds me to embrace my quirks, find humour in the chaos, and never underestimate the healing power of laughter. The lessons Rufus taught me serve as a guiding compass on this relatable, absurd escapade we call life. Here is to Rufus, my friend, my mentor, and my eternal source of laughter, whose legacy lingers on through every chuckle I share. He transformed life into a comedy show and, in doing so, left a trail of laughter that echoes through my heart, reminding me that humour is a gift we can all partake in. Here is to climbing our metaphorical trees, this time with laughter as our safety harness.

Chapter 8:
Books That Changed My Life
Power of Reading – Unlocking Wealthy Ideas

The power of reading is a true treasure chest of wisdom, wealth, and maybe some wild characters who could easily inspire a collection of comedic tales. As I sit here gathering my thoughts, I cannot help but remember the countless hours I spent with my nose buried in a book, soaking up ideas that would make even a tepid accountant weep with joy. In fact, you might say that reading is the secret ingredient for cultivating an aristocratic mindset; without it, you are just trying to bake a cake with flour.

Picture this: a young Joe, back in Nimba County, eagerly flipping rough pages like a monkey unwrapping a banana. Little did I know then that I was planting a garden of thoughts that would later blossom into my "Millionaire Dreams." Each time I opened a book, it felt like inviting a new friend. Friends such as the late great Napoleon Hill seemed to speak directly to my inner millionaire. I still remember the first time I read *Think and Grow Rich*. It felt as if I had been handed a magic wand capable of transforming humble dreams into golden realities. But even magic wands come with a user manual, and I read that too.

Reading is where ideas sneak in like shadows during the day, gradually but profoundly. I would be reading about compound interest and, before I knew it, I was convinced I could challenge Bill Gates to a most-well-versed speller contest. "Compound interest? Ha! More like compound intrigue!" I would exclaim. A sense of bravado surged through me, fuelled by the characters I met along the way, each richer than the last. Sure, some of those characters made poor financial decisions (we all know the one whose investment strategy is like a toddler playing with fire). Still, they taught me valuable lessons. Never underestimate the power of an uneducated gamble, my friends.

One amusing takeaway from the books on wealth was how some people treat reading like a chore, preferring to scroll through social media instead. Don't get me wrong, I enjoy a good meme about "adulting," but memes do not provide the financial roadmap to success. They give laughs, yes, but when it comes to financial wisdom, I would much rather digest the plot twists of a good book than the latest viral cat video. It is like comparing a Michelin-star meal to a soggy French fry: one leads to success, the other leaves you sitting on the couch, wondering if your life choices need more flavour.

If you want to unlock the vault of wealth, my advice is to visit your local bookstore or library. You might find inspiration in self-help guides, but what is even better is a gripping biography about an entrepreneur who rolled the dice and came up golden. I remember reading about Richard Branson. His daring escapades made my attempts to sell candy on the streets of Monrovia feel like child's play. You must admire the audacity of a man who says, "I am going to start an airline," and then does it while skydiving. Can you imagine the board meeting? "So, how do we plan to increase our flying passengers?" "Well, first, we put them in a plane and jump out!" Pure genius.

In the later chapters of my reading journey, I became acutely aware of something: the books that shaped my mindset were not just about wealth in dollars. They also brought laughter and a keen understanding of human nature. The financial gurus I read often hid nuggets of wisdom in their personal stories. It was not only about investments or forecasting; it was about how to bob and weave through life's punchlines. That is where real wealth lies, understanding people, money, and how to laugh your way through the process.

So, my dear readers, if you ever catch yourself without a penny in your pocket, rest assured that you can still be wealthy. Go ahead and read as if it were your job, even if it is just to avoid making dinner for the family. Remember, every book is an investment waiting to pay off, and you do not need a Wall Street broker to remind you of that. Embrace the power of reading, and before you know it, you will be playing your financial cards right. Just do not forget to save a joke or two for when things get tough. Your inner millionaire is patiently waiting for you to open the next chapter.

Books That Shaped My Mindset:

Books are silent companions that have shaped my journey from the rolling hills of Nimba County to the bustling streets of Australia. It is funny to think that my obsession with reading began not out of sheer interest but out of sheer necessity. Imagine a kid with big dreams, sitting in a room with a roof so low it barely brushes your hair. That was me, desperately looking for ways to escape my humble beginnings without hyperventilating from bookish terms. Little did I know that flipping through pages would open doors wider than the ones that led me to the bakery for fresh bread.

One pivotal book that stands out in my memory is *Rich Dad Poor Dad* by Robert Kiyosaki. This delightful book had me slinging one minute and shaking my fist in the air the next. I frequently found myself shouting, "What do you mean, poor dad?!" at my existential angst while recognising a glaring truth: financial literacy can be a wild ride. It was like attending a thrilling lecture on financial independence, but instead of a stuffy professor, Kiyosaki came equipped with wit and engaging stories that practically slapped me awake. Who knew learning about assets and liabilities could provoke such a visceral reaction? I kept thinking, "If only poor dad had invested in that land instead of me!" That book became my financial bible.

Then there is *Think and Grow Rich* by Napoleon Hill. Ah, my good old pal Hill! You know you are in deep when your friend's library starts including books that make you think "rich" and "think" deserve awards for best pairing. Hill's stories had me giggling like a kid whose big brother had just revealed where he hid the best candy. I would be reading about burning desires, faith, and persistence, right in my modest little room, and it felt as if the universe conspired to make me a believer. There is something about those words that grips you and makes you think, "If this applies to them, why not me?" I walked away with a newfound sense of purpose, feeling like I could bust down the doors of the nearest bank and ask for a loan based solely on the audacity Hill instilled in me.

Of course, *The Millionaire Next Door* offered quite a humbling experience, mainly because I often pictured my neighbours as millionaires lounging around in swimming pools that looked like small oceans. Robert H. Frank and Thomas J. Stanley made me realise that wealth is not just about flashy cars you see on social media. It is about living below your means, because you do not want to be that person showing up at a party in a brand-new suit while holding a bag of 'noodles on sale'. That cringe-worthy scene had me examining my own spending habits, at least until I reached for my emergency stash of peanut butter as a comforting snack.

Let us not forget the entrepreneurial treasure chest that is *The 4 Hour Workweek* by Timothy Ferriss. Who would not want a life that resembles jet-setting while sipping a piña colada on a beach? Ferriss practically slapped me awake, showing that I could stop dwelling on work and start living. He was a maestro orchestrating a symphony of ideas, such as outsourcing tasks so efficiently that your neighbour would start questioning whether you had sold your soul to the productivity gods. I eagerly tried applying some of those ideas; my friends laughed, and there I was, attempting to delegate washing dishes to the chickens in the yard. Did I achieve the lifestyle Ferriss espoused? Not quite. But I had a good laugh and even convinced a chicken to help pick up the scraps.

Books like these have shaped my mindset dramatically. They taught me that wealth is not about the zeros in your bank account but about knowledge, understanding, creativity, and yes, a sprinkle of audacious humour. I have realised that constantly feeding my brain with new ideas allows me to constantly evolve, a journey where even failure becomes a delightful lesson, such as learning how not to cook rice without burning it. I am still making my way through, recognising that every book adds fuel to my fire of ambition. So here I am, a proud advocate for reading, convinced that the world of books holds the keys to unlocking the million-dollar dreams lurking in each of us. Grab a book and discover the secrets that will tickle your funny bone while building your dream empire. After all, if you cannot laugh your way to wealth, are you even doing it right?

Lessons from Financial Gurus and Their Stories:

Financial gurus are like wise owls everyone wishes they could be friends with but can barely understand. Their stories are filled with anecdotes that can make your hair stand on end, like the time Warren Buffett bought a company because he liked the taste of its ice cream, while simultaneously telling everyone to read more. I often wonder whether these gurus have secret wands hidden under their suits or if they simply earned their wisdom through tea with the universe, accompanied by a few doses of reality. On my quest for financial enlightenment and a bit of comic relief, I discovered gems in the quirks of their tales.

Take Robert Kiyosaki, for example. His "rich dad" and "poor dad" dichotomy rings true, especially because I have a cast of characters in my life that resembles a soap opera more than a financial seminar. He advises surrounding yourself with people who encourage you, not those who throw cold water on your dreams while offering a bowl of cold porridge. That resonated with me as I recalled a beloved family member saying, "Joe, maybe being a millionaire is not your calling, maybe you should just become a professional chicken whisperer." Little did they know, my aspirations included visions of success that did not involve scaring farm animals.

Then there is Dave Ramsey, who would probably argue with a squirrel about savings. His story of rising from financial distress is like a dramatic hallmark movie. He teaches that debt is like that annoying friend who overstays their welcome: it takes more than your time and resources before you realise the toll it has taken. His "baby steps" approach made me chuckle, as I often picture myself crawling across a giant balance sheet rather than taking any real steps towards financial independence. I can still hear my mother saying, "Joe, baby steps for you are still giant leaps for the rest of us!" But dear friends, hear me when I say this: if a "baby step" towards wealth is all it takes, I will do the cha-cha with every dollar I make.

And then there is Tony Robbins, whose stories are a whirlwind of motivational confetti. Have you noticed how he always seems as if he has had seven espressos? Robbins can make a person believe that merely believing you are a millionaire can make it happen. I remember his lesson about turning "CAN'T" into "CAN." Initially, I was sceptical, but I gave it a try. I marched around my apartment shouting, "I CAN be a millionaire!" while my curious neighbours must have thought I was auditioning for a role in an overly dramatic play. Over time, the more I asserted my riches, the more ideas started flowing. Next thing I knew, I was scribbling business plans on deli napkins, which, ironically, was not the best place to write down thoughts about being rich.

Let us not overlook Tim Ferriss, who condenses the life lessons of hundreds of people into a 200-page book. He gives the impression that if I delegate all my tasks, I could live on the beach eating coconuts while my financial empire runs itself. In reality, coconut water would be the only thing I would be drinking. Trusting a tech-savvy parrot to manage your online investments is not quite as reliable as it sounds. However, I did get inspired to outsource my grocery shopping, and I will be darned if that was not the best decision I made in 2021. Let us leave the parrot to take care of the investments.

Ultimately, the stories from these financial gurus often highlight more than just wealth. They teach resilience, creativity, and contentment. If Richard Branson can swim with sharks while starting Virgin Records, then perhaps I can also politely ask a few chickens to help me with my online sales strategy. The blend of humour and life lessons reminds us that, while the path to wealth may be strewn with bizarre encounters, it is our creative thinking that gets us through it, all while chuckling at the absurdities we encounter.

So next time you pick up a book by these financial giants, remember their tales. Somewhere among them lies your own comical journey to success. Laughing at their wild experiences, and perhaps even your own, may just pave the road toward realising your million-dollar dreams, one ridiculous venture at a time.

The Importance of Continuous Learning:

Continuous learning is the magic elixir that keeps our brains from turning to pudding while giving us that extra edge we need in this chaotic world. I often joke that if knowledge were a currency, I would be swimming in pennies while everyone else hoarded gold bars. Who needs wealth when you can have all the trivia the world spills out? Continuous learning has not only been the beacon illuminating my path to success, but also the reason I can continue conversing with friends without sounding like a social robot malfunctioning mid-sentence.

As I reminisce about my humble beginnings in Nimba County, it strikes me that learning was not a luxury but a necessity. My parents would often say, "Joe, if you want to avoid being poorer than a church mouse, you'd better start reading!" Their sentiments were clear: knowledge is power, and it is not merely a cliché; it is practically a mandate for survival. Little Joe transformed from an ordinary child into a learning machine, fuelled by the belief that every morsel of information was essential for the incredible journey toward financial success. I even found joy in unexpected lessons, like discovering you can learn about personal finance from cooking. That is right! Efficient cooking methods can come in handy when balancing meal prep and budgeting. Psst, you can save time by tossing ingredients into the air and letting gravity do the chopping (kidding, you may want to avoid that).

Let us be real: in a world where technology evolves faster than a toddler can consume snacks, continuous learning keeps you awake at the wheel. Whether it is new financial apps, investment tips, or strategies for offering chicken diplomacy at the local market, keeping my knowledge fresh has been both a gritty adventure and an unholy handshake with creativity. I can still recall the day I learned about cryptocurrency. It was like discovering that my old Nokia phone could transform into a smartphone with a rational leap of faith. Sure, I may not have fully grasped "blockchain," but who knew learning could lead me down a rabbit hole of virtual coins and memes? Now, I can enjoy spirited debates about Bitcoin at Sunday brunch with friends who still think Wi-Fi is a type of fish.

One of the greatest beauties of continuous learning is how it breeds adaptability. Look around! The world changes at lightning speed, and if you blink, you might find yourself on the wrong side of the road. In my nursing career, learning about new technologies and methodologies is not only encouraged but expected. The ability to pick up new information and adapt has allowed me to connect with my patients in ways I had never dreamed of. To use a humorous metaphor, it is like getting to know a fruit in a smoothie. Everyone is doing it until you throw in avocados for that fancy health kick, and suddenly, everyone must adjust their perspectives. Continuous learning has not only transformed my career but also endeared me to patients with delectable smoothie-related chatter.

Continuous learning does not have to feel like a second job. Once I started treating it as an enjoyable pursuit, akin to soaking up the sun at a beach, the world became a treasure cove of experiences. How cool is it to learn about marketing categories while in line at a café, perfecting the art of stealthily eavesdropping on business discussions between sips of chai? With each interaction, I learned something new, laughing at how humble internet rooms sometimes became the best classrooms I had ever experienced. I cannot tell you the number of times I have ended up in deeper-than-expected conversations while waiting for coffee, little realising I would gain valuable financial insights while trying to conceal a crumb from a cone stuck to my cheek.

In the end, continuous learning is about flexibility, humour, and finding joy in the process. The takeaway is simple: when we invest time in upgrading our knowledge and skills, we build a resilient foundation for success while simultaneously seeing the humour in the challenges that come our way. You never know when a new nugget of wisdom might sprout wings and help you unexpectedly fly toward your goals, or at least offer comic relief in an otherwise extraordinary journey.

Let us embrace this marvellous adventure called continuous learning. Whether you are reading books, watching tutorials, or even hosting trivia nights with friends, know that you are not just feeding your brain but cultivating a powerful arsenal of knowledge that can guide you toward those millionaire dreams, one laugh at a time. When life throws lemons at you, you will be ready to make lemon meringue pie, sold at an outrageous markup. Cheers to learning, and may the laughter never end.

How to Start Your Own Financial Library:

The financial library is a sanctum where dreams are monetised, motivation is ignited, and every book has the potential to catapult you from the couch to beachfront bliss. I still chuckle at the idea of my humble bookshelf back in Liberia, adorned with volumes filled with wisdom, books stacked in a way that resembled an art installation rather than organised literature. But do not let my past chaos deter you. Let me share some steps to create your own financial library, one that may just become the envy of local squirrels. Who knows, a few might even come knocking, asking for tips on investing in acorns.

First, set a clear vision for your library. Think of it like planning a theme party. You would not invite fifty guests without knowing the theme, right? What is the purpose of your financial library? Are you looking to master investing, understand entrepreneurship, or simply build a nest of wisdom mixed with humour? Maybe you want a place to tuck away your secrets for balance sheets and cheap laughs alike. Whatever your motivation, having a clear vision helps maintain focus as you curate your collection. I assure you, my library went from 'financial chaos' to 'financial haven' once I discovered what I wanted to achieve. The more I homed in on my mission, the fewer random cookbooks on sushi I ended up with.

Now for the fun part: gathering your books. You can happily cash in your treasure chest of change from under the couch, but the quest for knowledge does not have to break the bank. Online platforms like eBay, thrift shops, and local libraries often harbour hidden gems waiting to be unearthed. Every time I rented a book from my library, I half-expected them to hand me a suitcase as well. How much could this knowledge change my life? Venture forward, my friend. Search second-hand shops and garage sales for those quirky finance books whispering, "Pick me, and I will tell you the secrets of the universe."

Do not shy away from a digital library either. Nowadays, eBooks are manna from heaven for aspiring readers. Websites like Project Gutenberg or Open Library have a treasure trove of free content waiting to be explored. A wise saying rings true: there is no such thing as too many books, especially when you can download them for less than the price of artisanal coffee. The only downside? If you are reading on a tablet during breakfast, you might spill orange juice on it, which becomes a new book: the "Orange Juice Book."

Once you have your collection started, make it aesthetically pleasing. Organising your books on glorious shelves can bring immense joy to the heart. I recall the days of colour-coordinating my shirts, believing it automatically bolstered my finances. While I was at it, why not do the same with books? Think of categories like *Budgeting for Dummies*, *The Art of Investments*, or *How to Play the Market Like You're in a Game of Snakes and Ladders*. Whatever suits your style, unleash your creativity. The library should be a visual feast that makes you want to dive in headfirst.

Next, let us talk about nurturing that library. Much like how plants need water and sunlight, your financial library thrives on attention and care. Regularly assess your books, refresh the collection, pitch out those dusty volumes you have not touched in ages (donate them somewhere useful), and replace them with new titles that will pique your interest. This requires regular "weeding" and "planting," but it is not as messy as it sounds. I dubbed my reviews "The Great Financial Cleanout," where my friends and I would gather and swap books over lively discussions about their merits. Spoiler alert: we often ended up laughing more than we cleaned.

Finally, invite a community around your library. Surrounding yourself with like-minded individuals fosters inspiration and can amplify your reasoning. Host monthly book parties, or be the caffeinated guru at your local coffee shop, where discussions bounce around like popcorn. As you share your insights, hidden treasures often arise from other radars, unearthing ideas that make you reconsider your entire financial approach. Before long, your library might evolve into a thesis worthy of publication.

Creating your financial library stores knowledge and contracts a world filled with possibilities and laughter. Each time you add a tome, you take a step closer to your millionaire dreams, armed with hilarious anecdotes and profound wisdom. Let us not forget the vibrant, confident atmosphere you can create while assembling a space that reflects you, the aspiring entrepreneur and reader. Grab that spark of ambition and start building your sanctuary of knowledge. Soon, you may find yourself nestled between pages of limitless potential, and maybe even a mischievous squirrel or two seeking your wisdom. Let us get reading, my fellow financial adventurers.

Chapter 9:
Diving into Public:
A Different Kind of Health

The Importance of Public Health in Community Development

When we talk about the foundation of a thriving community, the first things that come to mind are usually roads, schools, or maybe, if you are particularly optimistic, a budget for local dance parties. But let us be honest: without public health at the heart of community development, everything else is just a beautifully painted façade hiding a crumbling skeleton. Picture this: a community with excellent schools, lively parks, and roads wide enough for a marching band, yet half the people are sick and the other half are dodging healthcare like it is contagious. That is what we are trying to avoid. Let us chat about why public health is as vital as the coffee I need to fuel my vigorous dreams of becoming a millionaire.

Public health is the invisible superhero of our communities, transforming the mundane into the magnificent with very little fanfare. Imagine public health as a diligent gardener, tending to the soil of society to ensure it blooms beautifully. Healthy communities can engage in activities with vigour, build businesses, and form relationships. Without solid health foundations, you have a community more likely to be bedridden than building the entrepreneurial empire everyone talks about. Health is not just about avoiding colds or maintaining a six-pack. It is about creating an environment where people feel motivated and empowered, motivation that translates into running a startup or spreading joy through laughter instead of sniffling and sighing on a hospital bed.

Furthermore, a community with a robust public health system can save heaps of cash—money that could go toward the latest smartphone or a dream holiday. An ounce of prevention is worth a pound of cure. When everyone in a community is educated about preventing disease, the need for costly medical treatments shrinks faster than my symptoms when I sneak a peek at a hospital bill. Health education programs can do wonders. These workshops teach people to choose kale over cupcakes or check their blood pressure instead of scrolling social media notifications. Investing in public health early can spare a community the pain of emergency room visits later.

Now, let us highlight my favourite subject: economic productivity. When people are healthy, they can work, think, and innovate without feeling like they have been hit by a bus. A sick community is like a car running on fumes. It might move slowly, but it is nowhere near top speed. By investing in public health initiatives, a community paves the way for an agile workforce, flickering like a light bulb at full wattage, which in turn draws investors like moths to a flame. Picture potential investors walking through the community. Instead of dodging coughing fits or the smell of sickness, they see joggers, fresh entrepreneurs, and cheerful faces. Who would not want to jump into such a sparkling environment?

Public health also fosters community pride and cohesion. People are more inclined to support one another, share resources, and establish connections when they feel part of a healthy ecosystem. You see this at local festivals, farmers' markets, or nightly community soccer matches. When everyone is healthy, the dances are bouncier and laughter echoes louder. The buzz generated by a harmonious community attracts attention, leading to a sense of belonging richer than my grandmother's palm oil stew, an authentic recipe for wealth beyond figure digits.

Lastly, let us not sugarcoat this: public health can be hilariously prone to the ironies of human behaviour. Something funny happens when people become health-conscious; suddenly, everyone is a nutritionist. Your neighbours will flood your ear with unsolicited advice on avocado consumption while you are just trying to enjoy your deep-fried plantains. But that is the beauty of public health. It enables small interactions over neighbourly fences and kitchen counters, which might lead to friendships or those awkward moments where you politely smile while someone declares beloved fried snacks the "enemy of the healthy."

Next time someone asks why public health is a cornerstone of community development, you can chuckle and highlight all its delightful paradoxes. It is not just about avoiding sickness. It is about weaving a rich tapestry of wealth, camaraderie, and resilience, letting every thread sing or dance its way to a promising future. Securing your health is the new "get-rich-quick" scheme the world did not see coming.

Lessons from My Nursing Career:

As I navigate the bustling world of healthcare, armed with my stethoscope and an absurd number of pens in my pockets, I have learned far more than just how to calculate a medication dosage or bandage a scraped knee. Nursing, my dear friends, is like attending a never-ending circus. There are thrills, spills, and acts I never imagined I would witness. Each day offers a fresh repertoire of oddities, where colourful characters from all walks of life converge to remind me of the absurdity and beauty of being human.

So, let me share some priceless lessons from my nursing career that go far beyond the clinical manuals.

First, let us dive into the importance of humour. In the world of nursing, laughter is essential, and trust me, if you cannot find humour in the chaos, you might end up curled under a hospital bed in the foetal position. Whether it is a patient bracing themselves for an injection or bewildered family members insisting they are "just here for moral support" (which usually means they will eat all the free food and confuse the scent of hand sanitiser with baked bread), humour can be the antidote to anxiety. I have learned to wield laughter like a weapon. It does not matter if someone is shouting about a misplaced IV line or insisting their "vital signs" are psychic predictions. Cracking a joke can break the tension faster than a nurse's instinct to locate the nearest caffeine source.

Next, let us talk about resilience. Nursing teaches resilience like nothing else, especially when you find yourself running in circles at 3:00 am, wondering whether it is reality or a delirious dream fuelled by too much coffee. There is a saying: "If you want to know what a person is made of, watch what happens when they are under pressure." And there is plenty of pressure. You learn to balance heavy emotional loads, navigate high-stakes situations, and find your footing on floors slipperier than a cartoon banana peel. Nursing has taught me that when the chips are down, you must pick yourself, and your patients, up, dust off the disappointment, and march forward. I have witnessed fragile lives become beacons of resilience, inspiring me to grab life by the horns and steer through challenges with the determination of a runaway goat.

Speaking of runaway goats, let us talk about the art of multitasking. In nursing, it is a language all its own. You learn to juggle medications, patient preferences, family concerns, and your own sanity at the same time. I have checked a blood pressure while instructing someone to stop spinning around in a wheelchair like it was a carnival ride. Skills learned on the nursing floor translate easily to everyday life, such as managing chaotic family dinners or holiday disasters when everyone mysteriously brings the same dish as last year. Multitasking is not merely a skill. It is a survival strategy, and I carry it confidently into every endeavour, especially when pursuing my dream of wealth.

Lastly, patience, that elusive god of virtues, has been both a friend and a foe. In nursing, real-time patience is vital when frustration simmers just beneath the surface. Whether a patient insists on having their snack at the unbreakable 2:00 pm despite being NBM (nothing by mouth), patience must be practised. I have learned that sometimes the best medicine is a willing ear and a few deep breaths in the face of seemingly irrational demands. Patience ties us together in this wild tapestry of life, guiding us not only through hospital corridors but also through life beyond those walls.

My nursing career has been my Everest, filled with trials and triumphs, a journey that even a million dollars could not fully define. The lessons I have gathered are not superficial. They form the bedrock of my dreams, emboldening my quest to foster health, wealth, and laughter throughout my journey. So the next time someone says, "I should have gone to med school," remember that sometimes the path less travelled leads to true wealth, meaningful wins, and the occasional giggle while delivering a bedside joke.

Navigating Financial Stress in Healthcare:

Financial stress in healthcare arises when the love of saving lives collides with the reality that bills do not pay themselves. As a clinical nurse, I can assure you that wandering hospital corridors can feel like participating in a game show where the prizes are buried beneath red tape and dollar signs. It is like playing Monopoly with real money and the constant risk of landing on "hospital fees" one too many times. Fear not, though, as I will guide you through the tangled world of navigating financial stress in healthcare while attempting to keep your sanity intact.

First on this rollercoaster is the dubious art of budget jiu-jitsu. Healthcare budgets often feel like puzzles missing half their pieces, frustrating and absurd, much like attempting to cook a meal using only ketchup and crackers. You quickly learn that creating and sticking to a budget is as vital as administering CPR. One wrong move and you can slip into debt faster than a patient can say, "I thought this was covered!" Prioritising expenses is essential, from medical supplies to food, especially if you have ever tasted hospital cafeteria lasagne. Saving lives while protecting your savings is a balancing act that would surprise anyone. Who knew nurses would also need an MBA?

Then there is the delightful world of insurance claims. If you think navigating a maze is difficult, allow me to introduce insurance bureaucracy. Securing approvals can feel like trying to convince a car to take a bath. You submit a claim only to receive a denial letter that might as well be written in ancient hieroglyphs. "Ingenious," I think, staring at stacks of paperwork and wondering whether documenting a patient's last meal choices is truly necessary to approve a heart-stopping MRI. Sifting through policies while keeping patients calm is a genuine test of endurance. Sometimes it feels as though you need the skills of a Bollywood dancer to twist your way through those claim forms with grace.

Now, as we wander further down the bank account path, let us talk about advocacy. Financial stress is not just about numbers. Advocating for patients includes guiding them through the murky waters of medical costs. Many patients do not understand their options, such as whether they truly need the deluxe corner room. Nurses often become financial superheroes, sharing information about assistance programs or pharmaceutical discounts. There is nothing quite like seeing a patient realise they do not need to sell their beloved cat to afford their medication. Moments like these reaffirm why we do what we do, even amid financial turmoil.

Then there's the dark horse of healthcare finances: student loans! Ah, yes, financial aid that feels like a villain in a superhero movie. While we're out here saving lives, we've also acquired astronomical debt that could fund a small country in Africa (or at the very least several rounds of iced coffee). Navigating these financial responsibilities while trying to maintain a sense of normalcy can resemble walking a tightrope—a tightrope made of G bills, loans, and late-night ramen dinners. I often joke that my degree is printed on fancy paper, but the ink isn't worth much compared to thefinancial stress it induces! But fear not, fellow financial tightrope walkers; reeking forgiveness programs or income-driven repayment plans can help fight that burden.

Finally, let us embrace the most amusing solution to financial stress: humour. During the most chaotic shifts, embracing absurdity is essential. If there is a spill or a hilariously miscommunicated medication order, laugh it off. Sharing stories with colleagues helps dissolve stress and reminds us that even amid the whirlwind, there is room for light-heartedness. Humour can act as a bandage for harsh realities, turning "I just emptied the point-of-care glucose meter instead of the sharps box" into an impromptu comedy routine.

Navigating financial stress in healthcare can feel like trying to catch a noodle with chopsticks in a windstorm, but remember you are not alone. With creativity, resilience, and humour, we persist through the sparkling chaos of healthcare. So the next time the billing department feels like a black hole swallowing your dreams, take a deep breath, adjust your stethoscope, and dance through the chaos like the financial rock star you are. Life, and healthcare, should always leave room for laughter, even in the face of economic uncertainty.

Creating Opportunities through Health Initiatives:

Creating opportunities through health initiatives is like hosting a potluck dinner where everyone is invited, and the only entry fee is a little innovation, genuine commitment, and perhaps an unquantifiable amount of caffeine. Trust me, I know all about navigating the murky waters of public health. It often feels like rowing a canoe made of cardboard while dodging the waves of real-world challenges. Yet amid those waves, opportunities bob up like beach balls at a summer parade, and I am here to show you how to catch them with the right mindset.

Take a moment to picture your community. Perhaps it is a vibrant place where neighbours exchange greetings, or more likely, a place where everyone is perpetually busy and glued to their smartphones. Health initiatives act as the glue that binds people together, much like a peanut butter sandwich, without the frustration of it sticking to the roof of your mouth. When you implement health initiatives, you are not merely setting up programs. You are orchestrating a dance of opportunity where local businesses, schools, and healthcare providers come together. It is a choreography that requires coordination, community spirit, and the occasional misstep, much like an amateur dance-off at a wedding.

One of the most significant opportunities arises from preventive health programs. Prevention in healthcare is like finding a discount at a trendy smoothie bar you thought you could never afford. It allows you to enjoy health benefits without draining your bank account. By educating communities about nutrition, exercise, and overall wellbeing, we help individuals avoid potential illnesses while cultivating an environment where wealth grows from the seeds of good health. Health fairs, workshops, and cooking classes can spring up like mushrooms after rain, creating opportunities for local entrepreneurs to showcase their offerings, whether that is kale chips or quinoa pudding. These initiatives often attract service organisations or businesses eager to collaborate, improving public health while strengthening local economies.

Another sparkling gem in the treasure chest of health initiatives is community engagement. You see, engaging community members allows them to take ownership of their health, like a toddler with a too-big cookie. When community members are motivated, they can run programs or facilitate discussions that promote collective growth. Think of it like planning a seed; the initial effort feels challenging, the watering seems pointless at times, but with dedication, it bursts forth into vibrant fruits. Engaging people in their health challenges and empowering them to find solutions together can unleash a wave of creativity that emerges as community gardens, walking clubs or local health coalitions. Suddenly, everyone's invested and before you know it, your neighbourhood resembles a vibrant marketplace on a sunny day.

Additionally, let's not forget the fantastic partnerships that can stem health initiatives, like a giddy marriage of convenience between organisations that share a common goal. When businesses and community agencies collaborate on health initiatives, the possibilities are endless! a local gym that partners with a nearby grocery store to promote healthy eating and exercise. Now you've got discount smoothies for every workout completed—and who doesn't love that combination? Organisations that team up can leverage their strengths, whether it's educational outreach or financial support, creating a synergy that benefits everyone involved. You get more bang for your buck, and the community reaps the rewards of improved health and happiness—all while humming along to the sweet sounds of camaraderie.

Now let's sprinkle in a bit of the lighter side. Think about those hilarious moments that can arise from community health events—like the competitive spirit that often emerges during a fun run or the delightfully awkward dance-offs at health fairs. These comedic connections can foster relationships that go deeper than surface-level dialogue. After an event, the conversations don't just fade like the scent of healthy kale; they evolve into friendships, collaborations, and even new businesses sprouting like little entrepreneurial sprouts. Who would've thought that a health initiative could ignite entrepreneurial passions, pushing individuals out of their shells faster than adding hot sauce to bland food?

Ultimately, creating opportunities through health initiatives is about more than structured programs. It requires adaptability, resilience, and a healthy dose of humour. It is about recognising opportunity, making choices that change lives, and planting hope within communities. The next time someone points out barriers to health, remind them those barriers can become stepping stones to wealth, in spirit, community, and joy. By building connections and strengthening collaboration, we transform communities into thriving ecosystems where wellbeing fuels creativity and success. After all, community health initiatives are not just about staying alive. They are about living fully, one joyful and laughter-filled moment at a time.

The Future in Public Health and Wealth Creation:

As I sit here sipping my morning coffee, which might as well be liquid gold given my ambitions, I cannot help but feel that we are standing at the edge of an exciting era in public health and wealth creation. The future is not simply around the corner. It is bursting through the door like an overenthusiastic relative at a family gathering, loud, unpredictable, and holding a bowl of questionable potato salad. But let us clear the table, because the trends shaping public health and wealth creation are far more appealing and promise to leave us well satisfied.

First, let's talk about technology. It is like I need a new dictionary to keep up with the buzzwords flying around these days. From telemedicine to health apps that track everything, from your heart rate to your stressed-out emojis, the future will see an exhilarating blend of traditional healthcare with cutting-edge innovations. Imagine bustling through life while a tiny device on your wrist whispers reminders to breathe, stretch, or even knock off those extracted snacks. With the rise of digital health, education will have unprecedented opportunities to offer wellness resources that empower people to take charge of their health without breaking a sweat, or if they do, they can log it on their fitness apps.

Furthermore, we're turning public health into a collective endeavour! The tan-Ire will have communities actively collaborating on health initiatives, rather than relying solely on the "experts" in white coats. This isn't some dystopian nightmare where zombies overrun the hospital because someone misread Google Search suggestions. No, I'm talking about empowering individuals to share insights, resources, and experiences. Think neighbourhood health potluck gatherings—where for each bowl of goodness, someone shares practical knowledge about health living, nutrition, and financial wellness. It's a lovely idea, and certainly better than arguing over whether pineapple belongs on pizza (it does, by the way, fight me). A communal approach to health will undoubtedly nurture health creation by building bonds that stand the test of time, like Grandma's legendary stew recipe.

Another promising trend is the increasing focus on mental health and the removal of long-standing stigma. This is where genuine progress is being made. Mental wellbeing is beginning to integrate into every aspect of life, much like food somehow occupies every corner of my fridge. Organisations are recognising the importance of employee mental health and introducing wellness programs at an impressive pace. These initiatives improve productivity, encourage clear thinking, and foster innovation, creating an environment where businesses can thrive. When people feel supported and positive, creativity has room to flourish.

Sustainability also plays a vital role in the future of public health and wealth creation. Healthier environments support healthier people, and wealth naturally follows. Investing in sustainable health solutions and environmentally conscious practices benefits both the planet and the economy. Green initiatives attract consumers who value ethical choices, whether that involves buying local produce or choosing biodegradable products. Businesses that prioritise sustainability create conditions where health and wealth can grow together, a combination that even the most cautious budget would applaud.

Let's not forget the rise of personalised healthcare in the future of public health. No longer will our healthcare be one-size-fits-all; it'll be tailored, just like the beautiful tuxedo you rented for your cousin's wedding. With advancements in genomics and data analytics, health initiatives will begin addressing specific community needs rather than forcing people into cookie-cutter programs. That means targeted interventions that can potentially solve problems at their root. You may find your town thriving, as local businesses tap into this personalised wave. Local health practitioners can identify community-specific concerns and craft tailored solutions that drive both health and local economic growth!

Lastly, there's an incredible opportunity through philanthropy and charitable organisations! In a world inundated with technology, all organisations will have the opportunity to invest in health initiatives that cater to marginalised populations. Health disparities will be addressed, and as communities' rally for inclusivity, unique avenues for wealth creation will flourish. Imagine the business opportunities smouldering in projects aimed at providing access to healthcare for underserved communities; here, we truly break down barriers

So, my friend, the future trend in public health and wealth creation looks promising and bursting with potential. As we step into the vibrant world, let's embrace innovations, collaboration, sustainability, and the power of mental health. Together, we can shape the future where health and wealth intertwine to create a dazzling sunset. After all, we deserve a world that celebrates the vibrancy of life and wealth, filled with laughter, prosperity, and a bowl full of your grandma's famed potato salad. Cheers to that.

Chapter 10:
Roots and Routes: Culture and Commerce

Understanding My Cultural Heritage

Understanding my cultural heritage is like having a front-row seat to the greatest spectacle on earth, complete with costumes, dance routines, and, of course, the occasional chicken running through the scene. As a proud member of the Mano tribe from Nimba County, Liberia, my roots are deeply woven into traditions, storytelling, and plenty of laughter. Growing up in Liberia was not just about dodging potholes or mastering the art of saying "hello" in every possible dialect. It was about embracing a rich tapestry of customs that shaped my understanding of wealth, community, and the occasional mischief.

My cultural heritage taught me lessons about wealth long before I ever saw a dollar bill. We did not have much in the way of material possessions, but we had stories in abundance. Elders in the village would gather the children, mostly because they had no idea how else to keep us quiet, and entertain us with tales of our ancestors and their heroic feats. These stories were our version of TED Talks, filled with wisdom, humour, and unforgettable moments that left us wanting more. They spoke of legendary warriors who defeated lions not with swords, but by scaring them away with nothing more than a thunderous sneeze. Imagine that.

Through these stories, I learned that wealth was not measured by the number of cows someone owned or the shine of their sandals, but by the strength of community ties, shared laughter, and kindness scattered like confetti at a wedding. Every visit to my grandmother's house left my pockets full, not of money, but of good advice, fresh bananas, and the crucial lesson that you should never look a goat directly in the eye, unless you are ready for trouble.

But do not get too comfortable with all this warmth. There was a time I witnessed my aunt wrestling a chicken over my grandmother's prized cassava. That alone deserved its own cultural festival. Armed with a frying pan and fierce determination, she chased that chicken around the yard like she was competing for Olympic gold. Moments like these remind you of the pure absurdity of life. They also taught me that ambition comes in many forms, sometimes it is simply about protecting what the household considers priceless.

When I transitioned from Liberia to Australia, I stepped into a world that felt like a dream and a shock rolled into one. In Australia, you can ask for bush tucker at a fancy restaurant and be met with expressions usually reserved for marriage proposals to kangaroos. Still, my cultural roots acted as a compass, guiding me through the maze of modern life. I realised my heritage was not something to hide away in a dusty trunk, but a practical toolkit filled with lessons for success in business, relationships, and everyday life.

Along this journey, I discovered that many principles from my cultural upbringing were remarkably adaptable. The focus on community, respect, and humour became part of my business approach. Who knew that making people laugh could be a pathway to prosperity? Back home, we simply called it humour. Here, it is known as branding.

If my ancestors could navigate hardship while cracking jokes during elephant hunts, then surely I could carve my own path through laughter and cultural authenticity. Understanding my cultural heritage has become a way of turning laughter into connection. It has allowed me to blend ancestral wisdom with modern business practices. Yes, I still believe I might one day become a millionaire, dashboard chickens included, but I now understand that real wealth lies in heritage, shared laughter, and lasting memories. It is a million-dollar mindset shaped by yesterday's experiences. And if my grandmother were here, she would certainly demand her share for all this advice. My biological mother turns 101 in November 2025. God bless you, Mum.

The Impact of Globalisation on African Businesses

Globalisation is the fancy word that sends shivers down the spines of village elders and leaves market sellers scratching their heads. As someone who has witnessed its effects on African businesses firsthand, I can say it is a wild ride filled with highs, lows, and an unexpected number of TikTok dances.

You might be wondering, What does globalisation even mean? Is it like the world decided to hold hands and sing "Kumbaya" while sipping chai across continents? Well, sort of. It refers to the phenomenon where business culture and economies start blending together like an unholy smoothie made of avocado toast and Eba. But while globalisation has opened doors and created opportunities, it has also raised some eyebrows— and I don't just mean the ones you find on the chickens my aunt chases in the backyard. In Africa, the impact is multifaceted. Imagine you are a local seamstress in Liberia, expertly stitching clothes that are as colourful as your aunt's five-tiered wedding cake, complete with intricate details. You've been making outfits for weddings and special occasions because, let's be honest, who can resist the joy of looking fabulous in a bright red lappa? Then globalisation comes barging in, armed with "fast fashion" brands—suddenly, your beautiful, handcrafted garments are competing against clothing made in factories where workers haven't seen daylight in years. Uh-oh! It's like watching a monumental wrestling match between David and Goliath, except David forgot to come in with a slingshot.

Some businesses struggle under this pressure, while others adapt with impressive creativity. I once met an entrepreneur who showcased traditional African clothing online and found an international audience hungry for authenticity. Her business flourished while I struggled to sell my comedy book at family gatherings. With access to the internet, business owners can reach customers worldwide. A handwoven basket made by your grandmother in Liberia can find its way to a yoga enthusiast in Australia, all while you enjoy palm wine back home.

Still, challenges remain. Trade agreements, tariffs, and international shipping can feel as confusing as convincing an elderly relative to join Facebook. Small businesses often find themselves vulnerable to global market forces, much like that unfortunate chicken fleeing my aunt's frying pan.

Then there are social media influencers promoting African culture after a brief online search. While intentions may be good, watching someone attempt Afrobeats dances in mismatched attire can be cringe-worthy. Yet globalisation also allows African culture to shine on the world stage, one viral moment at a time. Think of it as a digital cultural festival where people learn, laugh, and occasionally step on each other's toes.

Ultimately, globalisation has the potential to be both a blessing and a curse for African businesses. It can pave the way for new opportunities or leave some traditional practices behind, much like my old flip-flops. The world is changing, and we have to adapt like eggplant in a pot of stew. As businesses evolve, my hope is that we can hold onto our cultural identities while embracing the advantages that globalisation offers. Because. Nothing says "you are part of the global village" like realising that Ma Karma's incredible lapper is suddenly trending on Pinterest and selling out faster than hotcakes! All jokes aside, it's all about balance—finding that sweet spot where tradition meets innovation, ensuring that our culture not only survives but thrives in this hyper-connected land of opportunity. Eat your heart out, globalisation! We're not going down without a fight—or at least, without a good laugh!

Balancing Tradition and Modernity

Balancing tradition and modernity is like performing acrobatics on a tightrope made of goat hair while wearing flip-flops. It is thrilling, entertaining, and slightly terrifying. As an African who journeyed from the lively streets of Nimba County to Australia, I can say this balancing act requires adaptability, humour, and the willingness to keep moving even when everything feels unsteady.

In Liberia, where I spent my formative years, tradition was our compass. From the age-old stories shared under the stars by elders to the grand celebrations filled with drumming circles and, more importantly, delicious food, I learned to appreciate the wisdom and richness of our customs. Yet in a world that never seems to slow down, those traditions can sometimes feel like an anchor dragging behind while you are trying to speed ahead in a motorboat. How do you honour the past while embracing the rapid changes of modern life? It is an age-old question, one that often leaves me scratching my head as though I am battling a particularly stubborn tick.

I fondly remember running barefoot through red dust and helping my mother prepare cassava dough for our traditional GB. It was a time when community truly mattered, and everyone knew who to consult when you had a bad cold or a love jinx. The answer was usually the wise grandmother who lived at the edge of the village. However, when I transitioned to life in Australia, I realised I could no longer rely on folklore and herbal remedies to cure my woes. Modern medicine became my trusted ally, complete with antibiotics and neatly scheduled appointments.

Then there is marriage in our culture, a truly beautiful institution. Beyond the drumming and celebration, marrying within your culture is deeply respected, like belonging to an exclusive club. But the modern world arrived with dating apps and social media, turning romance into a process of swiping through potential partners as if choosing which rice to cook for dinner. Gone were the days when parents played matchmaker and village gossip paused briefly while someone took a sip of palm wine. In Australia, I often listen to love stories that sound about as graceful as a goat attempting ballet. They are amusing, refreshing, and also deeply confusing to my traditional sensibilities.

In my search for balance, I discovered that blending tradition with modernity brings its own rewards. Traditional ceremonies remain a source of pride, but now they can be live streamed for aunts who could not travel from Liberia because they refuse to leave their beloved goats behind. Everyone can attend the celebration, no matter where they lay their mats. Modern technology allows elders to share timeless wisdom while younger generations add their own flair, reminding me that whether you are in Nimba or Sydney, a well-timed dance can bridge cultural gaps faster than you can ask for a plate of jollof rice.

That said, I will not pretend it is easy. One moment you are at a polished office function where people sip lattes and discuss investments as casually as market prices. The next, you are wondering how to incorporate traditional rice ceremonies into a corporate presentation. "Mr

Dahn, shall we discuss risk management while celebrating the new harvest?" It is a challenging pitch, to say the least.

As I continue balancing the old with the new, I have come to see modernity as a tool rather than a threat. The key lies in blending ancestral wisdom with contemporary ideas. It reminds me of how my grandmother encouraged experimenting with GB soup, adding new ingredients instead of rigidly following tradition. I can only imagine her reaction if she knew I now use cayenne pepper from an Australian supermarket rather than fresh pepper from home. Still, it is about blending flavours and creating something meaningful from both worlds.

So here I am, walking the tightrope between tradition and modernity, holding a goat in one hand and a smartphone in the other, laughing my way forward step by step. It is a reminder that even in a rapidly changing world, who we are lives on through our stories, handwoven garments, and dances that bind us together as one extended family, no matter where life takes us.

Harnessing Cultural Assets for Entrepreneurship

Harnessing cultural assets for entrepreneurship feels a bit like being a magician, the kind who can turn a chicken into a fine meal while dodging a flying flip-flop aimed by an aunt at a mischievous cousin. Growing up in Liberia, I was surrounded by cultural riches, from ancient tribal wisdom to the infectious rhythms of our music. These assets were not relics of the past, but powerful tools waiting to be transformed into opportunity. In a globalised world, it is our responsibility to embrace these cultural gems and become the entrepreneurial forces we are meant to be.

Cultural assets are like my grandmother's secret GB soup recipe. Every ingredient matters, and everyone has their own way of mixing it for the best result, ideally without burning their tongue on an overly enthusiastic pepper. In Liberia, storytelling was our original form of marketing. Picture an elder sharing a thrilling tale while children clung to every word. Those moments taught me persuasion, audience connection, and the power of narrative. Today, in business, who needs a dull PowerPoint when you can weave generations of wisdom into your pitch and captivate an audience faster than a goat sprinting through a party?

Take arts and crafts, for instance. I once met a craftswoman in my village who could turn simple palm fronds into beautiful works of art. When I suggested selling her creations online, she looked at me as though I had proposed teaching a goat to perform ballet. Yet once she experienced online sales, her scepticism turned into confidence. Suddenly, palm-leaf baskets were selling faster than Uncle Nyanquoi whenever food was cooking. It struck me then that the craftsmanship embedded in our culture gives businesses an edge that factory-made products simply cannot match.

Cultural assets also foster community, which is entrepreneurial in itself. Behind every successful business is a network of support, collaboration, and more than a few spontaneous karaoke nights. No one succeeds alone, especially not while eating a meat pie in isolation. The bonds that hold our communities together can translate into strong business partnerships. Think of a modern version of bartering built around skill sharing. You teach me basket weaving, and I will teach you how to dodge flying sandals at weddings. Together, something remarkable can be created.

Now, let's talk about food—how can I not? Food is a universal language, a great equaliser of all humans and the best form of cultural expression: memorable! The culinary delights of Liberia, from spicy pepper soup to the ID-smacking taste of fried plantains, can spark joy in hearts across borders. Creating a food business that celebrates our rich culinary heritage, we introduce the world to the tantalising flavours of Africa while making a profit. Perhaps I could launch a food truck called "Joe's Jollof Jam" that travels the streets of Sydney, spreading delicious love one plate at a time. After all, who doesn't want to know that they're eating history served with a side of laughter?

Let's not forget about our traditional customs and ceremonies. We can market them—not just as heritage experiences, but as unique selling propositions that attract tourists eager to learn about our culture. Picture it: a lavish festival featuring drumming, dancing, and head-knocking competitions that both honour our roots and showcase our entrepreneurial flair. Just imagine the eclectic mix of tourists trying their best not to embarrass themselves with their dance attempts—I'd charge a small fee for that view alone!

In the end, harnessing cultural assets for entrepreneurship means taking pride in who we are and where we come from, while thoughtfully integrating that into the modern world. It is about turning stories, art, food, and community spirit into ventures that reflect our identity. Whether selling handmade goods online, opening a restaurant, or simply sharing our stories, our heritage deserves to shine brighter than Aunt Zina's hidden stash of palm wine at family gatherings. Each cultural asset adds depth to the entrepreneurial journey, helping us create something truly our own, blending tradition with innovation in a way that leaves the world inspired, entertained, and perhaps a little hungry.

Creating a Culture of Innovation in Commerce

Creating a culture of innovation in commerce is a bit like attempting to bake a cake in the middle of a dance party. It is full of excitement, messiness, and the undeniable chance of ending up with a frosting-covered face. Please do not misunderstand me. While I may be navigating the world of business, I firmly believe that innovation is crucial. It is the secret sauce that can turn a bland soup of traditional practices into a fiery, mouth-watering stew bursting with flavours from all over Africa, perhaps with a side of Grandma's famous hot pepper sauce to spice things up.

In Liberia, the concept of innovation was not just about digital apps and TikTok dances. It was an understanding that problem-solving and creativity could emerge from even the direst situations. Picture this: an enterprising friend of mine decided to turn old flip-flops into fashionable handbags. That is right. Instead of tossing them away like yesterday's leftovers, she crafted beautiful accessories that were not only stylish but also saved a few unfortunate souls from slipping on wet roads. Innovation, at its core, is not just about having an idea, but about flipping expectations and redefining what is possible.

To foster a culture of innovation, we must embrace collaboration. Think of it as forming a committee of noisy chickens and wise elders brainstorming around a communal pot of soup. Each person brings their own spices to the mix. I have come to realise that the magic happens when we open our ears and close our mouths, and truly start listening. Conversations can lead to groundbreaking ideas, whether it is adjusting business models or introducing a spontaneous dance break to lighten the mood. Who knows? A quick shimmy might inspire the next brilliant marketing idea and remind us not to take ourselves too seriously.

Furthermore, let us explore one of the primary drivers of innovation: failure. Failure is like an annoying younger sibling who keeps tagging along. Unwanted at times, yet deeply educational. When I first launched a comedy book about wealth, I naively believed everyone would instantly become a fan of joy, laughter, and self-help. Instead, rejection greeted me like an unexpected visit from the in-laws. Yet in those moments of embarrassment and frustration, I learned valuable lessons. The best ideas, and often the best jokes, come from the worst failures. That lightbulb moment came when I adjusted my marketing approach, shared my misadventures, and wove them into my story. Without failure, innovation would struggle to grow.

Technology also plays a vital role. It is the icing on the cake, or perhaps more accurately, the slapstick moment that keeps us alert. Consider the opportunities it offers: e-commerce, social media, and the ability to connect globally. I learned the hard way that technology can be as treacherous as a goat on a slippery rooftop. Entertaining, yes, but also risky. Still, my vision for an innovative culture lies in embracing and mastering these digital tools. Imagine combining traditional selling methods with modern technology, such as live-streamed rooftop events featuring local businesses. That sounds like a business model worthy of a celebratory glass of palm wine.

Flexibility is another key to promoting innovation. The business landscape is constantly evolving, and at times it feels like living inside a giant kaleidoscope. Flexibility encourages experimentation, challenges old norms, and invites new approaches at every turn. Creating a workspace where people feel comfortable saying yes to bold ideas is essential. Some suggestions may feel like an uninvited goat crashing an important meeting, but chaos can occasionally spark creative brilliance in the most unexpected ways.

Lastly, we must not overlook the importance of community among entrepreneurs. A chicken does not lay eggs alone. It needs its flock. Sharing experiences, insights, and inspiration creates a powerful network that amplifies innovation. Group brainstorming sessions can lead to surprising breakthroughs and lasting friendships, even if they begin with heated debates about whether jollof rice or fried plantains stole the show. When we celebrate each person's contribution, we weave a rich tapestry of creativity that fuels innovation.

In conclusion, creating a culture of innovation in commerce requires nurturing an environment where creativity flourishes, accompanied by laughter and the occasional spontaneous dance. By embracing collaboration, taking failure in stride, leveraging technology, fostering flexibility, and nurturing community, we can cultivate a fertile ground for new ideas and opportunities. So, grab your aprons, invite over many of your entrepreneurial friends, and let's dance our way to a marketplace where vibrant cultures are celebrated and innovation reigns supreme. The rest of the world will be wondering how we managed to combine the chaos of chicken-goats and the brilliance of serious business into a ground-breaking show.

Chapter 11:
Setting Goals That Stick

The Importance of Clear Vision

Imagine waking up in the morning and realising you have misplaced your glasses. You know you need them to see, but trying to navigate the world without them is like trying to find the last piece of a jigsaw puzzle in a room full of Lego. It is a confusing mess, and you can end up tripping over your dreams, quite literally. This is what living without a clear vision is like. A clear vision is not just about having a goal. It is about being able to see the road ahead, the destination, and all the twists and turns along the way. Without that clarity, you might just end up adding unintentional acrobatics to your résumé.

Growing up in Nimba, Liberia, I learned early on the importance of having a vision. Even my uneducated parents were, in many ways, dream architects. They would mark areas they wanted to turn into farmland four to five years in advance, even if the land was slightly unstable and involved a questionable number of palm trees. My mother, Ma Zogbelee, always emphasised that if you do not have vision, you might as well be a chicken running around the compound, clucking away but going nowhere fast. Her vision for me was simple: education and upward mobility. Her message played like the soundtrack of my life on repeat. Son, if you can dream it, you can do it. And yes, I dreamed. I dreamed of becoming a millionaire so I could finally afford a lifetime supply of fufu and palm butter soup.

Having a clear vision is like having a GPS without the usual hiccups, no annoying recalibrations or sudden rerouting. It is about knowing exactly which direction you want to go. In my own quest for wealth and wisdom, I decided early on that healthcare would be my path. This is ironic because, as a child, I could not even handle a mosquito bite without crying for my mother to rescue me. Yet here I am, pursuing a master's degree in public health while working as a clinical nurse. Vision is not about being perfect. It is about seeing your goal and understanding that the journey may be filled with bumps, hiccups, and yes, even the occasional dance party.

Now here is the kicker. Your vision should be bold. I am not saying you should wake up one day and decide to swim across the Pacific Ocean wearing nothing but a snorkel and blind determination. That kind of vision needs serious revision. What I am saying is dream big. If you aspire to be a millionaire, visualise what that life looks like in vivid colour. Imagine the cars, the homes, and even the endless supply of "I want to be a millionaire" T shirts. This dreaming phase is where you can let your imagination run wild, just do not let it run into traffic.

A clear vision also helps with accountability. Think of it as hiring your own personal cheerleader, the one who does not just wave pom poms but actually keeps you honest. When someone asks, "What is your vision?" and you can confidently recite your ambitions faster than you can say "palm wine entrepreneur," it keeps you committed. You become motivated not only to work towards your dreams but also to share them with others. Sharing your vision is like handing out tickets to your personal concert. People show up to support you. Just be careful not to invite too many people to the front row. That space should be reserved for true fans, like family or close friends, who may or may not say "I told you so" when things go sideways.

Sometimes, however, we get so caught up in our vision that we forget to enjoy life's quirks along the way. For me, laughter makes the journey to millionaire status far more enjoyable. Picture this. I once tried to set my business goals right after a high caffeine breakfast of Liberian coffee and plantains. I had so many ideas flying around that I nearly started a revolution in the cereal aisle. So while clarity is essential, remember that the road may feel like a roller coaster, and laughter is your safety harness.

Ultimately, a clear vision serves as the roadmap to achieving your dreams. It steers you away from distractions and guides you towards your goals. It is not about perfection. It is about progress. So grab your compass, put your glasses on, and let us navigate this journey together. Who knows, we might stumble upon a million dollar idea, or at the very least, share a good laugh along the way as we aim to become the richest intentional comedians around.

Creating SMART Goals

Now that we are energised about the importance of having a clear vision, it is time to put that vision into action by creating SMART goals. And no, I do not mean high fiving your goal setting buddy while wearing cool shades, although that does sound tempting. In this context, SMART stands for Specific, Measurable, Achievable, Relevant, and Time bound. If you want your dreams to flow smoothly, like palm wine at a celebration, you need a solid plan.

Let us start with "Specific." When you set a goal, you need to be sharp and focused. Saying "I want to be rich" is as vague as a mother asking if you want second helpings of cassava leaf. You understand the intention, but specifics matter. Instead, say, "I want to make $50,000 from my online business by next year." Now that is clarity. It is like going to a buffet. You cannot just say you want food. You have to choose what you want, otherwise you might end up with boiled spinach when you were really hoping for fufu and spicy stew.

Next is "Measurable." If you cannot measure it, how will you celebrate it? It is like throwing a birthday party without knowing if anyone is coming. When I turned thirty, I wanted to know exactly how many people were enjoying the barbecue. Your goals should include clear metrics. Instead of saying "I want to increase my savings," say "I want to save $200 every month." That way, you can check your progress and do a little victory dance every time you hit your target. And yes, dancing is encouraged.

Now we come to "Achievable." It is great to aim high, but let us stay realistic. Jumping off the roof will not help you reach the stars. If I had set a goal to become a multi billionaire in one year by selling banana chips from my backyard, you would rightly suggest I cut back on caffeine. Banana chips are wonderful, but that goal would not be practical. A better approach is starting a small business while continuing to work as a clinical nurse. Good goals challenge you, but they should not require you to break the laws of physics.

The next element is "Relevant." You might dream of becoming a world class tightrope walker, but if your vision is to build wealth through public health, that goal is completely off track. Choosing relevant goals ensures you are moving towards your bigger picture. I have always focused on goals that support career growth, knowledge acquisition, and community impact. When your goals align with your vision, your chances of success increase dramatically.

Finally, there is "Time bound." Every meaningful goal needs a deadline. Without one, goals can drag on endlessly. Setting a timeframe creates urgency and keeps you motivated. If your goal is to save $200 every month, decide when you want to reach $2,400 and mark it on your calendar. That deadline might have you racing towards your savings jar like a squirrel preparing for winter.

So there you have it. Creating SMART goals is not about tossing ideas into the wind and hoping for the best. It is about building a practical roadmap with clear signposts along the way. Remember to celebrate every small win. Each milestone deserves recognition, whether it is a mini dance party, a bowl of palm butter soup, or a new T shirt that proudly declares, "I am pursuing my millionaire dreams."

In conclusion, creating SMART goals is like building a successful business with limited resources. It is simple, practical, and essential. Make your goals specific, measurable, achievable, relevant, and time bound. Before you know it, you will be living your millionaire dreams, armed with laughter, discipline, and a guidebook written by yours truly, Joe Robert Saye Komadan. Now, who is ready to get SMART?

Strategies for Effective Planning

Alright, folks, let's dive into the delightful world of planning, where chaos meets clarity and dreams have a fighting chance of becoming reality. If you have ever formed wild ambitions without a plan, you probably felt like my uncle trying to catch a chicken at a family barbecue, full of energy but completely lost. I have learned that effective planning strategies are essential if we want to avoid chaotic fiascos and actually move towards our millionaire dreams.

First, let's talk about something I call "the big picture". This is more than a fancy phrase that sounds impressive at dinner parties. It is essential. The first strategy for effective planning is visualising the destination before mapping out the route. You would not set off on a road trip to an unknown place without a map, even if that map came from a tourist who left their glasses at home. So draw your big picture. What do you want to achieve by the end of the year? A thriving business? A wardrobe full of T shirts declaring, "I'm on my way to millionaire status"? Make it bold, colourful, and exciting. I even recommend sketching it out. Grab markers, sticky notes, and let your creativity run free. Your big picture should make you excited to wake up each morning, as if someone has hidden a pot of gold under your bed.

Next, break that vision into bite sized pieces, much like dividing a serving of cassava leaf rice the morning after a big night out. I learned the hard way that trying to tackle everything at once is a recipe for disaster. Think of it like attempting to eat an entire bowl of GB, also known as Gaingbah or African cassava fufu, in one sitting. It does not end well. Instead, identify key milestones that move you closer to your destination. If you are planning to launch an online business, break it down into clear steps. Research your target audience, build a website, create social media accounts, and then market your launch. Each action should be distinct yet connected, like links in a chain guiding you towards that pot of gold, without the risk of indigestion.

Flexibility is another vital part of any planning strategy. Life has a habit of throwing curveballs, such as unexpected family gatherings or discovering a new favourite snack. While it is important to have a solid plan, you must be ready to adjust. If your marketing strategy is not delivering the expected results, do not panic. Adapt your approach. You might try running an online giveaway or testing a new promotional idea. Flexibility allows you to respond to change and seize new opportunities. It is like dancing at a party. You do not want to be the person who cannot keep up when the DJ switches from reggae to hip hop.

Accountability is another strategy I cannot stress enough. Having someone on your side matters. Otherwise, the only audience for your business ideas might be your cat, and they rarely offer useful feedback.

Consider forming an accountability group with friends or family where you can share goals and track progress. Picture everyone gathered together, snacking on plantains and cheering as milestones are shared. When one person's excitement spreads, it lifts the entire group, creating energy similar to a lively market day.

Scheduling is just as important. A well structured timeline is like the secret ingredient in your grandmother's stew. It brings everything together. Take your collection of goals and add deadlines to each step. This keeps motivation alive. Use a calendar, digital tool, or colourful planner to map out when you want to achieve each milestone. I once convinced myself I could manage without a schedule, and that week turned into chaos that even my mother's prayers could not fix.

Finally, do not forget self care in the middle of all this planning. Sometimes we chase our goals so intensely that we forget to breathe. Schedule time for rest and enjoyment as part of your plan. Treat it like a business expense, because your mental wellbeing is priceless. Whether it is a walk in nature, a visit to the market, or enjoying your favourite snack, taking care of yourself boosts creativity, sharpens focus, and prepares you to face challenges more effectively.

In conclusion, effective planning is like laying a strong foundation for a house. You would not want your dreams collapsing during the first storm. By embracing the big picture, breaking goals into manageable steps, staying flexible, holding yourself accountable, scheduling wisely, and prioritising self care, you create a plan that can withstand pressure. Planning is not meant to restrict you. It is meant to empower you. So gather those markers, sketch your vision, and let us start mapping out the joyful journey towards your millionaire dreams. Who is ready to dance their way to success? I know I am.

Tracking Progress and Adapting

Alright, my ambitious dreamers, let's dive into the lively world of tracking progress and adapting along the way. If planning felt exciting, execution is where the real adventure begins. Tracking progress is like keeping score in a game. You would not celebrate too early only to realise the other team has just scored. This is the moment to roll up your sleeves, stay alert, and assess how far you have come on the journey towards your millionaire dreams.

First, let's talk about measurement. When you set out on this journey, you need clear metrics to track progress. Just like calculating how many plates of jollof rice I can finish in one sitting, the number is impressive, but not the point, you need to know what success looks like. Are you saving $200 each month? Excellent. Are your online sales steadily increasing as well? If yes, you are sailing smoothly towards your destination. If not, it may be time to adjust your strategy.

Tracking progress does not have to be boring. In fact, it should be fun. Create a colourful chart to monitor your goals. Add stickers, symbols, or doodles that proudly announce your achievements. I once made a progress board that looked like a bustling marketplace, complete with celebratory stick figures for every completed task. Watching those little drawings pile up gave me enough motivation to charge into the next goal with unstoppable energy.

That said, tracking progress also means facing challenges honestly. When things do not go as planned, and trust me, they will not, adaptability becomes essential. Think of yourself as a bamboo tree that bends with the wind rather than a rigid oak. There is no shame in adjusting your approach. I have seen business ideas collapse faster than a poorly made piñata at a birthday party. When I first launched my online store, my product photos looked like they were taken with a potato instead of a camera. Sales dropped quickly. Instead of quitting, I sought feedback, improved my visuals, and kept refining my approach. Eventually, I felt like a film director carefully crafting the perfect shot for my brand.

Adapting effectively means creating a feedback loop. This is simpler than it sounds. It involves checking your progress regularly, not just once a month while relaxing with palm wine. Schedule weekly or fortnightly reflection sessions. Ask yourself what is working, what is not, and what new ideas could help you move forward. Whether through self reflection or trusted feedback from others, staying open to constructive criticism is vital. And if friends start offering advice like fruit flying in a busy market, take what resonates and leave the rest behind.

Equally important is celebrating small wins. Every step forward deserves recognition. When you reach a milestone, reward yourself. Enjoy a movie night, your favourite snack, or even a dance session in your living room. These celebrations lift your spirits and remind you why you started. I have turned my living room into a makeshift nightclub just to celebrate a month of consistent saving. And while the universe may not send a confetti cannon to your house, the joy you create for yourself is more than enough.

Tracking progress and adapting is not just about reaching the destination. It is about staying engaged, learning from the journey, and enjoying every step along the way.

Lastly, remember that tracking is a time for reflection, not harsh judgement. The road to success can feel like riding a rollercoaster, complete with twists, turns, highs, and lows. Do not be hard on yourself for not getting everything right. Instead, adopt a curious mindset. Ask what needs to change without turning self reflection into an excuse to sink into regret over past decisions. Mistakes are simply stepping stones for learning. Every stumble is an opportunity to grow wiser and stronger.

In conclusion, tracking progress and adapting is not just about keeping ambition alive. It is an art that requires creativity, flexibility, and encouragement. Celebrate your successes, adjust when life throws challenges your way, and remember to enjoy the journey. So grab those charts, gather your cheering squad, and let's keep the momentum alive. Together, we will move closer to that million dollar dream, one dance party at a time.

Celebrating Success and Learning from Failure

Ah, the sweet nectar of success. There is nothing quite like it. It is like taking the first sip of fresh palm wine at a family gathering. It warms your heart and reminds you of all the effort that went into earning that moment. But before we get lost in celebration, let's talk about its equally important companion, failure. And no, I will not sugarcoat it. Failure is not comforting or cosy. It is more like that cousin who shows up uninvited and reminds you of your most embarrassing memories. Still, both success and failure carry powerful lessons and deserve equal respect as the balance of life.

Let's start by savouring success. There is nothing quite like the moment when hard work pays off and you finally say, "Yes, I did it." Whether it is reaching a long term savings goal, launching your first product, or hitting a career milestone, every achievement deserves celebration. Think of success as your generous grandmother offering you the biggest slice of cake on your birthday. Why would you ever refuse it? I always encourage celebrating wins, no matter how small they seem. Even finishing a project or writing a chapter is reason enough to acknowledge yourself.

Let me share a quick story. When I finally launched my online business, the day felt huge. Everything was prepared. I had my best presentation ready and a motivational playlist that could energise an entire army. And then I tripped over my slippers during my victory dance and landed flat on the floor. Instead of letting embarrassment steal the moment, I laughed until tears came. That fall became part of the story. It reminded me that success often arrives with a bit of chaos. From that day on, I promised myself to celebrate the wins and embrace the awkward moments that come with them.

Of course, where there are highs, there will be lows. Now let's talk about failure, the equivalent of burnt cassava sitting on the kitchen bench. It is tempting to hide it and pretend it never happened, but failure is one of life's best teachers, even if it has a sharp sense of humour. I have had my fair share. My first attempt at running a public health communication workshop was more circus than seminar. It was messy, confusing, and full of laughter, but it taught me invaluable lessons about preparation and audience engagement.

When failure shows up, pause and reflect instead of sinking into despair. Ask yourself what you can learn. Do you need to adjust your approach? This is the time to seek feedback from trusted people, because no one succeeds alone. Failures are not permanent. They are temporary obstacles that guide growth. When I miscalculated parts of my business strategy, I invited friends over and turned the experience into a feedback session over jollof rice. We laughed, analysed what worked, and improved what did not. Turning failure into a brainstorming session can be surprisingly powerful.

A key part of celebrating success and learning from failure is developing resilience. When things fall apart, give yourself grace. The journey is not linear. It can feel like running a marathon while dodging unexpected obstacles. Acknowledge the setback, but do not let it define you. What defines you is your ability to adapt, rise again, and keep going. Each setback is a step forward in disguise.

Also, take time to appreciate the people who support you. Share your victories with those who helped you reach them. Doing so strengthens bonds and builds lasting support systems. You will be surprised how many meaningful connections grow through shared laughter, honesty, and both success and failure.

In conclusion, life is about balancing the sweetness of success with the lessons of failure. Celebrate wholeheartedly, laugh at your missteps, learn from every experience, and invite others to walk the journey with you. With the right perspective, both triumphs and challenges enrich your life. So let's raise a glass, enjoy the moment, and dance through this blend of wins and lessons, knowing they are both essential on the path to becoming the millionaires we aim to be.

Chapter 12:
Investing in Relationships

Understanding the Value of Networking

Networking. A single word that can make or break your journey faster than a politician changing sides. Understanding the value of networking is as important as knowing how to cook rice without burning it. In my search for wisdom and a decent cup of coffee, I learned that connections are not just helpful. They are powerful. Think of them as a strong current that carries you towards opportunity while you navigate life's unpredictable waters.

At its core, networking is about who you know and how you build those relationships. It is like using your mother's secret recipe when you want to impress guests. If you want your dreams to take shape, you must engage in conversations, even the awkward ones. Yes, this includes small talk. Whether you are chatting with someone at your local café or debating whether pineapple belongs on pizza, these simple interactions often lead to unexpected opportunities. While you are trying to seem interesting, remember that others are doing the same. That shared effort is where connection begins.

In today's fast paced world, building a network is essential. A weak network is like wearing flip flops in the rain. It is risky and uncomfortable. A strong network, on the other hand, is like sturdy boots that help you move forward with confidence. It is not about collecting as many contacts as possible. It is about building meaningful connections. Seek people who can guide you, challenge you, open doors, and share real knowledge. It is not a secret society. You simply need to remember names, values, and what matters to people.

Diversity is also vital. If your network looks the same everywhere you turn, it is time to broaden it. You would not watch the same movie on repeat, so why limit yourself to the same perspectives? Connecting with people from different cultures and backgrounds expands your thinking and opens doors you never knew existed. My move from Liberia to Australia showed me the power of diverse relationships. The mix of ideas, experiences, and viewpoints enriches both personal and professional growth. Plus, who else will introduce you to the hidden gems of the city if not your multicultural circle? Embrace the variety, just as you would enjoy both a comforting bowl of pepper soup and a classic Australian meat pie.

Of course, it is not enough to simply add people to your address book and think the job is done. Relationships need care, just like a well tuned engine. Regular check ins, a simple "How are you?" message, or even sending a funny meme can make a big difference. Keeping your network active does not mean becoming the social star of the year. It simply means showing genuine interest in people's lives. People remember those who truly care. You also never know when an old contact might be holding a great opportunity.

Using social media for connection and growth is also important in today's digital world. Platforms like LinkedIn, Facebook, and Twitter are modern marketplaces for sharing ideas and building relationships. However, it is easy to get distracted by endless scrolling and entertainment. Be intentional with how you use social media. Treat it like a virtual office. Share useful content, engage thoughtfully with others, and make it clear that you are open to meaningful connections. One simple conversation could lead to a collaboration, a job opportunity, or even a good laugh that brightens your day.

In summary, understanding the value of networking is not just about attending events or enjoying fancy drinks, although that can be a bonus. It is about building relationships that offer support, guidance, and opportunity on your journey towards financial success. Take the initiative, follow up, and show real curiosity about others. Your next breakthrough might be just one honest, laughter filled conversation away.

Building Meaningful Connections in Professional Life:

Building meaningful connections in professional life is like carefully constructing a fantastic jigsaw puzzle. You've got to find the right pieces. And if you try to force a corner piece into the centre, you'll just create a mess—trust me, I tried. During my sojourn from Liberia to Australia, I learned the intricate dance of transforming random acquaintances into enduring relationships that could sustain me through gut-wrenching challenges and exhilarating triumphs alike. So buckle up, dear readers, because this ride through the realms of professionalism isn't just a slog through LinkedIn profiles; it's a wild adventure woven with humour and warmth!

Have you ever attended a networking event where it felt like everybody was vying for a marquee spot in the next big blockbuster? I sure have! Conversations often felt like a weird auction where people exchanged cards instead of bids. You know, "I have a degree from Harvard, do you have?" It took me some time to realise that shoving your down someone's throat isn't effective. Building connections by introducing your authentic self, sharing laughter, and creating Stories that last far beyond the stale refreshments of a networking soirée. About finding common ground, whether that's bonding over a shared vision for soggy sandwiches or celebrating your mutual passion for a good dad joke.

Don't underestimate the power of authenticity; it's the glue that holds relationships together! Picture this: you're at a work event, desperately trying to impress a potential mentor, and instead of being yourself, you start reciting facts about your industry that even Google would roll its eyes at. —There's nothing more cringeworthy than seeing someone squirm trying to be someone they're not. The real magic happens when you showcase your quirks. I'm a clinical nurse by day and an aspiring author by night. I've also been known to crack self-deprecating jokes about my attempts at an elaborate Liberian dish—spoiler alert: it ended up looking like an experiment gone awry. When you embrace your true self, it opens doors. People love connecting with the human side of you, the one who intentionally burnt the rice but still has great stories to tell.

Now, as I navigated this colourful bamboo forest known as the professional landscape, I realised that diversity is the seasoning that any dish needs to be fulfilling. While it's tempting to surround yourself with people who think just like you, it'll transform your conversations into a monotonous hum of boredom. Seek out different perspectives, backgrounds, and experiences. In the professional realm, these colourful reactions can illuminate an entirely new blueprint for your career. Be a wise older colleague who has seen it all or a fresh grad with sparkly eyes;

every person holds treasures in the form of knowledge, stories, and sometimes even life-altering advice.

Next came the act of nurturing connections. Picture this: the winter of 2020 hits, and I'm reminding myself that maintaining relationships isn't just about sending a birthday card once every five years, though even that took some practice. It's about regular touchpoints and sincere dialogues—like asking a friend how their project is progressing, sharing a helpful article, or perhaps even being the first person to like their latest social media post. Trust me, it isn't as complicated as you might think. Just sprinkle a little kindness and humour into your interactions, and watch those connections blossom like flowers in springtime!

And speaking of springtime, let's talk about advocacy! Yes, I said it. Being an advocate means going the extra mile—not just for yourself, but also for those around you. When you support the endeavours of others in your network, they're more likely to return the favour. I've seen it firsthand, such as during a challenging time when I stumbled upon an opportunity that was ideally suited for a former colleague. Passing that torch illuminated both of our paths! When you help others achieve their own goals, you also lay the groundwork for mutual growth—a beautiful dance of reciprocity.

Finally, in this whirlwind of building connections, don't forget to have some fun! Crack jokes, share incompetencies, and revel in the light-hearted moments that arise over a coffee. Connecting with others is not just about cold calculations and strategic planning. It's about sharing laughter and even engaging in light-hearted negotiations about whether "chicken cr fish" will somehow secure that promotion. So, embrace the joy of building meaningful connections. Whether they lead you to wealth, wisdom, or a delightful new perspective, remember that a professional life enriched with genuine connections is bound to sprout opportunities like weeds in an unkempt garden! Now, go forth and make those connections! Just don't force any puzzle pieces together; it tends to cause more chaos than clarity!

The Art of Small Talk: Turning Conversations into Opportunities:

Small talk—the fine art of conversing without really saying much at all! It's like trying to describe a Liberian hot pepper soup without ever mentioning the soup. We've all been there, standing awkwardly in a corner, cringing at the idea of initiating what feels like a verbal game of Twister. Your elbow is tangled in one vague topic, while your foot is stuck in the "how's the weather?" conversation! But let me tell you, dear friends, small talk is not only a necessary evil; it's a secret weapon that can transform bland interactions into golden opportunities faster than you can say "business casual.

The first lesson I learned about small talk is that everyone is an expert in the nuances of awkward silence. You know that uncomfortable moment where your brain throws a circuit breaker, and suddenly, you're contemplating the meaning of life instead of what's happening at the cookie table? But here's the kicker: it takes just a sprinkle of confidence and authenticity to turn those cringeworthy pauses into gateways of connection. Instead of fretting about what to say, shift your focus to the person in *front of you! Are they wearing that brilliant shade of orange because they have a sunny disposition, or did they just lose a bet? See? That's a conversation waiting to happen. Asking open-ended questions that invite creativity can often lead you to unexpected pathways. Who knew that a bright tie could lead to a discussion about their trip to the Australian Outback?

Now, let's flip the switch on the classic, "How are you?" question, which becomes the professional equivalent of wallpaper—nice to look at, but one's actually paying attention. Instead, consider kicking it up a notch! What if you ask, "What's the most adventurous thing you've done recently?" This is the kind of question that often catches people off guard. Suddenly, you've engaged them, but you've also invited them to share a story that reveals their character. Did they recently try bungee jumping while blindfolded? Bingo! You have transformed a mundane moment into a riveting exchange! It's here that you may uncover unique viewpoints, life experiences, and even a future = partner-in-crime for your next venture.

Small talk doesn't have to be a chore; think of it like creating a mosaic. We're gathering colourful tiles—fragments of life's experiences—little bits of laughter and anecdotes. Why do I say this? Because the more stories we share, the more we paint a picture of who we are and what we stand for. A chance to swap stories about our families, backgrounds, and daily life quirks can turn those early conversations from boring monologues into lively exchanges full of laughter and sympathy. My grandfather once told me that people are like stories waiting to be told; you just have to ask the right questions to unravel them. So, break open those tales _like the most exciting mystery novel!

Now, let us talk about the beauty of humour. When you weave laughter into conversations, you create an invisible glue that brings people together. Who does not enjoy a good chuckle? During my own networking experiences, I discovered that sharing light-hearted jokes about my own mishaps helped break the ice instantly. One time, I mistook laundry detergent for cooking oil and ended up with a soup that could frighten even the bravest soul. The result was genuine smiles and hearty laughter. Humour disarms people, creates comfort, and shows that you are relatable. And if you can make someone laugh, there is a good chance they will remember you. Just be careful not to let your jokes flop like poorly cooked fufu, the kind that collapses despite your best efforts to make it fluffy.

That said, humour works best when it suits the audience. You would not tell a ghost story at a child's birthday party, would you? It is important to read the room. At a corporate gala, delivering punchlines as if you are on a comedy tour may not land as well as expected, unless you are aiming to be remembered as the person who made the CEO lose their appetite. As you refine your small talk skills, remember that listening is just as important as speaking. Conversations are a two-way street. If you are too focused on planning your next joke, you might miss insights that could open doors you never imagined. Active listening allows you to respond thoughtfully. If someone mentions a hobby or interest you share, take the opportunity to explore it further.

In conclusion, mastering the art of small talk transforms ordinary conversations into powerful opportunities for connection and collaboration. Embrace the awkward moments, as they are part of the journey. With confidence, humour, and genuine curiosity, mundane chit-chat can become meaningful conversation. The next time you find yourself standing awkwardly at an event, take a deep breath, smile, and step into the conversation. Every great opportunity begins with a simple hello and a touch of humour. You may surprise yourself and perhaps even gain a new friend or future business partner along the way.

Creating a Diverse Network: Bridging Cultures and Communities

Creating a diverse network is like cooking the perfect pepper soup. Every ingredient needs to come together in harmony to create something truly special. Limiting yourself to familiar faces and ideas is like preparing a single-flavour dish that leaves your palate, and your network, craving adventure. My experience has shown me that embracing cultural and community diversity is not just beneficial but essential for personal and professional growth. So, grab your metaphorical cooking spoon and explore this rich pot of possibilities.

Moving from Liberia to Australia was a real eye-opener. It felt like stepping into a bustling market where every stall offered something unique. Some of the most valuable lessons I learned did not come from textbooks, but from conversations with people from different backgrounds. Those awkward silences we often fear can easily be filled with stories that reveal new ways of seeing the world. Every person carries a collection of experiences shaped by culture, tradition, and family quirks. If you only met people who liked vanilla ice cream, you would miss out on flavours like mango, coconut, or chocolate fudge. Diversity invites us to explore beyond the familiar.

Building a diverse network does not mean becoming a cultural expert overnight. It begins with openness and a willingness to engage with people outside your usual circles. I often find that conversations with those who hold different perspectives deepen my understanding of the world. It feels like stepping out of a quiet library and into a lively festival filled with sounds, aromas, and laughter. Whether someone is from a different age group, nationality, or industry, connecting with them can lead to surprising insights. Learning how to break the ice often uncovers incredible life stories or innovative ideas that help solve challenges you are facing.

You may wonder how to start these conversations without sounding rehearsed or awkward. The answer is to keep it simple. At any gathering, shared interests are usually closer than they appear. Rather than diving into heavy topics, start with something universal, like food. Everyone eats. Ask about family meals or share a funny story about a mystery dish you once tried. These light conversations often lead to deeper understanding and lasting connections.

As your network grows more diverse, you become a cultural sponge, absorbing experiences that broaden your perspective. Growing up in Mano culture taught me the value of family and community. Connecting with others expanded that understanding even further. My Australian friends, for example, have shown me how a barbecue can become the centre of every celebration. From vibrant markets in Liberia to sun-soaked picnic spots in Australia, life is a celebration woven through shared traditions. Being part of a diverse community means embracing those contrasting lifestyles and learning how each is woven together to create the intricate tapestry of the human experience.

One cannot deny the challenges that may arise while bridging cultures. Mismatched humour, cultural faux pas, and perhaps a dismal attempt at understanding regional dialects are bound to happen! But truly, the laughter you share through these moments often becomes the glue that cements relationships. Sharing stories of my own missteps or even cringe-worthy moments has usually led to people recounting their own "oops" stories. We unfold our layers, and suddenly, we're not just individuals; we're fellow humans who have navigated the same turbulent waters of life. That's the kind of connection that can transform a diverse group of people into a thriving network!

Ultimately, your vibrant network of diverse individuals will empower you to think critically and creatively. They will inspire you to make connections that you previously thought impossible. By understanding different cultures, ideologies, and experiences, you prepare yourself to face challenges with a myriad of perspectives. In this fast-paced world, adapting and thriving in diverse environments is crucial, and it starts with recognising the beauty around us.

So, my dear readers, embrace the kaleidoscope of cultures we live in! Say "hello" to someone new, try out a recipe from a different cuisine, or earn a few words in a language that intrigues you. In doing this, we form magnificent bridges, cultivating an enriching environment where ideas flow freely, just as the stories of our lives. Diversity isn't just a buzzword; it's a celebration worth indulging in. Let's turn our networks into an aromatic feast where every spice adds depth, flavour, and magic to our collective journey.

Leveraging Social Media for Connection and Growth:

In this digital age, leveraging social media for connection and growth feels a bit like cooking under pressure—if you can navigate the chaos, you can create a feast! Gone are the days of writing lengthy letters and sending them through the postal service, slower than a snail on vacation. Today, social media platforms are the highways of human interaction, a virtual bazaar, offering exciting and dynamic opportunities to connect, collaborate, and showcase your talent. Trust me; it's more exciting than a one-legged chicken wearing a tutu! So, let's dig deeper into how we can cultivate flavourful connections and growth using these digital landscapes.

First thing first, social media it isn't just about posting cute pet pictures or sharing last night's dinner that faintly resembled gourmet art. While those things warm our hearts, it's crucial to approach these platforms with intention. What do you want to achieve? Are you looking to foster genuine connections, grow your professional brand, or perhaps gain insights from others in your industry? Once you scope out your goals, you can tailor you online presence to reflect that. Set up your profiles like you're organizing a vital meeting—a little polished, highly engaging, and unmistakably YOU Who wouldn't want to engage with a charismatic persona that oozes warmth, humour, and a pinch of mischief?

Next comes the age-old mantra: "Engage, don't just exist!" Social media isn't a silent film; it thrives on interaction. Bombarding your friends with self-promotional posts doesn't cut it. Instead, dive into the comment' section! React to others' updates, share their content, and engage in conversations that spark joy—or at least intrigue. Imagine walking up to someone at a party versus sitting in the corner scrolling mindlessly; the former opens avenues for delightful conversations, while the latter shrinks your social persona like a deflated balloon. When you take the effort to genuinely engage with others' posts, it adds delightful colour to you: connections, turning them from acquaintances into allies.

Social media can also be a treasure trove of learning opportunities! Follo• influencers, industry leaders, and thought provokers to fill your feed with insightful content. And let's not forget the glorious utility of hashtags— use them like a chef uses herbs! They help you discover communities within your niche and get your content noticed by others. Picture it like attending a massive potluck; you don't just want to fill your plate with your own dish. Explore what others have brought to the table, and don't hesitate to share your creation! This active participation helps foster a sense of camaraderie and presents you in a light that encourages growth— not just personal but also communal.

Now get ready for my favourite part, captivates and connects! Your social media posts are proverbial invitations to the banquet table, so make sure they embody your unique essence. Aim for authenticity and make it relatable by inserting personal stories, sprinkling in humour and leaving the boring corporate jargon in the documents folder. I mean, let's face it, we have all read about the "synergy" and "paradigm shifts" one too many times. Let's serve the delicious narrative instead. You can capture hearts with a vibrant story about an embarrassing work blunder or a moment of triumph in your career journey. Vulnerability leads to engagement, and suddenly, your followers are not just spectators but active participants in your narrative.

But let's not forget about collaboration—it's the secret ingredient that ups the dish! Social media is brimming with like-minded individuals -c to connect, so why not seize the moment and hop on a collaboration? Whether it's co-hosting a webinar, collaborating on new endeavours, or a good ol' Instagram live session, teaming up with others amplifies reach and brings distinct perspectives into your work. You create a form that's rich in knowledge, experiences, and networks to help another grow. It's like combining two fabulous recipes to whip up a monster of amazingness—everyone wins!

Lastly, monitoring your progress on social media is essential. Just as you should taste-test your dishes, it's crucial to analyse your engagement metrics. What types of posts resonate the most with your audience? Which strategies led to connections or new business opportunities? Adjust and pivot accordingly. Keep your social media dynamic and fluid, constantly adapting to your evolving aspirations.

In conclusion, leveraging social media for connection and growth is an opportunity served fresh every day. With intention, engagement, and authenticity, you can create a vibrant networking space that appeals even to the fussiest participants. So put on your best networking suit and step into this digital journey with confidence. The table is set, the audience is waiting, and with a dash of humour and empathy, your digital kingdom is ready to grow.

Chapter 13:
The $100 Mindset:
Thinking Small for Big Dreams

When I first heard the phrase "think big," I assumed it was another clever slogan used by motivational speakers to sell expensive coaching packages. If thinking big meant sipping champagne on a private jet while wearing sunglasses indoors, then I was sweating like a goat in a sauna just imagining it. But here is the surprising truth. Sometimes, thinking small is the fastest way to reach those big dreams spinning around in your head like mosquitoes at a family reunion.

Let us talk about the $100 mindset. When money is mentioned, we are often told to invest big for big returns. But what if the real magic begins when you focus on just $100. Yes, that same amount you might casually spend on tips or an overpriced coffee. It may sound unimpressive, but it is often the smartest starting point for an entrepreneurial escapades.

Imagine this: instead of dreaming about launching a colossal tech startup with a budget that would make Jeff Bezos blush, you start with the humble ambition of using a crisp $100 bill as your launch pad. I can already hear the sceptics, "But Joe, that's not enough to even get a taco stand!" Well, sometimes the best recipes start with just a pinch of something marvellous!

The $100 mindset teaches us to view problems more like jigsaw puzzles -not as full-blown disasters. For example, when I arrived in Australia with nothing but my luggage, children and dreams bouncing like kangaroos, it hit me: I didn't need to own a thriving multi-million-dollar business to make an impact. I just needed to make good use of the limited wisdom resources circulating within the Australian outback and mingle like old Grandma at a church potluck. You know, enterprise on a plate!

Think about it! With just $100, you can start a service oriented business—perhaps lawn mowing, where you don't even own a mower yet, but have a can-do attitude and a few friends trying to earn some extra cash. Vineyard needs some fluffing and ding-a-ling. What starts as your pal's could morph into a neighbourhood landscaping empire with just a bit of hard work! This is what I call entrepreneurial alchemy: turning potatoes into mashed masterpieces.

For many of you, this idea may feel comically absurd. I mean, who wants the '$100 Business Guy' when our world is filled with glitzy Instagram influencers flaunting their private jets? Well, let me tell you, my fellow weaver, when you start to learn the art of "small thinking," you're embracing the journey rather than focusing solely on the ATM numbers. Carving out small successes leads to bigger lessons, and you might even get to enjoy a few quiet tacos along the way instead of yearning for the whole grand fiesta.

In the realm of wealth creation, $100 is definitely not a "one size fits all" ß=ion, but it can serve as the ideal starting point. It's your invitation to enter your imaginations, brainstorm like a squad of caffeinated squirrels, and find treasure lurking where you least expect it. Sometimes, the smallest can launch the most outrageous journey—ask my cousin Alfred; *turned a $100 bet on a local chicken race into the most excellent fried chicken —e I've ever tasted. And look where we are now—one step closer to while suspiciously eyeing Colonel Sanders.

So, dear reader, as you ponder your dreams, I implore you: put on your smallest thinking cap and embrace that nifty $100 mindset. You just discovered that the truest riches lie not in the size of your aspirations but in the size of your tenacity, realism, and willingness to embrace the immensity of creativity within the confines of that modest sum. The road to world-changing wealth doesn't always have to be paved with gold; sometimes, it's just a few dirty coins in your pocket and an epic spirit willing to hustle for happiness. Look out, privilege—Joe's bringing the charm of the entrepreneurial revolution, one $100 dream at a time!

Finding Opportunity in Everyday Life:

You know, a wise man once told me that opportunity is like the wine, it's always blowing, but you have to be the one to open the window. For my fellow aspirational millionaires—you can take that quite literally! If you find yourself cloistered in a cubicle, hoping for an escape route, raiding the office fridge for last week's leftover pizza (that might even be a finance broker's gold mine), it might be time to rethink your next move. Trust me, as someone who migrated from Liberia to Australia with a head full of dreams and a pocket full of lint, I'm here to tell you that opportunities can be found in the most unsuspecting places.

Let's explore how we can turn our mundane moments into money-making adventures! It's as simple as looking around: the supermarket, your neighbourhood park, even your roommate with a failing plant (hex there's a business idea brewing there). The world is a ripe fruit tree, waiting for someone to pluck the low-hanging fruit! Take that supermarket as an example. Do you ever notice how they have those samplers wandering around, offering you mini awkward bites of crackers? Well, befriend those folks. Next time, bring your best look of youthful enthusiasm and strike up a chat. Who knows? Maybe they'll offer you their sampling gig and inspire your culinary career. If nothing else, you've scored free snacks, and in this economy, that's no laughing matter!

One day, while waiting at a bus stop (picturing myself casually tapping the essence of success), I noticed an elderly lady struggling with a handful of grocery bags that could rival a family-sized serving of burritos. Sow, one might say, "Joe, just mind your own business!" to which I pondered, "Aha! An opportunity!" I offered to help her lug those bags to her house, and through chit-chat, I found out that she had an unused Fage just brimming with collectibles! Collectibles people! I gave her my mighty pre-caffeinated veins and in return received a lead for the type of measure that would make Indiana Jones toss his hat in the air. Turned out, I was sitting on a goldmine, and here I was, the superhero of grocery lugging.

Now, let us not forget about social media. The digital world is full of opportunity. Everyone on Facebook seems to be an expert at something. I once saw a friend train his dog to take selfies, and now that dog has over 100,000 followers. Opportunities exist all around us within our social circles. Sharing experiences, even the most unusual ones, can connect you with people who may be just bold enough to collaborate on something truly brilliant. So next time you are scrolling past posts about cats or avocado toast, look closely. There may be a hidden opportunity such as cooking classes, dog walking, or even plant recovery services.

Then there are local community events like farmers' markets, exhibitions, and even questionable bake sales. They might sound dull, but they are full of potential. Every one of these events offers a chance to connect, learn, and test ideas. I once sold handmade postcards at a local art fair using what I generously call my artistic skills. I may not be a millionaire yet, but I certainly built connections with other vendors. The key is to stay tuned into your community and its needs. You never know when a small idea might grow into something bigger.

In truth, the world is filled with small opportunities hidden inside everyday activities. The secret is to take part in life rather than simply observe it. Pay attention to the small signals around you. Your local barista might be sitting on a great business idea, or the neighbour who constantly struggles with their garden could be your first client.

At the end of the day, if wealth creation is a dance, then let us not just do the cha-cha in our dining rooms but tango through the streets, parks, and supermarkets, embracing every opportunity like they're good friends who have come to stay a while. Remember, life is a game of chess, not just checkers—look for openings not just to win but to innovate, collaborate and connect! You might just set yourself on a trail of innovation, inspiration or at the very least, get a free lunch out of kindness. Now that's a win-win situation.

The Art of Negotiation: Making every dollar count:

Negotiation—the ancient art of making every dollar count while flexing your verbal dexterity like a master sushi chef wielding a sharp knife. If there's one thing I've learned in my quest from humble beginnings to the land of Australia and beyond, it's that negotiation is not just a skill: It's an essential survival tactic. Whether you're haggling for the price of a product at a roadside stand or trying to convince your toddler that broccoli isn't actually the vegetable equivalent of little green monsters, mastering the art of negotiation can make or break your expedition to wealth.

I remember my first attempt at negotiation like it was yesterday. I must have been about eight years old, trying to convince my mother that if she took care of all my chores, she would pay me in my favourite currency: gifts! Somehow, I could use slick words, maybe a little negotiation magic, and voilà, I'd have an endless toy collection! Looking back, I have to admit, I was about as effective as a cup without a handle at boiling tea. But here's the thing: every negotiation, be it with mother or potential investor, is a learning opportunity wrapped in an awkward social experience.

The cornerstone of any successful negotiation is researching your subject matter. Don't walk into these situations as blind as a bat in a blackout! Whether it's about knowing the latest price of avocados (who knew they could compete with small nations in price?) or understanding how much your services are worth, knowledge is power, my friend! A wise negotiator doesn't just rip the price off the wall like a kid at the candy store; they come with data and polite assertiveness. Trust me, no one wants to feel like a leaky faucet during negotiations.

Let's not forget the power of charm. Now, I know some of you may not see yourselves as the charismatic types—maybe you're more on the quiet •e, or perhaps your idea of charm usually involves monkey impressions. Let me tell you, being genuinely likable can get you far! Small talk has been known to open more doors than a professional locksmith. Picture yourself chatting up the manager of that store where everything is overpriced, and suddenly, you turn on that Joe charm. Who knows, maybe they'll be feeling generous, and before you know it, you'll be walking with discounted gadgets of bulk oranges for the price of three. Smiles go a long way—especially if they're accompanied by compliments about someone's incredible tie or well-coiffed hairstyle!

Then we have the magical powers of timing—much like the wizards in movies who can freeze people in place. You don't want to negotiate when everyone's over the last box of doughnuts, nor should you engage when your opponent's face looks like they've just bitten into a sour lemon. Timing is my friend! Capitalise on moments when the other party may be feeling emotionally charged. A friendly smile and some light-hearted banter can do wonders when it sets you up to claim that extra discount or that last seat on the bus without additional fees.

Now, let's talk about the power of silence. Ever notice how silence can make you feel just a bit awkward? Like you've been caught in a staring match with a pigeon at a park? In the realm of negotiation, that silence can be a secret weapon. When you say your piece and then sit back, it forces *other party to fill the void. When your counterpart realises they can't just walk away without addressing your concerns, my friend, you've mastered the art. Watch their face as they internally scramble like a chicken trying to miss the road without getting hit. Suddenly, they may even offer you a price that makes you raise your eyebrows like an over-caffeinated squirrel—yes, the magic of a good pause!

In the end, trust your gut, and know that negotiation is frequently a matter of finding the right balance. If the conditions aren't acceptable, feel free to decline. The next bargain is always nearby, potentially in a back alley next to the individual selling "used" garden gnomes, or wherever your search for a good deal leads. It's smart to know when to hold, fold, or just eat your vegetables!

So, whether you're negotiating discounts on plant pots, squeezing profits from business deals, or charming your way through life, remember that negotiation is both a science and an art. It's about understanding people, knowing what you want, and transforming connections into profits! Practice, and by weaving in a sprinkle of humour, who knows? You might become the negotiation master of your dreams—authentic, approach, maybe even a little bit legendary! Now, where's my broccoli?

Creativity over Capital: Innovative Business Ideas:

Creativity! That sparkling gem sitting somewhere between a wild idea and the audacity to believe it can earn you a living. When it comes to turning dreams into reality, I've learned that sometimes all it takes is a sprinkle of imagination combined with a dash of ingenuity—certainly more delightful than dollars! Having ventured from the vibrant culture of Liberia to the colourful streets of Australia, I've discovered that being innovative can pave a much sturdier road to success than simply dumping loads of cash into traditional ventures. So, dear readers, grab your imaginations and up—let's embark on a wacky journey of creative entrepreneurial gems!

First, we must debunk the myth that innovation requires a hefty starting budget. When I was in Liberia, I saw countless young people flipping the script on conventional businesses. Imagine a bicycle repair shop disguised as a friendly neighbourhood hangout. Those guys didn't need a fancy building or a gazillion shillings; they capitalised on their bike knowledge, socialising with the community over a brew of tea, and turned those dusty old bicycles into gold! Creativity was the star of their show, not shiny banknotes. Sometimes all it takes is a simple idea: leveraging what you already have and enhancing it with a twist of flair!

Another marvel of creativity is tapping into nature's never-ending resources. I once knew a fellow named Alfred who turned his absolute passion for gardening into a small yet thriving business. He wandered around his neighbourhood, collecting native seeds and plants from sidewalks and alleyways. With the right blend of fertile soil and good Liberian sunshine, he soon found that his backyard not only grew vegetables; it also flourished into a thriving garden shop, bursting with innovative ideas! Let's be honest, Alfred's entrepreneurial journey started with nothing but a shovel, determination, and the delightful scent of freshly dug dirt. No precious capital needed, just a heart and the will to cultivate!

Now, let us switch gears and bring some digital creativity to the table. The internet is the most accessible playground for aspiring entrepreneurs everywhere. Have you ever considered starting a blog or YouTube channel about the quirks of making plant-based Liberian dishes? Why not. With nothing more than your phone and your personality, you could attract hundreds, or even thousands, of curious food lovers eager to explore the wonders of cassava. No large start-up budget is required. All it takes is courage and a willingness to share your colourful culinary journey with the world. The best part is that your audience can help turn your passion into a monetised opportunity, much like the avocado toast everyone seems to be selling these days.

Another exciting option is creating handmade products. A neighbour of mine here in Australia once decided that his childhood hobby of crafting dreamcatchers could become something more. Using feathers and materials collected from local thrift shops, he started a small dreamcatcher business from his spare room. While the dreams themselves were sometimes questionable, the sales were surprisingly strong.

Creativity transformed an unused corner of his home into a thriving artistic space. It is proof that almost any space can become a creative headquarters.

Collaboration is just as powerful. Some of my favourite examples come from festivals and pop-up markets where entertainers and chefs work together to create vibrant, shared experiences. Imagine opening a small coffee stall and teaming up with a musician who plays instruments made from recycled materials. As people enjoy coffee and music together, both of you create something far richer than competing alone. Community grows, creativity flourishes, and profits rise naturally.

At the heart of this journey is one truth. Creativity matters more than capital. It opens doors and reveals opportunities hidden in unexpected places. Instead of letting a lack of money limit your dreams, lean into your imagination. Use it to shape your own path. If Alfred could collect seeds from empty plots and turn them into a plant business, there is no doubt that you can uncover your own potential. So here is my challenge to you. Think creatively, follow your passions, and embrace the delightful absurdity of turning the everyday into something extraordinary. Who needs a truckload of cash when you have an inventive mind and a sense of humour. If only my friend could finally create a creative dish involving broccoli.

Turning Challenges into Cash Flow

Let us be honest. Life is full of challenges. From missing socks to burnt dinners, and even global pandemics and complicated tax forms, obstacles have a way of appearing just when things seem settled. The difference is how you respond. While many people see challenges as setbacks, entrepreneurs often see them as opportunities. With flexibility and creativity, problems can be transformed into income.

One of my favourite examples involves my old friend Rufus Dokie, may he rest in peace. Rufus had a talent for fixing things, whether it was a squeaky door or a broken tool. One day, a heavy downpour flooded his small workshop in Liberia. Tools floated around, and the place looked like a scene from a disaster film. Most people would have given up, but Rufus saw opportunity.

Once the water cleared, Rufus launched a service focused on flood ready home improvements. He went around the neighbourhood encouraging people to prepare for future rain. His misfortune quickly turned into a successful business. What began as a disaster became a source of steady income through innovation and quick thinking.

I experienced something similar when I was struggling to stretch every dollar. Watching neighbours face similar challenges gave me an idea. I organised a local thrift market where people could exchange clothes, shoes, and household items instead of spending money. We called it Swap and Shop Day. The event turned our street into a lively community space where people shared goods, stories, and laughter. No money changed hands, yet everyone left feeling richer.

Even small inconveniences can become opportunities. One rainy afternoon, bored and restless, I attempted to bake a chocolate cake. It turned into a gooey disaster. Instead of giving up, I rebranded it as Chocolate Lava Surprise and sold it at community events. What started as a mistake became a popular treat and a lesson in creative thinking.

During the pandemic, many people faced disruption, but creativity flourished. A neighbour combined yoga with humour and launched online pyjama yoga sessions. It brought laughter, connection, and a sense of wellbeing during difficult times. What began as a way to help others became a successful venture.

Challenges are not roadblocks. They are detours that often lead to unexpected opportunities. The next time you face adversity, approach it with curiosity and creativity. With humour and resilience, even the toughest situations can become stepping stones towards growth and success.

Chapter 14:
Harvesting Natural Resources

Connecting with Nature as a Source of Inspiration

As I sit down to write this chapter, I cannot help but smile at how often we overlook one of the simplest sources of inspiration, nature itself. Trees, rivers, insects, and birds surround us, quietly offering lessons if we take the time to notice. Stepping outside is not just a break from routine. It is a powerful way to spark creativity and fresh ideas. If birds can soar with such confidence, surely we can lift our own ambitions a little higher.

Growing up in Nimba, nature was my greatest teacher. The forests, insects, and colourful birds shaped how I saw the world. They also taught me humility, especially when I realised chickens seemed to command more attention than my dance moves at community gatherings. Anyone who has watched a chicken strut knows exactly what I mean.

When I reflect on these childhood memories, it dawns on me that nature has a remarkable ability to spark ideas that can be transformed into profitable ventures. I once watched how ants worked together to navigate obstacles, and I thought, wow. If these tiny architects can strategise and collaborate, so can I. That observation sparked an "aha" moment and led me to explore team building in the most unexpected ways, such as creating relay races at family gatherings using buckets of sweet potatoes. Trust me, when food is on the line, you unlock a whole new level of creativity.

Connecting with nature also stirred my entrepreneurial spirit. One day, while reflecting on life near a babbling brook, not the kind that affects your credit report but the kind that makes you want to sip hot soup, an idea struck me. Why not use sugar from palm trees to create a rich syrup that could rival factory-made products? The taste could take you straight back to your grandmother's kitchen, filled with home-cooked jollof rice and the kind of comfort that makes you question why you ever strayed from the culinary path. Nature's abundance is a buffet of ideas waiting to be harvested, provided you are not too busy tripping over your own feet in awe.

As we dive deeper into this connection with nature, we must not forget its therapeutic side. I once saw my neighbour having a full meltdown over a lawnmower that somehow turned the yard into a shrubbery crime scene. While they were panicking, nature seemed to whisper to me, "Joe, take a deep breath and let the frustration drift away with the wind." The rustling leaves and the occasional croak of a frog remind us that we are all part of this vast cosmic theatre. Nature is everywhere, whether it is nudging you to call your mother back or reminding you to appreciate small things like rolling hills that do not judge you for wearing socks with sandals.

That said, nature can also behave like a cheeky performer that delights in our misfortunes. Just as you admire a sunset and watch seeds float through the air, a butterfly may decide your head is the perfect landing spot. It is an unexpected twist on a peaceful moment. Yet beneath the humour lies a rich source of inspiration. Nature invites us to laugh at ourselves while gently guiding us towards new creative paths.

In conclusion, connecting with nature not only fuels inspiration but also gives you unforgettable stories to share. Whether it is the absurdity of observing ants, sudden insights from breathtaking scenery, or laughter sparked by nature's antics, the ideas waiting to be discovered are limitless. So get outside, breathe in the fresh air, and see what imaginative and amusing ideas grow from your adventures. And remember, when life throws you a curveball, or a chicken, smile and let your imagination soar.

Identifying Natural Resources in Your Environment

Alright, my fellow aspiring millionaires and nature enthusiasts, let us explore the art of identifying natural resources in your environment. You might be thinking, "Joe, I can barely match my socks on laundry day, so how am I supposed to identify resources?" Do not worry. I am here to guide you, metaphorically speaking, unless you are dripping with sweat from a jog, in which case I will keep a respectful distance.

The first lesson is this. Natural resources are like that loud uncle at family gatherings. Always present, yet often overlooked. They include everything from the plants growing in your backyard to bubbling streams that may be home to fish plotting daring escapes. You do not need a doctorate in environmental science or a guidebook thicker than a dictionary. All you need is curiosity and a bit of courage. Just avoid poking suspicious mushrooms, as they might take you on an adventure you did not sign up for.

Take a walk around your immediate surroundings. You may be surprised by what you discover. If you live in Australia, as I do now, the diversity can be overwhelming. Kangaroos hopping across open spaces and towering gum trees make it clear that natural resources are everywhere. I would not recommend trying to catch a kangaroo for dinner unless you are prepared for the consequences. Some lessons are best learned from a distance.

For my brothers and sisters in Liberia, take a moment to admire the palm trees swaying in the breeze. It may be hard to imagine that a palm tree could be the start of an entrepreneurial journey, but consider the palm oil that can be produced. It can be used in cooking or transformed into handcrafted soaps with rich, natural scents. Just make sure you learn which leaves behave themselves and which ones explode into a confetti-like mess. Experience teaches quickly.

Let us also talk about herbs and plants that pop up in your garden. To many people, they look like unwanted weeds. To a creative mind, they are potential. When life gives you weeds, find out whether they can become herbal teas or natural remedies. I once wandered through my yard talking to plants as though they could hear me, only to discover that what I thought was a weed was actually my neighbour's secret ingredient for winning every argument.

Beyond plants, do not ignore what lies beneath your feet. Soil is a hidden treasure. Organic matter can be turned into nutrient-rich compost that supports a productive garden. Imagine vegetables growing so large that your neighbours start giving you suspicious looks and joking about record-breaking carrots.

Here is a personal tip. The most amusing discoveries often come from asking questions. Do not just observe your surroundings. Engage with them. Talk to locals and learn from their experiences. You may uncover stories about trees that offer comfort or rivers filled with fish that seem to have a talent for comedy.

As we wrap up this resource treasure hunt, remember that identifying natural resources is an unfolding process. Every leaf holds a story and every stream hides potential, as long as you are willing to become a nature detective. Be bold, laugh at the absurd moments, and embrace the surprises that come with exploring the outdoors. Your next big idea might be hanging from a branch, quietly laughing as you figure out how to reach it.

Creative Ventures from the Forest to the Sea

The great outdoors is where inspiration and opportunity bloom abundantly. From dense forests to open seas, nature offers endless possibilities for creative ventures. I firmly believe nature itself is the best business mentor. No formal degrees required, just raw wisdom and observation.

Let us begin in the heart of the forest, a place overflowing with potential. Have you considered eco-tourism? Imagine guiding visitors through the bush, sharing stories about plants, animals, and even the mythical creatures you swear you spotted once. If you can turn a squirrel into a captivating character, you will have your audience fully engaged. A strong sense of storytelling can transform a simple walk into an unforgettable experience.

There are also opportunities beneath the forest canopy. I once dreamed of becoming a gourmet mushroom supplier for high-end restaurants. Armed with enthusiasm and very little knowledge, I quickly learned that not all mushrooms belong on a plate. That experience taught me the importance of research. If you plan to explore this path, learn which varieties add flavour to a meal and which ones add drama to a hospital visit.

Nature offers lessons, laughter, and limitless inspiration. When approached with curiosity and respect, it can guide you from simple observations to meaningful and profitable ventures.

From the forest trails to the sun-kissed shores, we can transition into the realm of aquaculture, an elegant word for reaping the rewards of the sea. I still hear my mother's words ringing in my ears: "If you ever swim with fish, Joe, make sure you are not in a concrete swimming pool." Good advice, but did I take it to heart when I decided to explore ocean-related ventures? Imagine starting a coastal fish farm where you raise fish that taste so good they could make a Gordon Ramsay competitor weep. "What's that?" you say. "We have spicy tilapia that tastes like cloud nine?" You get the processing licences, and I will throw in the puns with your fish tacos. Talk about a winning partnership.

Not only is the ocean a buffet of delights, but it is also a vast canvas for creative ventures. Have you considered creating artisan sea salt? Yes, you read that right. With just a pot, a little seawater, and an inspired business mindset, you could produce your very own jars of magic. Trust me, if you label it "Joe's Salty Success" and market it as "The Best Salt from the Deep", people will line up for miles. Just make sure you do not accidentally sprinkle salt straight from an experimental batch onto someone's meal. There is no need to elevate culinary finesse through mistakes.

And who could ignore ocean art? I have a vision. As people stroll along the beach, they stumble upon the "Kaleidoscope of Seashells", a collection of beautiful wall hangings crafted from gathered shells. Imagine these pieces showcasing marine-inspired designs in homes across the globe and generating buzz for just $1,000. That sounds like a bargain. Who knew that casual beachcombing could evolve into an art exhibit born from an accidental idea?

Finally, let us remember that the journey does not always require grand ideas. Sometimes it is about embracing the little things, such as a spontaneous beach bonfire with friends or selling homemade herbal teas from forest ingredients at local markets. Share your passion and use the knowledge passed down through generations to turn quirky ideas into creative goods. By blending the beauty of land and sea, you can build a unique mix of ventures that reflect your personal style, creating opportunities as naturally as peas, or perhaps seagulls and pinecones. These outdoor inspirations deserve to be celebrated and shared with the world. So go forth and combine forest treasures with ocean wonders. You never know how creative gold might appear in the adventures ahead.

Sustainable Business Practices in Nature

Sustainable business practices are simply a polite way of saying, "Let's not ruin everything while trying to make money." In today's fast-paced entrepreneurial world, we often forget that we are borrowing resources from nature, not owning them outright. Mother Nature is not a vending machine where you insert money and walk away without consequences. She is more like a wise elder who reminds you not to make foolish choices. We have a responsibility to care for our planet while building innovative and profitable ventures, and sustainability is no longer optional. It is essential.

Let us begin by respecting the environment we rely on. Sustainable practices start with understanding where our resources come from. One powerful approach is agroforestry, which involves growing crops alongside trees. It allows productivity and environmental care to coexist. People often think they must choose between farmland and forest, but agroforestry shows us that both can thrive together. Imagine producing honey from bees, fresh fruit from trees, and crops that benefit from natural shade. Your land becomes both productive and environmentally balanced, earning goodwill from nature and your community alike.

Packaging is another critical consideration. In an eco-conscious world, relying on single-use plastics sends the wrong message. I once attempted to sell organic products wrapped in plastic, and the reactions alone made me reconsider my choices. Customers looked genuinely confused. Choosing biodegradable or reusable packaging is not just sustainable; it's a fashion statement that says, "I care!" Plus, imagine the accolades you'll get when you tell customers your product is so eco-friendly that even algae praises its cleanliness!

And let's not forget the magic of community involvement! Your business should feel less like a bottomless pit for profits and more like a gathering of those who gather to help each other flourish. The practice of involving communities can create sustainable symbiosis that resembles a dance party where everyone arrives, smiles, and most importantly, celebrates each other's successes—minus the awkward moments when your dance moves. When you employ locals, you're not only giving them a job, you're creating an ecosystem where everyone thrives together—strictly lone wolves allowed!

Moreover, be it craftsmanship or simple artwork, sourcing materials locally helps minimise that pesky carbon footprint. Why load your goods onto shipping containers bound for distant lands, only to have them surface at a fraction of the cost through the back of a questionable street vendor's truck? Instead, form partnerships with local artisans—whether they're weaving textiles or crafting furniture from reclaimed wood. YOLZ customers won't just appreciate your dedication to sustainable practice, they'll likely share amusing anecdotes about that artisanal chair made from driftwood they thought they could reserve for the living room, but you know better—it's always meant for that rickety porch!

Moving forward, it's vital to employ sustainable practices, and let's not gloss over the potential for a renewable energy source. How about solar panels? Yes, the sun has been the hottest news since the dawn of time! Harnessing that glorious ball of energy can reduce your utility bills and improve your carbon footprint faster than you can say "climate crisis." If you tell customers that they're supporting a business powered by sunlight (and not by a hamster on a wheel), they might even feel compelled to leave you a five-star review!

Lastly, we need to talk about waste management. Don't let food scraps or packaging just lie about like that mattress you're still avoiding from your college days. Instead, create a system where waste becomes a resource. Whether through composting or recycling, ensure that your operations leave minimal impact. I once made the mistake of tossing compost into a trash can while claiming an eco-friendly initiative." Needless to say, thx ended with me explaining to the cousins why the garden looked like it was auditioning for a horror movie!

In conclusion, sustainable business practices are not a passing trend. They are a commitment to the planet and to future generations. As we work towards profitability, let us also take responsibility for how we treat our environment. With creativity, accountability, and a sense of humour, sustainability can become a natural part of doing business well.

Your Personal Journey: Harnessing Nature for Growth

My friends, gather around as I share my personal journey, where growth meets nature and the occasional misstep turns into a memorable lesson. Growing up in Liberia, surrounded by the beauty of Nimba County, I learned early that nature was not just something to admire. It was a teacher, a companion, and sometimes a comedian ready to catch me off guard.

I remember my early years running through fields, climbing trees taller than my ambitions, and learning life lessons through experience. As a young Joe, I raced through the bush, fuelled by imagination, only to discover both joy and challenge waiting patiently. Years later, I found the courage to seek new opportunities beyond that landscape. When I packed my bags for Australia, I carried more than belongings. I carried the lessons nature had quietly placed upon me.

That transition felt like being uprooted and replanted in unfamiliar soil. The city moved to its own rhythm, chaotic yet intriguing. Over time, I began to notice that nature still whispered its lessons, even in urban spaces. Local parks became my refuge, places where I reflected, planned, and occasionally shared space with curious squirrels. One memorable encounter ended with a squirrel stealing my peanut butter sandwich. That moment taught me that not every partner in inspiration shares your priorities, especially when food is involved.

But here's the punchline: through nature's quirky ways, I unearthed opportunities I never saw coming. I took to observing the patterns of the seasons, noticing how trees shed their leaves to bloom anew, and reflected on how we, too, go through cycles of growth. What if I harnessed that ethos for my personal development? So instead of just dreaming about success, I started embracing those changes, nurturing personal growth as if it were a small plant needing sunlight, laughter, and the occasional dose of fresh compost—an odd analogy, but let's roll with it.

As I expanded my horizons, I began engaging in conversations with people around me about sustainable practices, ethical living, and finding ways to integrate our lives with nature. One afternoon, I stumbled upon an inspiring community initiative aimed at reclaiming green spaces. I threw myself headfirst into the project, and as we planted flowers and trees, I found my heart blooming as well. "Whoa!" I exclaimed in delight. "This is what growth feels like!" Not only were we beautifying our surroundings, but we were also nurturing relationships, cultivating friendships, and building community spirit that radiated through each rooted seed.

And oh boy, did I make some extraordinary friends in the process! One of my new buddies was an ornithologist whose fascination with birds made me realise something magnificent. Understanding the delicate balance between humans and nature was crucial to our collective prosperity. Who would have thought a few chatty birds could impart wisdom on wealth-building? I channelled that newfound inspiration, becoming obsessed with the idea that personal growth is inseparable from fostering a healthy relationship with nature. As the birds chirp away, they remind us that if you want to soar high in the business world, you mustn't forget your roots.

Soon, I transitioned from mere observation to action. I began exploring new ventures, blending my passion for health with a sustainable mindset, embodying the values instilled in me by nature during my formative years. Each new idea sprouted through my determination like a stubborn weed in a beautifully manicured lawn. Eventually, I incorporated those lessons into my business endeavours, crafting products that promote health while respecting the natural world around us.

In conclusion, embracing nature in your personal journey is the key to growth and opens the door to countless possibilities. It teaches resilience, adaptability, and creativity as we learn to mirror its dance with the changing seasons. So do not shy away from nature's hilarious quirks and profound wisdom; embrace them. When you align yourself with the lessons that come swirling in on a gentle breeze or crash like waves upon the shore, you will discover a kaleidoscope of opportunities unfolding before your eyes. Walk boldly and take charge, for growth is always within reach when you plant seeds of inspiration in the fertile soil of your life.

Chapter 15:
Mistakes Are Stepping Stones

Embracing Failure as a Learning Opportunity

Embracing failure might sound like inviting a long-lost ex to your family reunion, but trust me, it is one of the best life lessons I ever picked up. Growing up in Nimba County, I learned early that failure isn't just a possibility; it is practically a family member. My dear mama, bless her heart, once told me, "Joe, if at first you don't succeed, then you might just be normal." I took that to mean failure isn't the end; it is simply a detour on the path to success. Like most detours, it may lead you to unexpected places, sometimes the fridge for a midnight snack, but more often to invaluable insights.

Let me take you back to when I first thought I could become a millionaire. Armed with nothing but a dream and a t-shirt boldly proclaiming my aspirations, I decided to dabble in business. My first venture: selling homemade peanut butter. In theory, it sounded like a golden opportunity. In practice, it was a sticky disaster. Imagine my surprise when I discovered that no one in my neighbourhood shared my enthusiasm for what I called "Joe's Nutty Delight," especially after I accidentally added salt instead of sugar. The result? More "Joe's Nutty Disaster." That jar of peanut butter became a source of amusement and bewilderment. "Just add bread and make toast?" my friends said. "More like add an apology!"

I learned quickly that failure in that endeavour wasn't just about my cooking skills—or lack thereof. It was a lesson in market research. You cannot sell peanut butter to a community that lives off cassava and plantains. My foray into entrepreneurship taught me to pay closer attention to what the market truly wants. Sometimes, failure is the universe's way of telling you to pivot. I wasn't meant to be the next peanut butter mogul, but instead, something deeper was brewing within me: the art of listening and observation.

And what about when I took my passion for fitness seriously and thought I could start a workout program? Picture this: me, in my Nimba gear, leading a group of friends in a dance workout. By day two, everyone was more concerned with dodging my two left feet than sweating out their calories. I possibly invented a new form of exercise called "Oops!", which involved far more laughter than lunges. That failed dance program became a joyful reminder that sometimes, laughter is the best workout of all.

From those early days, I came to realise that each failure was a stepping stone toward greater self-awareness. Instead of giving up, I learned to embrace failure like my grandmother embraces her favourite bowl of rice. It was not something to shy away from but a badge of honour, a way of saying, "I tried and survived to tell the tale." Each misstep carved out knowledge, moulding me into a better leader and yes, even a more entertaining clinical nurse, as my patients will attest.

When I finally moved to Australia, I encountered a new set of challenges, each filled with potential pitfalls. Armed with the wisdom gained from my first attempts and escapes from peanut butter disaster, I strode forward. Each stumble became a learning opportunity wrapped in humility and, occasionally, embarrassment. Far from being roadblocks, those failures became humorous anecdotes I could share at gatherings to break the ice or liven up a conversation. After all, who doesn't enjoy a laugh at someone else's misfortune, especially when that someone is yourself?

So, the next time life throws you a curveball and you miss it, embrace it. Turn that faceplant into a dance move. Your mistakes may lead to the next big success—the hidden treasure in the ruins of your peanut butter adventures. The heart of every successful person is a library of failures that taught them to laugh and ultimately thrive. To err is human; to laugh at it is pure brilliance.

The Art of Bouncing Back

The art of bouncing back is a skill I have perfected over the years, like mastering dance moves that only make sense after one too many cups of Liberian coffee. Bouncing back is not just about resilience; it is about developing the spring that can launch you into your next adventure, even if you land on your backside more often than not. Today, I want to share the whimsical world of recovery, where each stumble is an opportunity for a leap, or perhaps a theatrical roll.

Growing up in Nimba, I quickly learned that life throws challenges like poorly aimed mangoes during mango season. Take my community poetry night as an example. I thought I'd channel my inner Shakespeare, but instead, I made everyone cry—not with laughter, but from the audible pain of my awkward rhymes. Picture me, standing in front of an audience of apprehensive friends, reading lines that sounded suspiciously like: "Roses are red, violets are blue, I'm still trying to figure out what adverbs do." I went home that night thinking my poetic career was over, but I still managed to orchestrate a remarkable recovery.

While sulking with a pint of ice cream, I realised something profound: everyone enjoys a good laugh. Instead of hiding under my covers, I created what I called "The Humour Rehabilitation Program." I invited people to a comedy night where my bad poetry became punchlines. It turned out that my ability to take a tumble and bounce back not only entertained friends but transformed failure into pure gold. Who knew that a line about adverbs could become a reflection on grammar as a form of physiotherapy for the soul?

Bouncing back requires a curious mixture of grit and the willingness to look foolish. I had my share of "look foolish" moments in Australia, a land where I occasionally confused the word "fairy" with "fair" while trying to order a dessert. Picture my face when the waiter gave me a blank stare, as if I had just suggested eating a mythical being instead of a lovely piece of pavlova. After my fair-fairy incident, I learned to own my mistakes. "If life gives you lemons," I'd say, "make lemonade, but first, remember to ask if the lemons are organic." Embracing humour became my secret weapon in the battlefield of setbacks, and I came to realise that laughter really is the best medicine, even for cultural misunderstandings.

But let me tell you, the bouncing back dance is not always sparkles and confetti. While pursuing my master's in public health, I faced rejection from rural programs. On the surface, I felt like a deflated beach ball at a kids' birthday party. I whined to my family in Africa: "Why do they not love me? Am I not educated enough?" But deep down, I knew each rejection was just a chance to pivot in my studies and figure out how I could contribute more meaningfully to community health. A week later, I reworked my applications like a chef perfecting a recipe. "Cook it till you can smell success," I told myself. I embraced the challenges and came back towards what felt like a million possibilities.

Whenever I found myself in a deflated state, I would sit back, reflect, and channel that into creativity. After all, one cannot build resilience without the broken blocks left behind. I took each setback and turned them into fascinating stories that redefined how I approached my next leap. My workstation, whether at home or in the clinical nursing station, transformed into a creative haven where failures became scripts for new beginnings.

So, my friend, if you find yourself wallowing in embarrassment, failures or setbacks, remember that adopting the art of bouncing back is the secret to prosperity. Sure, you might wobble a bit and stumble along the way, but keep laughing and keep trying. Embrace your inner trampoline; let those falls fuel your next leap, and maybe sprinkle some optimism along the way. Who knows, the next bounce might be the one that propels you into success—in the most entertaining way possible.

Transforming Mistakes into Motivation

Transforming mistakes into motivation is like playing a game of chess with life, if life were a particularly mischievous opponent who sneaks a few extra pawns into the mix. One minute you are confident in positioning your pieces, feeling like a grandmaster, and the next, you have accidentally sacrificed your queen through a sheer oversight. But fear not. Instead of conceding defeat, I have learned that those blunders are real plot twists, perfect for flipping the narrative and daring to make a bold comeback.

Let me take you back to my early days in Liberia, where I thought I could take on the world as a young entrepreneur. Armed with a bright idea and just enough savings to make me think I had it all figured out, I plunged into the wild and wonderful world of selling handmade jewellery. I thought, "Hey, what is more motivating than a touch of bling and a Samba rhythm?" Well, not only did my artistic abilities fall short, but I also mispronounced "bracelet" as "brainless" at the local market. "Trust me," I reiterated, "it is a limited edition, just like my common sense!" Unsurprisingly, the sales did not flow as I had hoped, and by the end of the week, I had just one customer: my mum, who felt obliged to support my venture and definitely had my genetics on her side for wearability.

I could have easily let that experience crush my entrepreneurial spirit, but instead, I doubled down and thought, "Why not laugh about it?" I transformed those cringe-worthy moments into a motivational montage. I started hosting hilarious craft sessions that embraced flops as part of the learning curve. Attendees and I would experiment boldly, stitching glitter onto unlikely materials and proudly sporting our brainless accessories. Yes, my market strategy evolved from "How many bracelets can I sell?" to "How many times can I make people chuckle?" Suddenly, my mistakes transformed into a community-building experience, creating laughter while "dazzling" the world with our absurd creations.

Fast-forward to my move to Australia, where I entered the public health field with that same mindset. I hit the ground running, brimming with enthusiasm—until I didn't. One day, while presenting a community health initiative, I spectacularly mixed up statistics on diabetes with an anecdote about delicious eclairs. "Eating sugar is like playing with…" I exclaimed, only to immediately realise how badly I had confused my audience. What felt like a train wreck at that moment turned into something beautiful. Instead of curling into a ball of embarrassment, I quickly turned it into an engaging discussion about healthy lifestyles, humorously comparing them to desserts. My blunder sparked a local initiative called "Eclair Awareness," a delightful ongoing motto combining education with events revolving around sugar moderation. Who knew that my mix-up would lead to a nutrition campaign built on laughter and camaraderie?

When I began working in clinical nursing, those lessons resurfaced even more. I recall a particularly challenging day when I accidentally switched 50 patients' charts, the kind of mistake that makes your stomach drop like a hot potato. Rather than wallowing in horror, I transformed it into a motivator for improvement. I created a new protocol for nurses that became widely appreciated, finally earning me the nickname "The Chart

Whisperer" instead of "The Chart Butcher." I went from being the subject of cringeworthy stories to being the go-to figure for organisational guidance. There is something satisfying about turning red faces of embarrassment into rosy applause.

Let us not forget the power of storytelling. I have always believed that sharing our blunders and failures is like handing out tickets to a comedy show. Everyone likes a good laugh while learning something valuable. By writing about my mistakes, I not only shed light on my journey but also equip others with the empathy and humour needed to tackle challenges. Nothing creates camaraderie faster than shared experiences while navigating a uniquely unpredictable journey.

So, if you find yourself caught in the delightful embarrassment of a mistake, remember that every blunder is an opportunity cloaked in motivation waiting to be unveiled. Transform that cringe into comedy gold and forge ahead to empowering lessons. Embrace your mishaps as fuel for the fire of inspiration, and remember that together we can turn slip-ups into stories that make the world a little brighter, with plenty of giggles along the way. After all, life is far more entertaining when we learn to laugh at ourselves, transforming every awkward moment into a stepping stone to greater heights, proper analytics, and dessert-laden banquets.

Stories of My Own Missteps

Let me take you on a thrilling rollercoaster ride through the amusement park of my life, where the ticket prices are paid in missteps, and I have racked up a frequent flyer number. My journey is not just a straight shot to success; it is packed with twists, turns, and plenty of moments where I thought I was the main character in a slapstick comedy. Welcome aboard as I share some of my finest misadventures that I now embrace like old friends.

First up, I remember when I decided to impress my friends with my cooking skills. Armed with a recipe for what I thought would be a delightful chicken stew, I invited everyone over for dinner—a casual gathering, or so I envisioned. As the intoxicating aroma filled the room, I began to feel like a master chef. Little did I know that my blending of spices had turned my culinary creation into something more akin to a potion than a dish. Then my friends arrived, and I proudly unveiled my "signature" stew, only for them to exchange glances that screamed, "Should we call the taste police?" The first spoonful sent shockwaves through the table. As my buddies bravely dove into the uneaten abyss, I coined the phrase "you need to chew courage" that night. By the end of the meal, my friends were talking more about the lows of taste than the highs of morale. It was a night of bonding over laughter as we experienced what I call "a culinary catastrophe," reminding me that my prowess in the kitchen was still a work in progress.

Fast forward to my adventurous days in Australia, where I thought I would impress the locals with my wit, capital W, rooted in my African humour. Picture me, the only man at a park barbecue, trying to strike up conversations amidst the sizzling of BBQ and laughter. "You think your kangaroo steaks are fancy? In Liberia, we throw a wild feast! Just last week, I cooked a feast with—" but the words barely left my mouth before I was met with a chorus of bewildered stares. They helped me build bridges of camaraderie, and I learned that humour has a language all its own. Just because my friends from Australia may never crave Liberian fish stew does not mean they cannot appreciate a good laugh about weird food.

Then comes the infamous "lost in translation" misstep during a public Seattle presentation. Oh, the agony! I stood before an audience, wearing my best suit, ready to share some dynamic statistics on health outcomes. Alas, in my enthusiasm, I used a phrase that made the audience burst into laughter: "We can all be 'hearty' and healthy if we watch our weight!" It didn't take long for me to realise that "hearty" sounded suspiciously like "party," igniting a roomful of laughter. I stood there, a deer in headlights, trying to understand why my commitment to communal health had turned into a call for a pizza party. To reconcile the laughter, I transformed the mistake into a mini dance-off right then and there. It was a mess that ended in victory; I garnered enthusiasm from colleagues who now had fond memories of my flair for both education and confusion.

Let's not forget my illustrious role as an aspiring public speaker. Between my first two attempts, I embraced the concept of "winging it" like an artistic flyer without a parachute. On my third attempt, I decided not to use notes—only to forget all my key points right on stage. I spoke about everything from mango diets to urban gardening—topics I had never planned to touch on. The audience was not sure whether they were attending a motivational talk or a peculiar seminar about tropical plants, but they laughed kindly, eager to indulge in whatever madness was unfolding. My failures sprouted moments of spontaneity that were far more genuine and exciting than monotonal anecdotes.

So, what have I learned from this delightful amalgamation of missteps? Embrace the fun! Missteps are like playful kittens—sneaky and sometimes unpredictable, but ultimately they invite joy, laughter, and opportunities for connection. Instead of running away from my blunders, I learned to cherish those moments, for they give me the ability to navigate life's complexities with resilience and humour. Every misstep has shaped me into who I am today, delivering valuable lessons wrapped flawlessly in laughter. It takes a lot of laughter to make me a millionaire— one funny story, one culinary disaster, and a dozen mispronounced words at a time.

Building Resilience for Future Success

Building resilience for future success is an art form I have come to admire and struggle with in equal measure. You would think that after stumbling my way through life with the grace of a giraffe on roller skates, I would have a foolproof formula ready to deploy. But the truth is, resilience is less about fancy formulas and more about embracing the delightful chaos, one splat at a time. It is about rising, sometimes like a phoenix, other times more like a slightly charred piece of toast that cannot be thrown out because you love it so much.

Growing up in Liberia, I often found myself perched on the sidelines of disappointment, mostly failing miserably at sports, knowing I could never master those epic basketball dunks. But instead of tossing my hands in the air and storming off in tears, I embraced my "unique talent." Picture this: me, the kid who fumbled every catch, making up reasons to cheer my friends. "Way to go! You're totally winning that game, for the team does not have me!" My ability to cultivate resilience through humour turned my failures into motivational pep talks. Rather than wallowing, I turned to cheer myself—and those around me—on, no matter how poorly performed. That sense of support built my foundation for resilience, something that I carry with me to this day.

Fast forward to my nursing days, where resilience would once again be put to the test. In one of my first shifts, I had a patient who freaked out over the possibility of needing stitches. As nausea washed over the poor soul, I promptly tripped over my own shoes while attempting to demonstrate my soothing techniques. Talk about a scene that could have graced a blooper reel! Instead of retreating to the nearest wall in embarrassment, I sprang up, dusted myself off, and promptly said, "See? This is why I am here! If I can survive that spill, you can too!" Laughter bubbled up around the room, instantly lightening the atmosphere. That moment of vulnerability only bonded us in shared laughter but reinforced the idea that building resilience does not mean you have to be perfect; it means you acknowledge the messiness of life with grace and a healthy dose of giggles.

In Australia, my foray into public health introduced another realm of challenges that tested my resilience. I vividly recall my very first community health fair, which, naturally, I envisioned would be a spectacle of unity and top-notch information. Instead, I miscalculated the number of resources we would need, leading to an epic shortage. The chaos unfolded as community members flocked to my booth like bees to honey. My mantra, remaining composed, was put to the ultimate test. In the moment of improvisation, I threw my hands up and said, "If there is one thing we can all take away from this, it is this: Always have more cookies—because everyone can agree on that!" Rather than letting my shortcomings derail the event, I turned minor failures into a unique discussion point, which brought smiles to everyone's faces and turned it into an unexpected bonding session.

Life is not about extremes; it is about the incremental steps we take to rise back up the ladder of success. I learned that genuinely embracing failure as a learning opportunity was woven intimately with resilience. From community efforts to professional outreach, I developed strategies for success based on humour and adaptability. For instance, I keep a "failure file"—a fantastical collection of my own mishaps, disaster dinners, and misjudged health presentations—documenting the mistakes and the humour that followed them. This file became a go-to reminder that even the most embarrassing moments have lessons. When faced with uncertainty, I would open it up for a hearty reminder that failure is just part of breaking through and resilience.

As I navigate my path, I find strength in knowing that setbacks are really just opportunities to recalibrate and try again, each time without skipping the laughter. There is a grace to resilience that lies in the ability to remember to frame our challenges as playful adventures; after all, who would not want to be the hero of their own sitcom?

So, the next time you find yourself facing an uphill climb toward success, do not trip over your self-doubt or worry about perfection. Instead, embrace the chaos with a hearty laugh and adopt a sense of playfulness. Every stumble, every pint-sized disaster is paving the way, guiding you on this unpredictable journey of life. Remember, resilience is not just the act of rising; it is about how you choose to rise, with a smile, a laugh, and the get-up-and-go spirit that you need to throw yourself into the grand adventure of becoming a better version of yourself. Who knows, you might discover a whole new brand of success waiting for you just beyond that next misstep.

Chapter 16:
Gratitude: The Silent Millionaire

The Power of Gratitude in Daily Life

Gratitude! That magical little nugget of wisdom that can transform a mundane Tuesday into a day worth writing home about. Let me tell you—back in Liberia, my mother always reminded me to be thankful for what I had, even if what I had was a half-eaten cassava leaf and some questionable fish. "Gratitude is the key to happiness," she would say, as I stared at the plate, wondering how I would ever survive. But hey, the very fact that she knew I was complaining was a reason to be grateful, right? At least I was not eating alone!

In the hustle and bustle of daily life, it is too easy to forget how powerful gratitude can be. We wake up, scramble to work, mutter curses at the traffic, and dive into our screens as if they are magical portals to a world where our to-do lists vanish into thin air. We become like the ultramarathoners of stress, dodging paperwork and Zoom calls as if they were Olympic events. But in the midst of all that chaos, donning seemingly invisible gratitude goggles can change your perspective faster than a caffeine binge.

Think about it: when was the last time you stopped to enjoy your morning coffee, not just because it wakes you up, but like a warm hug? Seriously, the first sip can feel like divine intention. It is as if the universe is dipping its toes into your soul, whispering, "You have got this, my friend." Grasping that first cup of coffee, with its rich aroma, like a perfume designed by nature itself, I cannot help but feel a bubbling sense of joy inside me. I would argue that without gratitude, life is like coffee brown water; with it, it becomes a delicious blend of purpose and caffeine.

And let us not forget those wonderfully quirky people in our lives, the characters that add flavour to our stories. Like my late friend Rufus, who I can say was nothing short of a walking comedy show. I still chuckle every time I recall his legendary attempts at cooking. He once tried to make a pancake, and I thought the kitchen was under siege! We were lucky to escape with our lives intact, but that catastrophe taught me the importance of humour in our shared struggles. I cannot help but be thankful for my memories with him, for funny mishap moments like these that remind me to appreciate these relationships and the delight they bring—even if that delight sometimes comes wrapped in floury disaster.

It is captivating how gratitude does not just elevate our mood; it creates a ripple effect, too. You might be surprised how a simple "thank you" can brighten someone's day. I remember one time at work, after a gruelling shift, I thanked a colleague who helped me out. That simple act generated a wave of good vibes that sent the two of us into an impromptu dance-off in the break room. Imagine that! Nothing says "Thank you for being awesome" like an awkward robot moving with questionable footwork. Gratitude, folks, has a way of forging connections that create unforgettable stories and comedy gold.

Now, if you think that gratitude is just a warm, fuzzy feeling, let me dust off the research for you. Studies have shown that people who practise it daily tend to have lower levels of depression, better relationships, and a stronger immune system. It is like gratitude is the hidden superfood of emotions. Talk about a healthy dose of wellness. So when life hands you lemons, think of gratitude as the tequila and turn that sourness into a fiesta. You drink it, and suddenly everything feels a lot brighter, and the world becomes a party rather than just another daily grind.

In conclusion, embracing gratitude in our daily lives does not have to be a chore; it can be the sprinkles on our cake, the cherry on top of every sundae. Whether you are thanking the barista for not burning your toast or celebrating a small achievement at work, gratitude is a charm that not only enriches our experiences but can also lead to laughter and stronger bonds. So every morning, as you trudge through the daily grind and your boss asks for metrics while wearing pants that look suspiciously like pyjama bottoms, take a moment to kick-start your day with gratitude. Let us be honest, happiness does not just happen; it is often part of the deal when paired with a grateful heart. Who knows? You might just find yourself grinning like a fool, ready to conquer the world or at least the next Zoom meeting.

How Gratitude Shapes Our Perspectives

Let me tell you about the mighty powers of gratitude and how it can reshape even the most cynical of perspectives. Picture this: I am standing in the middle of my usual morning chaos. It is like an orchestra of mayhem that never quite hits the right notes. My daughter is mastering impressions while my son is trying to convince me that breakfast consists solely of chocolate cookies. Meanwhile, my green tea, bless its soul, has decided to stage a rebellion against my taste buds. You could say my mornings are less "Zen garden" and more "wild safari." But I pause, take a deep breath, and remind myself to be grateful. The mere act of gratitude has the magical ability to adjust my mental lens—imagine a pair of rose-tinted glasses that does not require a dentist appointment.

First off, gratitude helps me flip the script on negativity faster than a pancake at a Sunday brunch. I recall a time when I was trudging through life, feeling like the universe had handed me lemons and then thrown them at my head. You know those moments when you are consumed by what is going wrong that you nearly miss what is right? But then, with a little ping of gratitude, I start achieving small milestones—like learning how to safely microwave water without creating an accidental science experiment. Shifting my perspective from "why is this happening to me?" to "what can I learn from this?" suddenly makes me feel like the protagonist in a blockbuster film rather than a background character in a sitcom where nobody remembers my name.

Not only does gratitude serve as a nifty mental reset button, but it also adds a delightful layer of humour to life's inevitable hiccups. Take family gatherings, for example—the joys of our eccentric relatives! My uncle Joseph Tokpah has a mysterious connection with every single conspiracy theory on life. Instead of feeling stressed about his ramblings about extraterrestrial beings vacationing in Nimba, I began to find the experience uproariously funny. "Thank you, Uncle Joseph, for the endless material for my future comedy routine," I would tell him. Gratitude transformed an awkward dinner into a laughter-filled evening. I am still convinced that he might be onto something, even if it is just the cotton tree he keeps eyeing like a hungry hawk.

But let us take it a step further! Imagine standing in line at the grocery store while the person in front of you is doing a full re-enactment of the history of their shopping list, competing with dramatic pauses and excessive hand gestures. Who would have thought that a mundane grocery trip could become an impromptu show? In that moment, rolling my eyes and feeling irritation bubble up like an improperly sealed can of soda, I took a deep breath and zeroed in on the humour. "Thank you for captivating my attention while my frozen peas go into a thaw," I thought, noticing how my perspective shifted from annoyance to amusement—finding humour where most would have found frustration.

This is the essence of how gratitude shapes our worldview: it dares us to see life through a lens tinted with optimism. It is like getting new sunglasses that magically smooth out the rough edges of our daily disruptions. The inevitable ups and downs become not just things to endure but experiences to embrace and learn from, even if those experiences include eating food I could not quite identify at a family potluck. When gratitude reigns supreme, we become less reactive and more reflective, permitting us to navigate life's curveballs, and oh, they can be unpredictable as wild monkeys on the loose.

And let me tell you, there is something liberating about acknowledging that we can choose our perspective. The next time I find a parking ticket on my windscreen, my brain instantly jumps from one thought to another: "Why does this always happen to me?" to "Thank you, Universe, for I need to work on my parking skills!" It is like coming to terms with the fact that while life may serve us uninvited surprises, it is our choice to either blow up like a balloon or float gracefully with laughter.

So let us champion the idea of gratitude shaping our perspectives. After all, if we can giggle our way through life's little inconveniences and shift our focus from grumpy to grateful, we will tackle challenges like a troupe of comedians ready to take on the world. That is a show that deserves its own standing ovation. So go ahead, my dear readers—embrace gratitude. It is the magic that transforms life's everyday absurdities into delightful discoveries and laughter. Now, who is up for some poorly shaped pancakes?

Practical Ways to Cultivate Gratitude

The secret sauce that can transform the tedious grind of life into a gourmet feast of positivity! Now, you might be asking, "How on earth can I cultivate this elusive gratitude in a world where a dog thinks my flower garden is its personal restroom?" Fear not, I am here to steer you toward practical ways to sprinkle those gratitude seeds and watch them blossom into an oasis of appreciation, even amid the chaos of life.

First up, let us dive into the magnificent realm of the gratitude journey. Picture it: a little notebook, just waiting for your brilliance to spill its pages like a toddler with a box of crayons. Every night before bed, jot down at least three things you are grateful for. I have found that no moment is too small, whether it is my morning coffee that tastes like the embrace of an angel or the miracle of surviving a family gathering without a "Do Not Talk About Politics" rule. I am penning it down. Before you know it, I am practically writing the next bestseller titled *One Thousand and One Grateful Thoughts: Dramatic Adventures of a Liberian Nurse in Australia*. Writing it down reinforces these moments and reminds me that, yes, there is plenty to be thankful for—especially as I watch my children and try to explain to their friends how they have a "crazy dad" who insists on "authentic" dance moves.

Now, let us talk about the art of thank-you notes—yes, they still exist in an age of emojis and chaotic group chats. Nothing says "I appreciate you" quite like a heartfelt, handwritten note. As a clinical nurse, I frequently thank my patients for their resilience and humour. After all, who else would willingly let me prod them with needles and keep a straight face during a bizarre medical history session about why Aunt Mildred thought wasabi was a vegetable? This small gesture fosters a connection that is more comforting than any round of antibiotics. Who knew gratitude could come with an added dose of healing?

But if you are thinking my approach is way too structured for your liking, let us bring in the wild and unpredictable world of spontaneous gratitude attacks. Imagine you are out with friends, and out of nowhere, you express how grateful you are for their friendship. Trust me, a well-timed compliment—even if it is about how they have mastered the art of making burnt toast—can unleash a torrent of laughter. Emit this kind of unforced, spontaneous gratitude, and you will feel like a comedic superhero spreading happiness while simultaneously confusing onlookers. Who does not want to shake up their environment with a healthy dose of unexpected kindness?

Have you ever thought of making a gratitude rock? Okay, hold your chuckles; I promise this is not just a hipster art project. Find a smooth stone—preferably one that is not a piece of your neighbour's missing garden gnome—and write a word or phrase on it that encapsulates your appreciation for something. Keep it in your pocket, and whenever you feel the urge to complain about that darned dog ruining your hydrangeas, hold that rock close. It serves as a tactile reminder of the good stuff. My rock's name is "Pelo," and he reminds me that things could be worse—I could be walking around with a pet iguana named "Gary" in a hat. Gratitude does not really care what form it takes; it just wants to be felt.

Let us not forget about volunteers—taking action is one of the best ways to cultivate gratitude. Volunteer, and you will realise just how fortunate you truly are. Some of my favourite memories come from working with community organisations that provide for those in need. It makes me feel that it is not just about what I have, but also about the chance to help others. Plus, nothing is more heartwarming and hilarious than participating in a bake sale where my cookies tasted suspiciously like bricks. Yet with laughter and camaraderie, I learned that a grateful heart beats strongest when shared, especially in the kitchen, where everyone has a disaster story to tell.

Lastly, embrace the power of presence. That is right. Put down your device and step away from the screen to engage with the world around you genuinely. As a nurse, I see countless individuals whose lives could teach us life lessons, fraught with moments of laughter, vulnerability, and resilience. By simply being present and actively engaging with the people around you—or even just the eccentric character who insists on telling their life story in the grocery store line—you recognise the beauty right in front of you. That joyful connection keeps the gratitude alive, making it a delightful contagion that inspires creativity and fosters memorable moments.

So, there you have it, my friends. Whether through journals, spontaneous eruptions, or the mystical power of gratitude rocks, there are countless eccentric ways to cultivate gratitude in your life. You will be amazed by the transformation. Before long, despite the chaos of daily life, you will find yourself laughing more, connecting deeper, and maybe even speaking graciously to that cannonball of a dog. Embrace gratitude, and you will be awash in positivity, camaraderie, and perhaps a newfound appreciation for burnt toast—life's little gems wrapped in chaos. Now, who is ready to grab a gratitude rock and get crafting?

Gratitude and Its Impact on Relationships

Relationships. Those beautifully crafted webs of human connection can sometimes feel like trying to untangle a bunch of earphones after a long flight. They are messy, they are challenging, and they can leave you with a headache that even a bottle of aspirin cannot fix. But amidst all that complexity, there lies a secret ingredient—yes, you guessed it: gratitude. When appropriately sprinkled into our interactions, gratitude can elevate relationships from "meh" to "magnificent." So grab a cup of your favourite beverage—I'll take a coconut-flavoured concoction—and let us delve into how gratitude plays a pivotal role in fortifying our relationships.

Imagine this. You are having dinner with your partner, and they are telling you about their day. It is easy to zone out of this moment, like a tranquilliser dart has just hit you. You start to nod, but your mind is racing toward the three episodes of your favourite show you missed. Then all of a sudden, gratitude kicks in, and you interrupt your daydreaming by fully engaging, maybe with a comment or two about how they deserve a gold medal for dealing with their boss's antics. Boom! Gratitude opens the door to deeper conversation and encourages that person to feel valued, like a prized trophy instead of yesterday's leftover meatloaf. It is those moments of appreciation that act like emotional fertiliser, watering the garden of your relationship to make it flourish.

Now, let us face it. We are all human, and humans have the wonderful ability to get on each other's nerves. You know those times when your sibling decided to use your toothbrush as a sword in an imaginary battle?

Ah, yes, sibling rivalry in full force. But let us sprinkle some gratitude on that toothbrush escapade. Instead of yelling and making threats that you will take their dessert privileges away, try texting them "Hey, thanks for being my partner in crime—even if you use my toothbrush to wage war." You might end up busting out laughing instead of pointing fingers. Gratitude creates a cushion that absorbs the shock of our little annoyances, allowing us to appreciate each other's quirks even when they are more annoying than a mosquito at a picnic.

What is even more remarkable is gratitude's ability to amplify the good times. Picture this. You are at a family gathering, and Aunt Togbeyee, who always brings a fruit mango salad that mysteriously has a 50% chance of being delicious or inedible, decides to bless you with her culinary creation. Instead of rolling your eyes, why not thank her for "taking one for the team"? Then you express genuine gratitude, which leads to positive reinforcement that transforms family gatherings into joyous occasions, rather than a battlefield of aggressive food critiques. Gratitude creates an environment where laughter flows naturally, and even Aunt Togbeyee's questionable fruit salad becomes a source of cherished memories rather than kidney stones in disguise.

It does not stop at family—our friendships blossom beautifully with gratitude, too. Think of your friend who always insists on splitting the bill, then grabs dinner even when they barely touch their meal. The next time you dine together, express gratitude by insisting on covering their half of the bill as a token of appreciation for their unwavering support through thick and thin, or through every slice of pizza devoured. This little act fosters reciprocity and reinforces your bond, making the friendship even more rewarding, like a double-cheese pizza topped with gratitude.

And here is the kicker: gratitude is contagious. Think about your workplace camaraderie. When you thank a coworker for their diligent effort on a project, even if you secretly wish they had not assigned the most chaotic role to you, it tends to spread like wildfire. They are likely to respond in kind, fostering a workplace atmosphere of teamwork and respect, which can turn even the grumpiest office into a cosy hub of collaboration. There is something to be said for creating a ripple effect of gratitude, sending waves of positivity that can soften the hardest of hearts, maybe even turning the person whose desk always looks chaotic into a marvel of efficiency.

So, what is the takeaway? Gratitude is more than just a warm feeling; it is a powerful tool that refines our relationships into something extraordinary. It transforms mundane moments into heartfelt experiences and fuels connection where annoyance once lingered. By infusing interactions—whether with friends, family, colleagues, or even that one aunt who insists on asking "When are we going to settle down"— gratitude reminds us of the value of being present, appreciating the quirks, and transforming the ordinary into the remarkable. So why not embark on a gratitude adventure? Embrace it, share it, and watch as your relationships bloom like tropical flowers in full spring. Now, if that is not a reason to raise your glass in gratitude, I do not know what is. Cheers to healthy and grateful relationships.

Sharing Gratitude with the Community

Community. What a beautiful thing it is, filled with quirky character, mismatched interests, and the occasional pie-eating contest where all bets are off. Sharing gratitude within our community is not just about being a friendly neighbour or smiling at a stranger. Those acts definitely count, but it is also about weaving a rich tapestry of connection and appreciation that can uplift an entire neighbourhood, all while being knotted together by shared experiences and the occasional mischief. Let us dive into how you can infuse your community with gratitude, spreading positivity like confetti at a child's birthday party, minus the cleanup afterwards, of course.

First, let us consider recognising the unsung heroes in our midst. You know, those outstanding individuals who work tirelessly behind the scenes, like the local librarian who keeps all the books tidy and occasionally entertains children with such captivating storytelling that it could rival the biggest Hollywood blockbuster. Imagine this. You walk into the library, and instead of just sliding by, you take a moment to thank her for the countless adventures she has provided without requiring an entry ticket. A simple gesture, perhaps bringing her coffee or writing her a heartfelt note, can make her day brighter than the fluorescent lights that illuminate those dusty shelves. When we shine our gratitude on these community champions, we foster a sense of belonging that makes everyone feel like they are part of something greater than themselves.

Now, let us talk about practical ways to channel gratitude into community service. Many hands make light work, right? Whether you are planting trees, cooking for a shelter, or even cleaning the local park where the neighbour's dog refuses to do its business because it knows it can get away with it, volunteering is a gateway to gratitude. Plus, the joy of giving back is a huge booster shot of happiness. Picture your community gathered for a clean-up event. One second, you are collecting litter and comparing questionable life choices, and the next, you are digging deep— which is a little harder than it sounds, let me tell you. But once you see that actual transformation, your heart swells with gratitude for every person you have met, the support you have gained, and even that rogue ladybug who decided to hitch a ride on your backpack. Each act of service is a celebration of connection, reinforcing that gratitude thrives in community efforts.

And who could forget community events? I still chuckle remembering a neighbourhood potluck where Aunt Gladys brought her infamous roll that had the potential to be a culinary thriller. I mean, nobody was sure what the ingredients were—secretly hoping it was not an old family recipe best left undiscovered. That night, I felt gratitude radiate not just for snacks but for the people who gathered there, each one a colourful brick in the mosaic that is our community. Organising or attending such events allows everyone to share their food, laughter, and stories, creating an ambience that elevates gratitude. Leave a note on each dish, thanking the person responsible for it, and magically, everyone ends up smiling. These moments nourish not just our bellies but our spirits, cooking up a healthy dose of camaraderie and connection to boot.

Now, let us not forget how sharing gratitude can also mean promoting local businesses. Next time you need to pick up groceries, consider checking out a nearby shop instead of heading to that big, flashy chain store that makes you feel like just another face in the crowd. Supporting businesses creates a ripple effect in the community, and taking the time to express your gratitude by leaving a positive review or sharing experiences on social media makes you a champion of local support. "Thank you for the delightful pastries that made me question whether I could realistically eat a dozen—wait, this is totally a one-person job." We are not just purchasing items; we are fostering relationships and preserving the vibrancy of our community.

It is also essential to create community gratitude boards or walls—not the kind that just collects dust, but the kind that brings people together. Set them up in a park or community centre, where locals can write notes expressing gratitude to others, share acts of kindness, or recommend someone for selfless efforts. Even a quirky tree branch can become a powerful reminder of appreciation. "Thank you, Bob, for always helping carry my groceries. Your dog looks at me like I stole its tennis ball." This kinship nurtures a culture of appreciation, giving a voice to people who often toil quietly in the background.

So, there you have it, fellow explorers of gratitude. Sharing gratitude with the community is about creating a positive environment where everyone thrives together. Whether it is recognising the local heroes volunteering, celebrating with potlucks, promoting small businesses, or creating a gratitude wall, these actions build authentic connections and foster a sense of belonging. And let us face it: if we can unite over Aunt Gladys's mystery casserole and that sticky note on the gratitude wall, we can certainly face anything. So go forth and spread that gratitude like a chef tending herbs over a bubbling pot. The aroma will waft throughout your community, transforming lives and leaving a lasting impact that is as delightful as your favourite dessert—no leftovers here.

Chapter 17:
Non-traditional paths to wealth

Finding your unique talent is like looking for the last piece in a puzzle. You know it is there, but sometimes it feels like it is hiding under the couch, sipping on a cold drink, and watching you struggle. Many of us wander through life feeling like we are just ordinary folk with a knack for misplacing our keys or tripping over invisible handles. But deep down, just beneath all that fabulous ordinariness, lies a glittering treasure trove of unique talent waiting to be unearthed.

Let us start with a short story. Imagine little Joe, a pint-sized version of my current self, trying to convince my playmates that I was the next Michael Jackson. I strutted, spun, and tried to moonwalk on the dirt roads while embodying what I thought was "Thriller." Let me tell you, if my dancing were currency, it would not buy a grain of rice. But as I failed about, unleashing enthusiastic but horrendous displays of creativity, I stumbled upon something I could make people laugh at. My dancing could be classified as comedy. I realised that my unique talent was not to be the king of pop, but rather the jester of Nimba. Sometimes, it takes catastrophe to illuminate our true gifts.

Finding your unique talent can be like trying to identify your favourite flavour of ice cream at the local shop—there are so many options the brain can short-circuit. The trick here is to embrace failure.

You see, so many people live in fear of not being good enough. They may shy away from pursuing their talents because they are afraid of falling flat on their face, and trust me, I have taken that plunge more times than I can count. My advice? Put on a helmet and jump into the pool of possibilities, or in my case, the "pool of silliness." Sometimes you will find hidden gems nestled between the snickers and side-eyes of others. Do not be disheartened by the occasional laughter; embrace it. You need to channel that energy into elevating your skills to the next level.

Next, a little introspection can work wonders. Ask yourself questions to uncover your unique talents. "What did my kindergarten teacher say I was good at?" or "Which delightful activities make me lose track of time?" It might surprise you how easy it is to uncover your unique talent if you listen closely. For instance, while I love writing, it was not until more than 50 people complained to family members about my unending jokes and anecdotes that I realised I could put pen to paper. I am not even good at writing, but spending five to eight hours doing it gave me the clue that I need to be an author. Suddenly, it was not just a tendency to annoy but transformed into a potential career. Opportunities sometimes knock, but other times, it is simply a note slid under the header, "You have got skills, my friend."

Consider looking within your circle. If your friends and family are giving you unsolicited advice on how real estate investment would be a great opportunity, they are probably right. Many of us overlook our talents because we are too busy comparing ourselves to the likes of Beyoncé and Elon Musk when we could be honing our own gifts. The beauty game of self-discovery lies in realising that you do not need to be the world's biggest star to face the biggest challenges. The world needs authentic, quirky, and versatile talents.

Lastly, let us not forget about feedback. Yes, I know, feedback can be more uncomfortable than a pair of badly fitting shoes, but think of it as your ultimate reveal party. Ta-da, you are great at…… Ask family, friends, or even the neighbourhood cat what they think your talent might be. You may be surprised that others see what you overlook. And remember, humour can be the sugar that makes this medicine go down. For example, you can gather feedback on your cooking by hosting a dinner party for friends. If they leave more on their plates than when they started, you may have uncovered why you should not open a restaurant.

Inclusion and finding your unique talent is a journey, sometimes filled with stumbling, falling, laughing, and occasionally even a little crying. Embrace the chaos and explore the hilarious mishaps along the way. Remember that every fantastic talent started somewhere. Mine began with a commercially bad dance move that warmed the heart of the audience. So think outside the box, take a chance, and be ready to discover the colourful, rich tapestry of your unique self. Your talents are not just something special; they are your ticket to creativity, wealth, and most importantly, a fulfilling and hilariously delightful life. Note, birds do not need a lesson on how to fly, fish do not need a lesson on how to swim, and so on. They only need the right environment. I do not want to be taught; your talent is something you are born with. You only need the right location. Let the world feed your talent before you leave.

Side Hustles: Your secret weapon

Side hustles are your secret weapon. Let me tell you, if I had a dollar for every time someone asked me about side hustles, I might actually be a millionaire. That is right, my friends. In this modern day and age, if you are not juggling at least two or three hustles, you might as well be living in the Stone Age while everyone else is riding flying hoverboards. Seriously, side hustling is like the secret sauce you sprinkle over your financial barbecue to make it sizzle with perfection.

Now let us begin by addressing the elephant in the room (and no, I do not mean your neighbour's dance moves). Why hustle on the side? Life has a funny way of throwing bills at you, like you are in a game of dodgeball. When I began my journey as a nurse, I had to face the harsh reality that my paycheck was not enough to fund my flaming desire to be a millionaire. Therefore, I dove headfirst into the thrilling world of side hustles, a place where both excitement and cash flow are of interest. From selling plastic bags on the street to offering my equally questionable public speaking and leadership skills in the community, I would try anything that pays a dime, as long as it does not involve singing in public.

Ah, but let us not sugarcoat it. Not every side hustle will make you feel you have just discovered the treasure map to a million-dollar fortune. In some cases, it may lead you down the path of absolute hilarity more than profitability. Take my stint as a cat groomer—yes, you heard me right. I thought experience growing up around cats and resisting the urge to bathe them would magically equip me with all the skills. Spoiler alert: cats did not want to be groomed. I ended up losing a few scratches and a tiny dose of pride. But hey, I got a funny story to share with my mates, who now call me the "cat whisperer of Nimba."

The secret to nailing a side hustle is finding what you enjoy while asking yourself, "How can I market this sheer brilliance?" Just think of yourself as a modern-day Robin Hood, but instead of stealing from the rich, you figure out how to turn your quirks into gold. Perhaps you have a gift for baking those mind-blowing cookies that make your neighbourhood's dietitian weep. Make that dough, pun intended, while people declare you the "cookie king." Or, if you are like me and have a knack for delivering dad jokes with impeccable timing, you could start a humour-based blog or YouTube channel.

To give you some insight, I once tried my hand at online t-shirt design. My t-shirts boasted the slogan "I Want to Be a Millionaire" on the front and my face on the back. Surprisingly, I did not sell a single one. My friends laughed, but let us be real, a laughing friend is still a friend. Embrace the awkwardness of every failed side hustle as an essential ingredient for a hilarious entrepreneurial narrative of your life. No risks, no funny stories, right?

Then comes the classic question: how do you balance full-time and side jobs without losing your sanity? Well, minimise time-sucking distractions, like scrolling through social media for hours while planning a side hustle. I mention this because I once created an Instagram account to showcase my epic meal prep, which was really just me preparing enough food for a small army. Instead of focusing on my hustles, I found myself drawn into the vortex of cat videos, dance challenges, and that one recipe video featuring a man making lasagna in a microwave. Trust me, unless you aim to be the next viral sensation, set specific hours for your side-hustle endeavours.

Also, try to connect with a community of fellow hustlers. I mean, what is more fun than sharing your experiences with those pursuing similar entrepreneurial quests? Find a local group or an online forum where you can laugh about your misadventures, brainstorm ideas, and perhaps plot a few "take over the world" schemes while you are at it. You might find that the world is full of creative people just waiting to collaborate.

Ultimately, side hustling can be everything from a gateway to true financial freedom to a glorious opportunity to add some excitement to your everyday routine. Embrace your quirky side, take leaps of faith, and remember to document every misstep and hilarious moment. You never know; that goofy side hustle might turn into the golden ticket. So gear up, my reader, and unleash your inner hustler. Who knows, maybe one day you will be the subject of an inspiring story—just make sure to laugh yourself along the way. After all, what is wealth without a whole lot of laughter?

Digital Opportunities: Skills that Pay

Welcome to the digital age, my fellow aspiring millionaires. If you are not tapping into the internet's untapped potential, you might as well be using a stone tablet to send emails. In our rapidly evolving world, the internet has not only redefined the way we communicate but has also opened a treasure chest filled with opportunities for those daring enough to dive in. Picture this: you can earn a living utilising your skills while sipping coffee in your pyjamas and dodging the chaos of the outside world. Don't pinch yourself; it is all very real.

Now, you might be wondering what skills are in demand in this digital realm. Let us start with the art of content creation, because who does not want to be a Kardashian for just a day? Well, maybe without the drama. With platforms like YouTube, TikTok, and Instagram, anyone with a smartphone can become a filmmaker, comedian, or coach, or all three if you really want to live on the edge. My interest in content creation began when I accidentally went viral for showcasing a five-minute recipe for boiled water—no one was more baffled than I was. But the reality is that behind engaging video, skills are waiting to be honed. Humour, editing, and storytelling can all turn your talents into cash.

Remember when websites were filled with clunky designs, like high school science fair projects? Well, in today's world, having an appealing website is non-negotiable, leading us straight to the world of design. If you have a knack for aesthetics and a little patience, you could be the hero saving struggling businesses from digital disaster zones. There is great money to be made in building sites that resemble anything but an unkempt jungle. And heck, if you can make a business look cool while they are staving off bankruptcy, they will not just pay you, they might even name a coffee after you.

Speaking of aesthetics, digital marketing is hotter than a summer in Liberia. Businesses are clamouring for savvy digital marketers to guide them through Facebook, TikTok, and whatever new platforms pop up overnight. Understand this: every "like," comment, or share is a direct path to profits. Armed with SEO skills, especially if paired with a sprinkle of digital creativity—think memes about the trouble of adulting—you can transform the fate of any company. Plus, seeing your ideas succeed is as satisfying as finding cash in your old jeans.

Oh, and did I mention freelancing? It is equally exciting, and whether you are good at graphic design, copywriting, or consulting—name it—the world of freelancing is waiting with open arms, a freelancer's mug overflowing with cheap coffee. Some freedom comes with being your own boss, though it often comes with the side effect of hunting for the next client in the dark corners of the internet. Just remember, there is a learning curve to managing your own schedule. Time management is a skill; try not to get sidetracked by the allure of cat videos while you are at it.

In addition to all this is the rapidly growing field of online education. If you have expertise in a particular area, there is a classroom full of eager learners ready to pay for your wisdom. Teaching languages, cooking, coding, or martial arts—the sky is the limit. Share your knowledge in online courses, webinars, or even create an e-book. Just make sure not to sign up for a class on "How to Avoid Cooking Failures" unless you want to be comic relief among anxious aspiring culinary geniuses.

But let me remind you, as bright as the digital opportunities may appear, it is vital to approach your new skills with gusto and a dash of humour. In this online hustle, people are drawn to authenticity more than perfection. So allow your quirky personality to shine through. Earn the respect of your audience and let them know they have stumbled into the magical land that is your world. Together, you will all rise.

In summary, the digital landscape is buzzing with opportunities just waiting for passionate individuals to jump in and cultivate their skills. Whether it is content creation, web design, or digital marketing, each avenue is a path where you could potentially turn hobbies into riches. Dive into the beautiful chaos of experimentation, gain insights from failures, and embrace the wild ride that is the digital economy. And who knows? You might find yourself thriving while still in the comfort of your pyjamas, laughing at how you turned your skills into cash, all while avoiding the cat in the other room.

The Power of Community-Based Ventures

Let me tell you, if you think that the secret to making it big lies solely in the echelons of corporate offices filled with plush chairs and espresso machines, it is time to climb down from that ivory tower and take a hard look around you. Communities are where the magic happens. Picture this: your neighbourhood is not just filled with neighbours who borrow your lawnmower and poke around for the juiciest gossip; it is an ecosystem ripe for innovation, collaboration, and entrepreneurial success. Yes, my friends, community-based ventures are the hidden treasure troves waiting to be uncovered.

Now, I know what you might be thinking: "Joe, we already have community potlucks, but that never turns out as planned!" Oh yes, who could forget those treacherous moments when Auntie Annie's fried okra soup made it to the table looking like it had been through a hurricane? But what the potluck reveals is crucial; it shows the importance of collaboration. Just as our family comes together to contribute their best and worst dishes to the shared table, we can pool our strength to create ventures that benefit everyone. When joining forces with your fellow community members, you are, in essence, sharing success. Believe me, nothing says prosperity like transforming a group of backyard BBQ enthusiasts into a thriving business, combined with a sense of pride and purpose.

Let us take a moment to explore some successful community ventures. For instance, have you ever heard of a community garden? That is right. A local garden not only provides delicious fruits and vegetables but also fosters a sense of belonging. It allows neighbours to bond over watering can battles and secret zucchini-growing competitions. By working together, a simple vegetable patch can blossom into a partnership opportunity, whether it is by selling produce at the local farmer's market or hosting a cooking class for forgettable dinner party guests. Helping people cultivate skills while scooping up organic vegetables can transform a neighbourhood in a way no installation of shiny mall kiosks ever could.

But it does not stop there. Think about cooperatives. A group of people pooling their resources to create something spectacular. Sounds like a dream, right? I mean, when did you last have a bartering session with a neighbour? "Hey, Barbara, you can have my collection of slightly used lawn flamingos if you give me a dozen of those fancy cheese wheels you make." Community cooperatives enable you to collaborate with your neighbours to produce goods and share profits, thereby evading the e-commerce machine. To see some roosters crowing about how they were part of the cooperative that provided artisanal cheese would be a sight to behold.

And let us not forget the digital age's twist on community ventures—local crowdfunding. As we scroll through our feeds, let us face it, few things are more satisfying than witnessing your neighbours band together to fund that quirky thing you thought only existed in a bad script. Imagine a group of locals coming together to raise money for public art installations. Everyone chips in, and suddenly your streets are filled with vibrant murals that tell the story of your community. People come to see the art, take Instagram photos, and giggle at the ship named "The Floating Fish" that no one really understands. This is what it means to work together.

Throughout my life, as I ventured from Liberia to Australia, I learned that enormous change often comes from grassroots movements. Small actions can lead to significant shifts. Community-based ventures are where we find unique solutions tailored for unique problems. You gather a group of people, each with something different to contribute, and you will be surprised at how many brilliant ideas emerge. A little spark can ignite a delightful bonfire of creativity.

However, never underestimate the power of laughter within community ventures. It can turn rivals into allies and feuds into laughter-filled moments. I recall the unforgettable neighbourhood calamity of "The Great Lemonade Stand Wars," which brought together competing families who, after trying to outdo each other's creations, formed a lemonade cartel. The laughter shared and friendships forged made them richer than any profit margins. That is the power of community, creating opportunities to transform chaos into connection.

In conclusion, community-based ventures are about utilising the power of collaboration, creativity, and a sprinkling of good humour. Rather than navigating your entrepreneurial journey alone, look around—your neighbours are your hidden partners and wild cards. Combine community talents and passions to create ventures that provide social and economic benefits. So next time you gather for a neighbourhood event, remember those laughs, shared stories, and even Auntie Annie's questionable dessert could be the spark for your next big surprise. Embrace this spirit, and who knows, you might find yourself leading an unstoppable community of innovative dreamers. Cheers to the power of community.

Exploring Local Markets and Services

Ah, there is something electrifying about wandering through the vibrant tapestry of local markets, where the air buzzes with laughter, the scents of delightful cuisines waft through your nostrils, and where you could potentially find everything from a pumpkin to a friendship bracelet made by artisanal squirrels. Yes, folks, markets are where the heart and wallet of entrepreneurial opportunism beats. If you have not immersed yourself in the charming world of local vendors, artisanal foods, and crafty folks hawking their wares, grab a reusable shopping bag and let us venture into the wild, weird realm of local commerce.

Let me share a little secret. Local markets are akin to treasure hunts. You never know what hidden gems you might stumble upon. I decided to explore my local farmer's market for inspiration. It turned into a mesmerising experience of delight and sheer confusion. From exotic fruits that looked suspiciously like they had come straight out of a sci-fi movie to handmade soaps that cost as much as my dinner, the variety offered was nothing short of astonishing. I could practically hear my wallet whispering, "Don't do it, Joe!" But lo and behold, one caught my eye. There it was, "Elderberry Elixir," touted to improve health and mood. How could I resist? Let us say my fascination with local entrepreneurial spirits skyrocketed that day.

The beauty of local markets is that they offer the chance to interact directly with the artisans behind the products. You can hear them explain why they started their businesses, and often they land a deal or two when they see your genuine interest. Remember my earlier fiasco? Well, I learned that if you chat long enough with the local shopkeeper, you might discover she once launched a cat rescue, resulting in an intriguing and slightly chaotic interconnectedness. Now that is a story worth sharing. Every vendor has a unique masterclass in entrepreneurship, and we can all learn something by engaging with them.

But wait, there is more. Local markets promote small businesses, which means shopping here supports the community. Have you ever craved cornbread, the kind that makes you feel sophisticated while secretly wearing pyjamas? By shopping at local markets, you are not only giving yourself a bakery experience that rivals the best French patisseries, but you are also boosting the local economy. It is like superhero economics— you are saving local bakers while munching on that chocolate croissant.

Cultivating local connections leads to discovering the services available in the community. Maybe you are not particularly interested in snacking your way through a local market, but why would you miss out on those samples? Dive into the services that the market offers. Most regional markets are infused with passionate people ready to share their skills. Consider finding a massage therapist who offers twenty-minute shoulder rubs that leave you feeling like you are floating on air, or a yoga instructor with classes suitable for everyone, from the nimble to the "I only stretch to reach the remote."

Networking is key, my friends. Witnessing local entrepreneurs interact can lead to unexpected collaborations. Picture this: I met a local artist at one such market who had a knack for painting stunning landscapes. Through our shared love of community, we organised classes in the park. Who knew that friendship could blossom from the eccentric pursuit of watercolour in the middle of a bustling market? Together, we painted the world one happy little tree at a time, attracting many other quirky souls.

Now, let us not forget the thrill of sampling. Yes, one cannot visit a local market and ignore the chance to explore new tastes. Be brave; try that strange spice no one can pronounce. You might just discover your new favourite. And while you are at it, do not hesitate to engage the vendor with your culinary skills. Who knows, maybe they will give you a few insider tips to up your recipes at home.

And now, the pièce de résistance. Exploring local markets encourages a sense of community. There is something magical about gathering with your neighbours, chatting, sharing recipes, and laughing at the kindly butcher's joke about a chicken crossing the road. It creates bonds, establishes friendships, and reminds you that we are all in this together. As I strode through my last market visit, I found myself delighted by the, for lack of a better term, weirdness that connects us. Crafts, food, and unique items made our neighbourhood an essential part of my heart.

In conclusion, the world of local markets and services brims with opportunities. Whether you are selling your amazing homemade salsa or attending art classes, you will not only be advancing your entrepreneurial pursuits but also deepening your connection to your community. So grab your wallet, folks. The excitement of exploration awaits. As they say in my neighbourhood, "get out there and mingle, but do not forget to sample the kola nuts."

Chapter 18:
Giving Back: The Real Measure of Wealth

Essence of Philanthropy in Africa

Think of philanthropy in Africa, and I cannot help but imagine a robust fufu rice simmering with all the right spices, inviting everyone to share. Just as every ingredient contributes to the rich flavour of that dish, every act of giving strengthens the fabric of our communities. Philanthropy in Africa is deeply rooted in our history, and much like the traditional dance steps that bring a village together, it is celebrated. It is about understanding that we are never alone on our journey of life; there is always someone who needs a helping hand or a kind word.

Now, you might envision philanthropy as a grand spectacle, with an ostentatiously wealthy individual dropping stacks of cash while a choir sings their praises. Sure, I have seen those powerful displays of charity where the philanthropist is greeted like royalty, and everyone dances. But here is the twist. In Africa, philanthropy is not just a parade of misty splendour; it is a humble, everyday practice that often goes unnoticed amid the flashiness portrayed in the media. It is simple. You do not have to be a millionaire to build a legacy of kindness. Just look at my mother, Helen SR. She has been the unofficial charity queen of our community, donating her time, resources, and love without expecting anything in return.

At its core, African philanthropy is about community and connection. It is about understanding that when the sun shines bright in one, it illuminates others as well. I remember a story from my village in the county where a family faced the dire consequences of a drought. Their food supply was smaller than a starving mosquito, and their cries travelled far and wide in a matter of days. What began as a simple call for help turned into a full-blown initiative. Neighbours gathered food, clothes, and the most precious of all—moral support. It was the proverbial village stepping in to care for its own. The community treated that family as part of itself, because, after all, a problem shared is a problem halved, and a meal shared is multiplied.

Millionaire Dreams: African Scheme

The laughter that erupted every time someone arrived at the house with a new bag of rice or a handful of cassava was like the sound of a thousand drums calling everyone to the dance floor. It was not just charity; it was a celebration of solidarity. People came together, telling stories, sharing jokes, and reminding each other of the merits of being part of something rather than focusing solely on ourselves. That is the essence I cherish—philanthropy as a party. Who says giving back must be sombre?

And let us not forget the proverb that says, "When there is a will, there is a way," unless, of course, you are trying to fix a broken generator. When it comes to philanthropy in Africa, there is always a creative solution around the corner. Community members gather for brainstorming, more energetic than a soccer match. How can we help? Perhaps a local fundraising event as elaborate as a World Cup, where you contribute a small amount and bring in the Mandingoes' drums to create a rhythmic atmosphere. You see, it becomes a form of fundraising as competitive as the locals' pride.

But do not get it twisted. Philanthropy is not just about building up our community's chocolate stash. It is a committed act of love and investment. In the long term, the focus is on creating pathways to sustainability, building a school, supporting local businesses, and investing in health initiatives. Even if my financial resources might currently resemble the bottom of a chicken coop after a heavy rain, I can still give back through my laughter, through the very essence of my being.

At the end of the day, philanthropy in Africa shows us how interlinked we are. With every act of kindness, we build a network of support that can uplift the most vulnerable among us. So, the next time you hear a wealthy tycoon bragging about their grand charitable donations, spare a thought for the everyday heroes. As I continue my journey with *Millionaire Dreams, African Schemes*, I am reminded that wealth is not just measured in currency, but in love shared, laughter harvested, and friendships nurtured. Philanthropy, my friends, is truly the heartbeat of Africa.

Personal Stories of Giving Back

Personal stories of giving back—where do I even begin? My life is a tapestry with vibrant moments that showcase the beauty of generosity, stitched together by threads of laughter. Occasionally, awkward silence creeps in when you realise you forgot to ask whether the recipient wanted rice or beans. But hey, that is the spice of life.

Let us sprinkle some colour on our first story. Back in Liberia, it was one of those happy days when my uncle, Joseph, decided to throw a party out of nowhere. It was a scorching Saturday afternoon, the air thick with the smell of grilling fish and the rhythmic thumping of a nearby drum circle. My uncle, a man known for his grand gestures and even grander expectations, had decided to celebrate… well, no one was quite sure what. Perhaps the arrival of the rainy season, perhaps the good fortune he had enjoyed at the local market that week. Whatever the reason, he had sent word out, summoning friends and family to his modest home.

My uncle, with a characteristic flourish, assumed that some of his friends whom he had invited would contribute to his party and shower him with gifts. Therefore, he announced, with a booming voice that carried across the bustling neighbourhood, that he would be donating to the local orphanage.

There were audible gasps, a collective intake of breath that rustled through the crowd like a sudden breeze. I swear if the universe could roll its eyes, it would have done just that. You see, in Africa, parties are not only about you; they are a grand celebration of who you are—a personal festival. It is a time for communal joy, shared food, and the unspoken understanding that you are supported by your community, who show up not just to celebrate, but to contribute. People come from everywhere to help you eat, whether they are invited or not. It is a culture of shared resources and collective responsibility. The number of people who showed up that day was more than the grain of rice my uncle cooked. The aroma of food, the chatter, the laughter, and the children running around—it was a true Liberian party. But my uncle decided to turn the tables, saying with a self-satisfied smirk, "What is a party without giving back?"

It was like a scene from a movie, where the protagonist suddenly morphs into a superhero. The sudden generosity, the public display of philanthropy—it was unexpected and, frankly, a little perplexing. He was trying to outsmart the system, the unwritten rules of the party. However, it was not enough for some of his angry and hungry guests, who, fuelled by disappointment and maybe a little resentment, ended up taking my uncle's pots, spoons, and even half a bag of his precious rice to their houses. A few of the more brazen ones even made off with a couple of his better cooking spoons. It was a sight to behold—a chaotic exodus of disgruntled guests laden with stolen goods. This experience taught me a valuable lesson, one that has resonated with me to this day. It reminds me not to throw a party if I am not fully prepared.

Creating Sustainable Change through Community Service

Creating sustainable change through community service—now, that sounds like a mouthful, almost as challenging as trying to pronounce "Sanniquellie" for the first time after a few drinks. But let me take you on a wonderful journey of how community service can transform lives, creating ripples of lasting change, whether you want it to or not. You could even call it the golden ticket to making our communities better while feeling like a superhero without the cape. However, it is pretty clear that in my case, flying would have been an issue—I am more of an earthbound character, if you catch my drift.

Take a look at my hometown in Liberia. We have always shared a sense of traditional community service, whether we liked it or not. I remember once our local school was notorious for its underwhelming conditions. It was so bad that I half-expected to find an ill-tempered goat living in one of the classrooms. Desperate for change, the residents organised a clean-up day. This was not your typical "bring-your-bucket-and-spade" affair; this was a "let us rebuild the future" extravaganza. With everyone from kids to grandmas unexpectedly armed with broomsticks and spray bottles, it was like a scene from a musical—everyone humming and swaying as they cleaned.

But while our hearts were in the right place, our skills were questionable. By the end of the day, the classrooms looked glittery, thanks to a generous appliqué of soap bubbles left behind by the rushing dancers—my very own soap opera unfolding right before my eyes. As we revelled in our perceived success, it dawned on us that cleaning was not enough. The school needed materials, teachers, and an ample supply of patience because, let us face it, students are not always the best at paying attention.

That is where sustainable change comes into play. It became clear to us that we had to think long-term, like planning a marriage proposal. You cannot just pluck a beautiful flower and expect it to flourish forever; you need to add water, sunlight, and a supportive community—okay, maybe not the bees, but you get the idea. So we decided to take it up a notch. We kicked off the *Adopt-a-Classroom* initiative, where community members could sponsor classrooms—think of it as a new-age version of fostering, but far less dramatic.

I vividly recall when one of my neighbours, Saye Gbah, showcased an unusual talent for multiplication. He was gifted in the art of hiring talented teachers, and soon enough, classes were filled with eager minds hungry for knowledge. It was heartwarming to see the children develop a semblance of understanding while Mr Saye Gbah reluctantly tried to teach them geometry. That man could not explain a straight line without linking it to an epic tale of his young days of dividing apples at the market, making the learning process both hilarious and enlightening.

Moreover, we formed collaborations with local businesses, creating a coalition stronger than my sister Rebecca's jollof rice at family reunions. Each partner contributed resources, skills, or even that random box of leftover stationery that had been lurking in the corner of their office. Suddenly, the school transformed from a speck of dust on the educational map to a beacon of learning. Children began to thrive, raising literacy rates far more dramatically than my failed attempts at growing hair.

We quickly realised that the key to sustainable change required more than just commitment; it needed a plan as intricate as sister Helen's family recipes. We set actionable goals, tracked progress, and celebrated milestones. Trust me, nothing beats the joy of seeing children excel, much like threading a needle while juggling three fruits at once. Community service was not just a flash-in-the-pan endeavour; it morphed into a thriving effort to improve lives through creative solutions.

Ultimately, the most important part of creating sustainable change through community service teaches one fundamental truth: we all have a role to play in our communities, even if it is part-time, like my successful career as a joke writer. From mothers distributing hand-me-downs to uncles planting trees, we learn that together, we can build a legacy—one that gives our children roots as sturdy as those hearty African trees. So roll up your sleeves, embrace the messiness, and let us keep doing what we do best, creating and fostering sustainable community change, one uncontrollable laugh at a time.

Ripple Effect: How Small Acts Can Create Big Change

The ripple effect. It is a concept so beautifully simple that it makes me wonder why they never taught us about it alongside the art of avoiding "that one uncle" at family gatherings. You know, the one who has opinions on absolutely everything, including the pasta you have chosen for dinner. But the ripple effect is far more important. It is like that first stone you toss into a calm river or lagoon, setting off a series of delightful waves that carry through the community. Who would have thought that a small act could cause waves of change, much stronger than my attempts at telling a joke in an elevator?

Let us take a stroll back to my days in Liberia—a time when the simple act of sharing a meal could send ripples through the entire village. I remember a particularly sweltering afternoon. A friend of mine, Nyanquoi Bebe, who has never met a piece of fried plantain he did not love, decided to host a modest gathering. He invited a few people over for what he claimed would be "just some light snacks" but ended up with an "all-you-can-eat" extravaganza that could challenge even an African wedding feast.

He prepared vibrant dishes: steamed jollof rice, groundnut stew, palm wine and enough plantains to rival the local market. But as our bellies filled, an extraordinary event unfolded. While devouring the delicious food and sharing hearty laughter, Bebe offered leftovers to his neighbour, who was in a bit of a financial pinch. This seemingly small gesture ended up sending ripples through the community. As the neighbour received the food, he could not help but share tales of his grandmother's recipes with others, inspiring them to come together for a grand culinary showcase of their own. Fast forward a week later, and there we were, dancing under the stars while wooden spoons and cooking pots clanged like a band warming up for a concert. It was magical. The event did not just bring the community together; it transformed it. Every small act of kindness generated excitement—each handshake and exchange of recipes sparked a newfound passion for home-cooked food. And guess what? It led to a food festival that not only delighted our stomachs but also strengthened friendships and encouraged local businesses to thrive. It was as if every spoonful of jollof rice came with a side of unity.

This ripple effect touches all parts of life. Imagine this: instead of just complaining about potholes, someone gathers a few friends for a cleanup day, like the Avengers, but instead of superheroes, we turn out as a ragtag bunch of well-meaning locals armed with shovels and brooms. Our crew of eager, stubborn folk, fuelled by determination more powerful than a double shot of coffee, took on the neighbourhood. As word spread, more joined in, strengthening community bonds until one day we unintentionally hosted a "let us save our streets" festival. Local shops jumped in with snacks, and suddenly, the event became a massive street party.

And let us not overlook the power of a single voice—the ability to inspire change with just a few words. I once watched my sister, Irine Saye, speak passionately about environmental preservation at a local gathering. She recounted how littering not only affects our planet but also diminishes our beauty. Suddenly, all eyes were glued to her enthusiastic hand gestures, and inspired individuals began to act. From creating neighbourhood clean-up campaigns to forming a community waste-recycling program, each call to action triggered new ideas. They thought, "If Irine can shout with passion, how can we not join her?"

Eventually, the ripple effect manifests in ways beyond our comprehension. Research confirms what we have known all along: one good deed often leads to another. Small acts of kindness have cumulative power; they can multiply and morph into something magnificent. I mean, look at our always-hungry local rooster that keeps following me around asking for snacks, and how every crumb I toss leads him to share his affection around the block.

So, my friends, remember that you have the power within you to create waves of change, just as you would toss that innocent stone into the water. Whether it is sharing a meal, cleaning the community, or being the voice of compassion, your small acts can set off a chain reaction that transforms lives for the better. You never know—what starts as a little splash might turn into a tidal wave. And in our case, if everyone gets on board, we might just host the most significant celebration this side of the river. So go ahead, toss your stone. The journey awaits.

Measuring the Value of Giving Back

Measuring the value of giving back is an art and a science, a delightful dance between what we believe our contributions are worth and the world's somewhat chaotic responses to our good intentions. Picture a teetering tower of jollof rice. It looks magnificent, yet one wrong move could send it crashing to the floor. That is how our efforts to give back can sometimes feel. We put in endless energy, only to wonder later if it was all worth it. But fear not, my friends, because today we will dive into the delightful work of metrics, value, and that unwavering belief: every spoonful of love counts, even if it occasionally resembles a heap of undercooked potatoes.

First, let us tackle the most glaring misconception: when you give back, you are not immediately endowed with a badge of honour. Sure, people will heap praise upon you like you are a celebrity at a movie premiere, and it feels fantastic. But then, after the applause fades, reality strikes. What is the real impact? Did the kids learn their multiplication tables, or did they just learn how to sneak a cookie before class? I remember volunteering at a local school, promising the children I would teach them about financial literacy. I strutted in with my best shirt, the one that still had a hint of palm oil from last week's feast, and a set of "exciting" lessons that turned out to be borderline snooze-fests. You can guess the outcome. The children learned to count in exchange for snacks, and I realised I probably should have brought more cookies.

When trying to measure the value of your contributions, you cannot simply look at the checkboxes on your to-do list and pat yourself on the back. It requires diving deeper into stories. This reminds me of my friend, Rebeca Saye, whose knack for storytelling is unmatched. During our latest charity event, she opened her mouth and spun a tale so vivid that the children in attendance suddenly thought they were superheroes saving their village. I realised that I cannot measure the impact of giving back with mere numbers; instead, storytelling can be the secret ingredient that adds flavour to our philanthropic endeavours. Those smiles and sequences of joy are what we need to embrace—real, immeasurable moments.

But let us also face the reality that numbers can indeed play a role. I mean, who does not love a good chart? Think of something simple: did you know that a single donation could help feed an entire family for a week? For our local initiative, we tracked how many families were helped through a system that made it seem like we were running a game show. We scored extra points whenever we exceeded our goal of feeding 200 families, and the applause echoed louder than the music at a Liberian street party. It was a simple way to measure our impact while giving a playful twist to an otherwise serious matter.

As we polished our methods, we decided to take it further. Growing these numbers displayed a tangible effect on our community's growth—I am talking bigger than Uncle Alfred's infamous birthday cake. We conducted surveys, engaged in dialogues, and, believe it or not, enlisted our young volunteers to help collect data. At first, it felt awkward, like trying to learn the cha-cha in flip-flops. Still, eventually, we became experts at collecting testimonials, photographs, and heartfelt moments that illustrated the changes we were making. It turns out, kids take fantastic pictures; not all superheroes wear capes—some wield smartphones.

Of course, the real challenge lies in keeping our eyes open to less obvious signs of impact. I recall visiting a local school two years after the initiative started. The children who had once been shy and withdrawn were now bursting with energy and ambition. One young girl, with glittering eyes brighter than my surprise at the size of Sister Helen's tracked-down cassava cakes, swarmed toward me. "I want to be a doctor!" she declared.

That single moment said it all. While I will never see the dollar value of this transformation, it reminded me how priceless every interaction and investment in kindness is. That is the hidden currency, my friends.

So, when measuring the value of giving back, let us embrace both the tangible and the intangible, the numbers and the stories. It is about recognising that every small act, every volunteering effort, and every heartfelt contribution contributes to a greater purpose. After all, while the world may not always hold a scale to quantify your impact, the rippling effects of your kindness will echo through the hearts of those you have touched. In the candid scheme of relationships, impacts, and laughter, success is less about statistical achievements and more about nurturing bonds—similar to that batch of jollof rice you held together in the pot despite the odds stacked against you. Now let us keep cooking up those hearty acts of kindness. May our contributions simmer, blend, and ultimately create a dish fit for every hungry heart.

Chapter 19:
Future-Proof Your Dreams

Adapting to Change: The Key to Survival

As I sit here in my cosy corner, sipping a cup of Liberian coffee that could wake the dead, I find myself pondering the fine art of adapting to change. There is one constant in life: change is about as reliable as a broken clock—at least it is right twice a day. But what does it really mean to adapt? I mean, aside from transforming into a chameleon to blend into different settings. Don't get me wrong, I love a good metaphor, especially one that includes cosy camouflage and colourful outfits.

Picture this: I am in Nimba, watching my grandmother try to use a smartphone. It is like watching a chicken trying to swim. Here is this woman who has spent a lifetime perfecting the art of planting cassava and making the best fufu in the village, and now she is faced with this little gadget that seems to have a mind of its own. It reminded me of the time I tried learning how to ride a bicycle. It did not end well, my friends. I had a knack for transforming bicycles into flying objects, often with my face as the landing gear. But with perseverance, and maybe too many flipped tortillas, I finally managed to pedal without flying headfirst into the dust road. That is the mark of survival—adaptation.

But wait a minute, hold on to your t-shirt. Adaptation is not just about changing our mode of transport or how we connect on social media. It is primarily about mindset. There is this saying that if you cannot change the situation, then change your attitude. I still remember my favourite shirt that said, "I want to be a millionaire," right there in bold letters. Curse it for not speaking volumes about my dreams. The funny thing is, I quickly learned that just wearing that shirt will not magically transform me into a millionaire. Who knew, right? So, I had to rethink my approach and attitude towards wealth, not as an end goal but as a journey, like learning to ride a bike again.

In Australia, everything is different. From kangaroos hopping around to the fact that they believe a meat pie is a suitable breakfast—it is true. The world keeps spinning, but one must keep up. Initially, I was like a gazelle on roller skates, trying to blend in at my nursing job. I faced some challenges that made my head spin faster than an African dance during a wedding ceremony. When I thought I had the hang of it, someone would throw me a curveball—a term here out of the blue. "Can you handle this acute situation?" they ask, and I would stare back like I was trying to read hieroglyphics. But over time, I learned to embrace these curveballs and sometimes hit home runs with them by adapting.

Let us not forget the wisdom passed down from my family, my mother, Zogbelee. She always told me, "When the river changes its course, you must follow." Ah, my mother and her analogies. I think that adapting to change does not mean simply reacting; it means your eyes are wide open, figuring out the flow, and sometimes finding a new route that leads to a better ocean—read: wealth, happiness, the good stuff. I have come to appreciate that the ability to adapt is like being a human yoga mat—stretching along with the whims of life while sometimes being a cushion for those who might need a little help landing.

Let us put this into perspective. Now and then, we must ask ourselves, "Am I just an iguana trying to swim?" If you can identify that you are hanging onto a branch in the metaphorical hurricane of life, it is time to adapt your grip, because that branch might snap at any moment. Embrace the challenge with a smile, maybe even a chuckle, because without laughter, what is life?

Ultimately, adapting to change is the secret sauce that keeps our entrepreneurial dreams from burning in the oven of stagnation. So let us buckle up and ride this rollercoaster together because success is not just about what you achieve; it is also about what you survive, adapt to, and learn along the way. So here is to changing lanes, finding our balance, and embracing every potholed road on this wild journey to millionaire dreams. Cheers.

Embracing Technology in Business

Technology. The magical realm where machines beep, people talk to devices that cannot talk back, and even the most traditional grandmas now video-call on Sundays instead of just shouting across the road. Who would have thought that the future would be so weird? But here we are, living in an age where embracing technology is as essential as wearing shoes when venturing outside—unless you are in Nimba, where flip-flops reign supreme. As I navigate my entrepreneurial journey, I have learned that technology is not just a tool; it is the magic wand that can turn ideas into gold.

Let us take a moment to acknowledge the awkward first encounters we all have had with technology. I still remember the day I attempted to set up my very first website. Picture me, a wide-eyed superhero with dreams of grandeur, trying to decipher coding like it was the secret language of the universe, only to end up with my website looking like a colourful disco party gone wrong. I felt like I had just entered a tech labyrinth where I could hear the Minotaur of Confusion lurking behind me, ready to devour my hopes of becoming a millionaire. But here is the kicker—after an epic battle that involved copious amounts of tea and the occasional hair-pulling moment, I emerged victorious. I learned that while technology may play hard to get, it ultimately rewards those brave enough to engage in its funky dance.

Now, embracing technology in business is akin to welcoming a cheerful friend who secretly harbours the keys to your success. Take social media, for instance. I mean, how else would I be able to share my "I Want to Be a Millionaire" shirt with the world and gather a tribe of aspiring millionaires across continents? It is a fantastic void-filler. Social media not only allows businesses to market their products and ideas but also provides a platform for authentic engagement. Nowadays, I can post humorous anecdotes about my misadventures in nursing, pepper them with pro tips, and suddenly it is like throwing a party where everyone is invited—from Liberia to Australia. Who knew sharing a laugh could lead to a network of connections that expand like a rubber band around a watermelon during a hot summer?

And let us not forget e-commerce. When I first heard the word, I thought it involved some secretive, ancient commerce society where billions of dollars were exchanged through grains of sand. But no. It turns out you just need a decent internet connection and a passion for trade. Opening an online store is like setting up a stall in an endless marketplace where customers can browse while still in their pyjamas. Do you know how liberating it feels to come up with the idea for a product and sell it without putting on proper pants? It is like saying goodbye to the trousers of despair. I dabble a bit in health-related products, tapping into my experience as a nurse. Who would not want to buy organic wellness tonics crafted by a clinical nurse with a flair for humour? It is like healing with a side of giggles.

Now, for the sceptics out there, I know some might argue that technology isolates us, replacing human connections with impersonal screens. But let us not be the grumpy kittens of the internet. Embracing technology can enhance those connections. Remember the last time you attended a virtual seminar on wealth creation? You got the chance to learn from experts, ask them questions, and connect in real time—all while sporting your favourite pyjama bottoms. That has got to count for something. I believe building communities, whether online or face-to-face, allows us to share our stories and experiences, learn from each other, and sprinkle wisdom like confetti throughout our lives.

Of course, technology also brings its fair share of quirky challenges. From the dreaded software updates that happen at the most inconvenient times to glitches that make you yell at your screen like it insulted your mother, the journey can be amusing, to say the least. I once spent an hour trying to figure out why my presentation was upside down, only to discover that my dog had somehow walked across my keyboard during a moment of inspiration. Animals in the business world, huh? They should come with a warning label.

In conclusion, as we dive headfirst into this tech-driven era, let us appreciate the weirdness, the laughter, and the occasional absurdity of it all. Embracing technology in business is akin to harnessing a superhero's superpowers—empowering us to reach new heights of creativity and connection while sometimes producing a gag-worthy blooper reel along the way. So, my fellow dreamers, remember to laugh your way through the challenges, embrace the uncomfortable, and let technology be the wind beneath your entrepreneurial wings. Here is to the exciting adventures ahead. Cheers.

Learning from Global Trends

Global trends. Those ever-changing waves of consumer behaviour, cultural quirks, and economic shifts that seem to sweep through our lives like a dramatic movie scene, most times with a plot twist that jolts us awake. I do not know about you, but I have come to appreciate the comedic ballet that these trends perform. Have you noticed how one minute we are obsessed with avocado toast, and the next, it is all about edible glitter? Sometimes, I feel like I am living in a kitchen on an international cooking show, trying to keep up with the judges as they critique my every culinary move.

When I first moved to Australia, I was astounded by how quickly things changed around here. One minute, I was sipping my Liberian coffee while flipping through a local magazine, and the next, everyone was talking about what was happening around me, adapting, and sometimes laughing it off.

One of the things I love about global trends is that they reveal a lot about our shared human experience. Every time I turn on the news or swipe through social media, I witness how interconnected we are, like a huge family reunion with people from all corners of the world. This moment of connection is decisive. When I see trends emerging from across the globe, I feel compelled to learn from them. And let me tell you, if there is one thing I have learned, it is that sometimes the silliest trends can lead to the most profound innovations. Who would have thought that a simple TikTok dance could launch a multi-million-dollar marketing campaign? I guess the lesson is: always be ready to shake a leg in the name of creativity.

Let us talk about sustainability. Take a look at how the world is shifting towards eco-friendliness. From reusable straws to plant-based burgers, it is as though we have all collectively decided to join a green revolution—almost as though we were reborn as conscious eco-warriors. But here is the humorous twist: many people are trying so hard to be sustainable that they end up living in a compost heap. You can practically hear them exclaiming, "Look at my hemp shoes! I am saving the planet!" But hey, if wearing someone's salad can save Mother Earth, who am I to judge?

On a serious note, it has inspired my own little business ideas. Maybe I should start selling "sustainable" fufu bowls crafted from recycled banana leaves. At least they would biodegrade better than my gardening attempts.

Then there is the trend of remote work, which has spread like wildfire and made our homes feel like the newest hip cubicle. Everyone seems to have turned their living room into their "office," complete with pyjama bottoms and a pot of coffee that has probably seen more action than the average workout routine. You know what that means for me? Embracing the power of the digital realm. I have discovered that learning from global trends allows me to incorporate flexibility into my work methods. A tiny twist here, an unexpected direction there, and voilà! Suddenly, I am completing complex nursing tasks while hosting a virtual workshop in my living room. Isn't it amusing how the home office can also double as a comedy stage? I cannot tell you how many times I have cracked a joke during a Zoom call, only to have my dog walk in, sit down, and steal the show.

Global trends also bring the unexpected joys of cultural exchange. I never knew that learning to appreciate different perspectives could be as refreshing as a cool breeze on a hot day. For instance, I have come to love the flavours of cuisines from around the world. One minute I am devouring a hearty bowl of jollof rice from West Africa, and the next I am eagerly experimenting with Australian meat pies—no judgment, please, it is all part of the learning process. Every bite is a lesson in globalisation, and every meal transforms my understanding of community and humanity.

In conclusion, embracing global trends is like strapping on a surfboard, ready to ride the waves of possibility. It keeps us grounded and agile, allowing us to pivot when the tide shifts unexpectedly. As aspiring millionaires, at least in spirit, with my trusty "I Want to Be a Millionaire" shirt in tow, we must stay open to learning from the world around us. So, my fellow dreamers, let us raise our coffee mugs to curiosity, adaptability, and the endless adventures that come our way. After all, laughter is the universal language, and adaptability is our ticket to the great show of life. Cheers.

Building a Resilient Mindset

The resilient mindset. The magical state of mind that makes you feel like a superhero, impervious to the curveball life throws at you, or at least dodging them in style. Let me take you on a journey through the wild yet humorous landscape of resilience, where mistakes become lessons and trials become triumphs. It is akin to life's ultimate rollercoaster, complete with stomach-churning drops and delightful loops. And believe me, it can be a scream.

Now, I must tell you a tale from my early days in Australia when I stumbled upon a massive life lesson while attempting to prepare a dish from my childhood—a Liberian classic, cassava fufu. Picture me standing in my humble kitchen, armed with all the fervour of a boy on his first day of school, ready to impress my friends with the glory of this traditional dish. In my excitement, I could skip a few steps and elevate this to "cooking genius" status. Wrong move. Not only did I end up with a pot of immense goo resembling disgruntled glue, but I also discovered that fufu can indeed be used as an adhesive for anything left unattended. Cue the laughter, my friends. However, this experience taught me something profound: when you tumble down, it is about picking yourself back up, dusting off the gooey remnants, and trying again.

Building a resilient mindset is about learning from those sticky situations (pun absolutely intended). You know what they say, "When life gives you lemons, make lemonade!" Well, let me tell you: when life gives you fufu, avoid the faux pas of overconcentrating on the failure. Instead, whip out your sense of humour. That is right, the cocktail of laughter and tenacity is your secret weapon. When faced with failures, I often find myself cleaning up the metaphorical mess with a smile, imagining how my culinary blooper reel would rate on a social media platform. It may not come out perfectly every time, but those moments teach us resilience and strength.

What is the secret sauce to this resilient mindset, you ask? It is all about perspective. I learned that I had to reframe challenges as opportunities for growth rather than viewing them as dead ends. For instance, take my nursing career—sometimes the night shifts feel tougher than an old rubber shoe, and getting up at 3 a.m. is nobody's idea of fun. But guess what? I flip that narrative by thinking of those moments as chances to prove my mettle. It is like life plays a game of chess, and the moment I see I am down a pawn, I shift my perspective and envision myself as the king, staying on the board. Suddenly, I am not just surviving; I am thriving.

Another essential aspect of resilience is embracing change. Life is like unpredictable weather in Liberia—one second, it is sunny, the next it is raining cats and dogs. You have to be like my favourite umbrella, the one that I keep tucked away in my bag; it is the very emblem of preparation. I have learned to flow with change rather than resist it, and that takes mental flexibility. I always recognise that, like my lovely friends who change hairstyles more often than the seasons change, adapting is vital. Every new shift, every twist in our journey, nudges us towards growth.

Let us not forget the importance of surrounding ourselves with positive vibes and cheerleaders. I mean, who would not want a crew that turns your failures into legends, celebrating your epic bloopers as if they were Oscar-worthy performances? It is my family who brings joy to my life— each laugh, each story of resilience shared at dinner is a reminder that we are all a work in progress. I like to see my relatives as my preferred form of therapy. They might not give clinical advice, but the side-splitting jokes and giggles build my resilient foundation stronger than the sturdiest fufu.

In the broader grand scheme of life, I have learned that resilience is not just about bouncing back from adversity; it is about how we respond to life's nonsensical moments. When you face challenges with a hearty laugh and dedication, you will discover that every setback pushes you closer to burgeoning success—like a seed pushing through the soil to reach the light.

So, my fellow dreamers, let us toast to building a resilient mindset, one laugh at a time. Recognise that setbacks are nothing but stepping stones draped in humour, and remember that every splash of gooey fufu adds texture to our remarkable story. Embrace challenges, cherish the absurd, and let laughter guide you through life's unpredictable dance. Here is to finding resilience in hiccups and undercooked fufu, my friends. Cheers.

Networking in a Dynamic Environment

Networking! The fine art of building connections, gathering opportunities, and creating a web of relationships that can, quite literally, make or break your dreams. It is like throwing a party where everyone brings a dish—some contribute gourmet delights, while others bring questionable potato salads. The trick is to graciously navigate through the chaotic buffet and make sure to taste a little bit of everything. And trust me, I have learned the ropes of networking in a dynamic environment— let us just say it is one wild, humorous ride.

When I first arrived in Australia, I felt like a lost puppy at the dog park. Here I was, this ambitious Liberian with dreams as grand as my T-shirt declaring "I Want to Be a Millionaire." I was excited but also a little horrified at the idea of networking. I walked into my first networking event like I was stepping into a wrestling ring—wide-eyed and a bit nervous, unsure if I would leave victorious or in tears. Let me tell you, my self-branded "millionaire" persona was slightly hindered by a perplexed look on my face when someone asked me about my "elevator pitch." I mean, what do you mean I have to make a speech about myself in 30 seconds?

But oh, did I learn quickly that networking is about embracing the chaos. I figured early on that successful networking is not about reciting a canned spiel; it is about authenticity and connection. My approach soon became simple: just be Joe. No pretence, no scripted speech, just a delightful mixture of laughter, charm, and a sprinkle of my favourite goat farming anecdotes (trust me, they go a long way). After all, if you cannot make someone chuckle, how can you expect them to remember you? I approached people, authentically curious, asking what sparked their interests while sprinkling in my own quirkiness. The more we laughed, the easier it became to create genuine connections.

One evening, I found myself chatting with a financial advisor who was keen to discuss the complexities of stock market trends. Now, here I was thinking, "What on earth is a hedge fund, and does it involve actual hedges?" But rather than break out in a cold sweat, I took a deep breath, complimented his tie (which was a vivid shade of turquoise—I mean, who would not notice that?), and then asked about his own journey. Suddenly, we were not just strangers at a networking event; we were two humans exchanging stories, sharing adventures, and perhaps discovering mutual interests. By the time the conversation ended, I walked away with valuable insights about investment and, believe it or not, a new friend.

Another significant lesson I learned about networking in a dynamic world is the importance of embracing diverse perspectives. One of the greatest strengths of a dynamic environment is its promotion of cross-cultural exchange. Having left Liberia and immersed myself in Australian culture, I began to celebrate the beauty of diversity in my network. While sharing stories of my upbringing, I learned about the experiences of those from entirely different backgrounds—their joys, their trials, and sometimes hilarious mishaps. Not only did it allow me to build better connections, but it also broadened my horizons in ways I never realised were possible. Who knew that someone's cake-baking disaster could be the bridge to a deeper understanding of resilience?

As I attended more networking events, I realised that the key to adapting in a dynamic environment is to be open to new people and experiences. For example, an international organisation where you meet people from different nationalities from all over the world. There is that old saying, "Don't judge a book by its cover," and oh boy, did I take it to heart. I came across the most eccentric characters at these events. From a self-proclaimed motivational guru who gave free hugs to a gentleman dressed as a giant avocado, I learned that everyone has something to offer. So instead of sticking to the usual suspects, I decided to entertain the absurd and have conversations that branched beyond the common clichés. Suddenly, the world opened up to me like a beloved family photo album—full of laughter, joy, and occasional eyebrow-raising moments.

Now, let us not forget the power of follow-up. You might have had a magnificent conversation at that networking event, but if you do not follow up, it is like buying a fancy fufu bowl without ever using it—what is the point? I made it a habit to pop a friendly message post-event, reminding new connections of our discussions or simply sharing a funny meme that tied back to our conversation. That is right; laughter transcends boundaries—it is the glue that sticks our relationships together.

In conclusion, networking in a dynamic environment is about authenticity, connection, and finding opportunities to laugh along the way. Embrace the eccentricities, celebrate the diversity, and always follow up with a light-hearted touch. So, strap on your socialising shoes, bring along your humour, and jump into that unpredictable dance of networking, because in this grand performance of life, the connections you make are what will take you to millionaire heights. Cheers.

Chapter 20:
Becoming Your Own Millionaire

Understanding Your Unique Value Proposition

When I first heard the term "Unique Value Proposition" (UVP), I thought it was just another piece of corporate jargon that people throw around to impress each other during meetings. You know, the kind of term that sounds smart but leaves you scratching your head, thinking, "What in the world are they talking about?" But here's the kicker: understanding your UVP is crucial to your journey to becoming a millionaire. It's not just for suits in high-rise buildings sipping overpriced lattes; it's also for you, me, and the friendly lady at the market who sells the freshest mangos in town.

So, what exactly is a Unique Value Proposition? Picture it like this: your UVP is the special sauce that makes your burger stand out in a sea of fast-food chains. It's what makes your idea or service irresistible to others. The beauty of it is that it can be as unique as an African dance move. I mean, have you ever seen someone try to do Zumba to the beat of traditional Liberian music? Hilarious! Just like that, your UVP needs to stick out in the marketplace so people can't help but notice.

You have to ask yourself: what makes you different? What skills or experiences do you bring to the table that no one else does? For me, it was a combination of my background in nursing, a deep desire to help others, and an unshakeable commitment to cracking jokes that brighten people's days. You see, I wasn't just a clinical nurse—we're talking about "MO' Money. MO' Laughter," a guy who helps people recover while making them chuckle. That's my UVP right there. It's like getting a hearty laugh while you get your blood pressure checked. Who wouldn't want that?

But here's the secret—developing your UVP requires some deep introspection. Think of it as a family gathering where Auntie Petunia is asking awkward questions like, "When are you going to settle down?" or "Why don't you have more hair?" You have to dig deep into your history, experiences, and skills and face them head-on, even if they make you uneasy. Reflect on your strengths and weaknesses. Are you a master at baking mouthwatering cassava leaves, or do you throw the best parties in your community? Find that one thing that makes you shine like the sun over the Liberian coastline.

Now, let's sprinkle in some humour because, let's face it, life is too serious. Think about the times you've failed. Maybe you tried selling "original" African print shirts that turned out to be "almost original" when people realised your aunt made them in her living room. That's a learning experience, my friend! Each failure adds depth to your UVP. It says, "Hey, I tried; I've learned; and guess what? I'm back with better designs!" Embrace that journey because that's what makes your story relatable and worth sharing. Your quirks, your misadventures—they all contribute to your navigational uniqueness.

Now, let's talk about your audience—who are they? Find your tribe! For instance, if you're offering health advice, make sure to tailor it to people who eat jollof rice for breakfast, lunch, and dinner. Build your UVP with them in mind. Speak their language, understand their needs, and make sure you serve them that special sauce that keeps them coming back for seconds. It's all about addressing the needs and desires of the people you want to connect with, and trust me, they'll appreciate you more for it.

Lastly, let's not forget the importance of communication—how you convey your UVP to others. Get creative! Write it on a T-shirt; shout it from the mountaintops (or the nearest village market). Tell everyone about it until they roll their eyes and say, "Okay, we get it!" But that's the point. It's not just about saying it once; it's about embedding it into the hearts and minds of those around you. Make them remember you for that unique flavour you bring into their lives.

So, there you have it! Your journey toward becoming a millionaire starts with understanding your Unique Value Proposition—the delightful blend of your skills, personality, and experiences. Embrace your quirks, laugh at your failures, and communicate it all with enthusiasm. And remember, whether you end up as the next millionaire influencer or a famous cassava leaf chef, your UVP is your secret weapon. Now, what are you waiting for? Go on and explore your unique flavour in this giant buffet called life!

Creating a Personal Mission Statement

The Personal Mission Statement—or as I like to call it, the "You're Not Lost, You Just Haven't Figured It Out Yet" statement. I remember the first time I encountered the concept. I was sitting in my friend Amara's living room, sipping some sweet palm wine, when he casually mentioned that he had crafted his own personal mission statement. At first, I thought, "What in the name of cassava is that?" But after a few more sips, his words began to make sense. A mission statement is like a guiding star that helps you navigate the often choppy waters of life. It's like having a GPS that reminds you which path to take when the only road you see leads you to Auntie Binta's notorious jollof rice… for the third time this week!

Creating your personal mission statement is a deeply introspective exercise that requires more thought than explaining to your aunt why you still don't have a spouse. It's about reflecting on your core values, your passions, and, most importantly, how you want to impact the world around you. Start by asking yourself some essential questions: What gets you excited? What do you absolutely love doing? And, if you could wave a magic wand and create a change in the world, what would that be? For me, the answer arose quite clearly from my love for nursing and my desire to uplift others through humour. Boom! There it was, right in front of me, like a perfect bowl of pepper soup on a rainy day—nourishing, comforting, and a little slippery if you don't watch out.

Once you've identified your passions, it's time to weave them into a mission statement that provides clarity, purpose, and maybe even a dash of humour. Trust me, life is too short to take yourself too seriously. My personal mission statement reads something like this: "To leverage the gift of laughter, health knowledge, and compassion to uplift my community, while also mastering the fine art of making a perfect jollof rice recipe." You see? It captures everything that I am passionate about and allows room for that hearty African meal that fuels my spirit (and I mean literally—it fuels my spirit, let's be honest).

This mission statement serves as my North Star. Whenever I feel overwhelmed—like when I accidentally mistook a bag of salt for sugar while baking or when I found out that making connections was more complicated than finding a needle in a haystack—I refer to my mission statement. It's a quick pick-me-up that reminds me of my true purpose. It lets me know that even if I burn the cassava cake, I can always come back to helping others with laughter. Instead of wallowing in despair, I hear my own voice reminding me, "Hey, you've got a mission, remember?"

You know, friends, creating a personal mission statement isn't just about nailing down a catchy phrase to hang on your wall and admire while sipping a cup of tea. No! It should resonate with you, almost like a catchy tune from that secret childhood campfire song you'd sing off-key with your friends. It should inspire you to jump out of bed every morning like you're running from a cockroach, ready to seize the day.

Now, you might be thinking, "Joe, why do I need such a statement?" Well, let me zoom in on that. A personal mission statement helps you make decisions. When faced with opportunities—like whether to attend a party or pass it for an online course in goat herding that could elevate your status in the community—you can refer back to your mission. Does this opportunity align with your mission? If not, then it's a no-brainer! You can save yourself from another night of standing in the corner with awkward small talk about the weather.

And here's a bonus: your mission statement can evolve! You might start off wanting to uproot the healthcare system in your town but then realise that your love for baking might be your true calling. That's okay! Adapt and grow. Life is all about experiences and surprises—like discovering that the mango in your smoothie was actually a banana. Life can be funny like that.

In conclusion, creating a personal mission statement is like building a roadmap to your dreams and is ultimately a divine act of self-love. So take out a piece of paper, a pen, and some palm wine (just kidding, or maybe not) and start crafting your own. Remember, your mission statement should encapsulate your essence and lead your journey toward realising your millionaire dreams. Go on! Embrace it! Your future self will thank you for it—preferably over a plate of delicious jollof rice.

Budgeting: The Foundation of Financial Health

Of a cockroach during a midnight snack raid. We've all been there, right? You get your paycheck, and before you even blink, it's gone—vanished like my aunt's famous jollof rice at a family gathering! But here's the secret I've learned: budgeting is the foundation of financial health, much like cassava is the foundation of a good Liberian meal. Let's dive in!

First of all, let's redefine what budgeting really means. It's not some evil, restrictive chain that keeps you from enjoying life; it's more like a friendly guide dog that helps you navigate your finances while avoiding the pitfalls of overspending. Think of it as a well-structured plan that keeps your finances from becoming a chaotic mess, akin to my attempt to sing four-part harmonies at church. You wouldn't want to end up sounding like a dying goat, now would you? Okay, enough singing metaphors (for now).

To begin your budgeting journey, you need to know where your money is going. Picture it like a game of hide-and-seek, but in reverse. Instead of looking for your cash, you need to retrieve every coin you've spent! Grab your bank statements, receipts, and maybe even that notebook where you scribbled down your millionaire dreams while stuck in traffic, because we all know one can dream anywhere! Create categories: housing, food (and by food, I mean regular groceries plus your midnight snack binges), transportation, entertainment, and don't forget that essential "clothes I don't need but can't resist" category.

Once you've sorted everything, the next step in budgeting is setting realistic financial goals. Whether it's finally taking that family vacation to Australia or starting your own handwoven bag business, having a target gives your budgeting a purpose. Personally, my goal was to sock away enough for a no-strings-attached annual trip back to Liberia, the kind of trip where you can escape the everyday hustle, enjoy delicious palm butter soup, and hide from Auntie Rose's unsolicited marriage advice. See how much more motivated you feel when your budget is tied to something exciting?

Now, let's talk about those unavoidable surprises life throws at you. You know, the ones that make you want to pull your hair out, like when your favourite shoe gets a tear right before your cousin's wedding, or when your car suddenly decides it prefers to be a paperweight. What do you do? You build an emergency fund! This is your financial lifesaver, a buffer that prevents you from going into a spiral of debt. Aim to save at least three to six months of living expenses, and trust me, when the unexpected hits, and oh, it will, you'll be glad you didn't spend that extra money on avocado toast!

Budgeting might feel constrictive; that's where the trick of 'wiggle room' comes in! Leave yourself a small allowance for spontaneous treats, because life is too short to avoid a good chin-chin snack. Maybe you can call it your "Oops, I'm Going to Treat Myself" fund. It's psychologically satisfying to know you can splurge occasionally without ruining the whole plan. Telling yourself you can't have any fun is like telling a lion to become a vegetarian, just not happening!

Also, technology is your best friend. Gone are the days of manual calculations while standing in line at the bank, looking as confused as a goat in a vegetable garden. Numerous budgeting apps can help you manage your finances. Download one, plug in your expenses, and watch as you become the budgeting genius you were always meant to be!

Lastly, remember budgeting is not set in stone; it's meant to be fluid! Your financial situation may change like the weather in Liberia, sunshine one moment, pouring rain the next. So, check in on your budget regularly. Tweak it, adjust it, and let it grow with you. If you find yourself overspending on fancy suits you never wear, maybe it's time to pivot toward comfy casuals that better match your vibe.

In conclusion, budgeting is the foundation of financial health and a pathway to achieving all those millionaire dreams. View it as your map leading you toward your goals while ensuring you enjoy the journey. With foresight, humour, and a sprinkle of self-love, you'll find that mastering your finances is not only possible but also a fun adventure. So take a deep breath, grab your budgeting tools, and get started! Your future self, balanced, thriving, and possibly enjoying some jollof rice, will thank you.

Developing a Growth Mindset

Ah, the elusive growth mindset! It's like that rare spice in your mother's cooking, a little bit can transform a regular meal into something divine. You might be wondering, "What is this growth mindset, Joe?" Well, my friends, envision it as the belief that you can continually improve and learn new things. It's that magical lens that enables you to see failures not as dead ends but as stepping stones to greatness. After all, who ever heard of a great chef who didn't burn their first batch of cookies, and let's be honest, who hasn't accidentally burned something? If you haven't, you might need to get out of the kitchen more often!

Developing a growth mindset begins with a simple twist in perspective. Instead of thinking, "I can't do this," try flipping that statement on its head: "I can't do this yet." That simple addition of "yet" is like adding a pinch of salt to your favourite soup; it evokes fresh possibility and ignites your motivation. Imagine if everyone in your life started using "yet", your heart would swell with joy as you encourage your cousin to finally learn to dance without stepping on toes, or give your neighbour the confidence to finally try his hand at gardening instead of just yelling at his plants.

But let's get real, embracing a growth mindset isn't always a walk in the park. It can feel as awkward as squeezing into those pants you wore before the holidays! There will be days when setbacks make you question your abilities harder than Auntie Grace questioning your romantic prospects. On those days, remember, setbacks are not only natural; they're essential ingredients in the recipe for growth.

Think of it like learning to ride a bicycle: you stumble, you wobble, you even fall, and then you get back up. And trust me, there's nothing quite like that feeling of finally zooming down the street with the wind in your hair, feeling like a superstar. Each time you fall and get back up, you're building resilience and confidence, without breaking a sweat! The same goes for adopting a growth mindset. Look at every setback as a step toward mastering your skills, like practising your Liberian pimento pepper sauce recipe until it's just right.

Another essential aspect of this growth mindset is embracing feedback. This isn't about letting people walk all over you or soaking in mindless criticism like a sponge; it's about constructive feedback that helps you realign your trajectory. Imagine if I had disregarded all the feedback I received on my book drafts: "Joe, this is nonsense!" "Why is the introduction filled with jokes about cassava?" Thank goodness I embraced feedback as I would my favourite pillow after an all-night shift! It led me to polish my writing and ultimately create something worthwhile, much like the second batch of cookies that didn't burn.

Don't forget the power of surrounding yourself with growth-minded folks. Your company matters, like choosing the right spices to complement your jollof rice. When you surround yourself with people who inspire and challenge you, it's like adding fire to your ambitions. You will find encouragement and motivation in their journeys, making it easier to navigate your path. Plus, who doesn't enjoy a good laugh over shared aspirations while feasting on chin-chin? You'll have a support system that lifts you higher, rather than a group of naysayers mumbling about why you'll never make it as a millionaire.

Finally, developing a growth mindset requires a commitment to lifelong learning. It's about being curious, hungry for knowledge, and open to experiences. Whether it's taking an online course, diving into self-help books, or joining a group, soak it all in. Chase knowledge down like a delicious cookout chicken that's just out of reach. Each bit of learning adds fuel to your dreams, igniting new possibilities that expand your horizons. You may find yourself stepping into new industries, making friends from all walks of life, or discovering a surprising talent for, say, motivational speaking (Who am I kidding? I still have stage fright!).

In conclusion, a growth mindset is more than just a catchy phrase; it's a transformative attitude that can redefine your journey. It helps you breathe deeply, channel your inner lion, and reminds you that you have the power to grow, learn, and roar your way to success. Now, put on your favourite shirt, grab that budget notebook, and let's conquer those goals together!

Taking Action: Your First Steps to Millionaire Status

Taking action! Now that's a phrase that sounds simple, yet we all know it's easier said than done. I mean, how many times have you told yourself you'd start saving, investing, or even writing that brilliant book about your journey to millionaire status? Then suddenly, a three-hour Netflix binge pops up like an uninvited guest at a family reunion, and all bets are off. Let's face it: procrastination has become as common as a power outage during the hottest month in Liberia. However, I'm here to tell you that taking action is the one crucial step you cannot afford to overlook on your journey to millionaire dreams.

First, start small and build momentum, like a toddler learning to walk. You wouldn't hand a child a unicycle and say, "Go on, get to the market!" Instead, let them take tiny steps until they can confidently strut their stuff down the street. Similarly, don't overwhelm yourself with massive goals! Start with short-term, achievable objectives that create quick wins. Write down three concrete actions you can take this week to bring yourself closer to your millionaire dreams. Whether it's enrolling in that online course you've been eyeing or learning how to budget your funds better, take that first tiny leap.

Once you've decided on your initial steps, create a plan of action and stick to it as if your life depended on it, because it really does! When I decided to take my finances seriously, I mapped out my journey like a treasure hunt: itemised my current expenses, set achievable saving goals, and even included fun little incentives, like treating myself to my favourite Thai restaurant every time I reached a milestone. Soon enough, I was surprised to find that indulging in treats became a powerful motivator to keep pushing forward. Who knew a little sugar could fuel dreams of grandeur?

But here's where it gets real, remember to hold yourself accountable! It doesn't matter if you're promising your family, friends, or even your neighbour's cat; share your goals with someone. This creates a supportive network that keeps you motivated. Accountability can be as simple as sending a text to a friend every week to update them on your progress, or, better yet, find a buddy to join you on your personal development journey. Imagine two determined friends tackling their financial goals together, swapping tips, sharing laughs, and, of course, indulging in the occasional plate of jollof rice as a reward. That's the kind of camaraderie that elevates your journey.

Now let's talk about the part that can feel as uncomfortable as wearing shoes two sizes too small: stepping outside your comfort zone. Taking action sometimes requires facing discomfort, which can be more challenging than persuading your relatives that you're serious about your career choices. But pushing through that discomfort broadens your horizons and opens doors you never knew existed. For instance, if you're terrified of public speaking, consider taking a small course or joining a local group. Watch as you transform from a shy wallflower into the life of the party, sharing stories about your million-dollar ambitions and making everyone laugh in no time!

Amidst the hustle, don't forget to celebrate your victories, no matter how tiny they may seem. One time, I managed to save a small amount after successfully negotiating discounts at local markets. Did I do a celebratory jig in my kitchen? You bet I did! Acknowledging your achievements, even if it's just sipping a cold palm wine while bragging to your friends, reinforces positive behaviour. So, go ahead: pat yourself on the back, grab a snack, and appreciate how far you've come.

Lastly, never underestimate the power of ongoing education. The world is constantly changing, and you need to keep your game sharp! Read books, attend workshops, or listen to podcasts related to your financial goals. You'd be surprised by how much resonates, inspiring you and expanding your perspective. Remember, knowledge is like the secret ingredient in your grandma's famous soup, it can elevate everything you do.

In conclusion, taking action may require guts, persistence, and a sprinkle of humour, but it is indeed the pathway to your millionaire dreams. Start small, create a plan, be accountable, step outside your comfort zone, celebrate your wins, and invest in education. You've got this! As you take those first steps toward financial health, imagine yourself standing on top of the world, sipping a refreshing concoction of your wildest dreams, with a plate of your best jollof rice on the side. Let's get that millionaire status, you're closer than you think!